deep down in the jungle

ROGER D. ABRAHAMS

deep down in the jungle...

Negro Narrative Folklore from the Streets of Philadelphia

ALDINE PUBLISHING COMPANY / *New York*

Again to the women
who have most affected my life:
my wife, Mary
my sister, Marj
and my mother

Portions of this work in earlier form have previously
appeared in *The Golden Log* (Publication XXX of the
Texas Folklore Society), *The Texas Studies in Literature and
Language, Journal of American Folklore*, and *Folklore In
Action: Essays for Discussion in Honor of MacEdward Leach.*

First revised edition published 1970
by Aldine Publishing Company
200 Saw Mill River Road
Hawthorne, N.Y. 10532

Library of Congress Catalog Card Number 78-124404
ISBN Cloth 0-202-01091-1
ISBN Paper 0-202-01092-0

Fourth printing, 1979

Designed by Cameron Poulter
Printed in the United States of America

Contents

v

Foreword

Deep Down in the Jungle became an indispensable work almost from the moment it first appeared in 1964. Its pioneering aspects were many: it was concerned with urban rather than rural folklore; it considered ghetto Negro folklore in depth; and it presented materials regarded by many as obscene, not in the usual cowardly bowdlerized way but in an honest unsensational scholarly manner.

In this revised edition, Professor Abrahams has updated his analysis and has included much more of his personal fieldwork experience than in the first edition. (It is almost as though he were inspired by one of the important stylistic features of the Negro folklore he analyzed in making such a remarkable shift from the objective "intrusive eye" of the conventional fieldworker's report to the more subjective "intrusive I" which is inevitably a factor in the actual recording of data by all sensitive fieldworkers!) There may be some readers familiar with the earlier edition who might have wished for even more revision, e.g., there is still the marked organizational division between analysis and raw, annotated but unanalyzed texts. However, the critical point is that there is analysis and interpretation, features all too rare in folklorists' presentations of their data.

The publication of this unique and important study in a relatively inexpensive paperback edition will make it more readily available to serious students of urban folklore and Afro-American culture. Hopefully, some of these students will go on to continue the dialogue begun by Roger Abrahams.

Alan Dundes

vii

Acknowledgments

So many people have given me help and encouragement in this study that it would not be fitting if I did not point them out at the very beginning. The one person more than any other responsible for the completion of this work is Gershon Legman. This study arose from some of the work in my dissertation. I sent him a copy of that collection and he answered voluminously and perceptively, providing me with questions and approaches that made me see at least a few of the trees in the forest, the ones I discuss here. Legman's immense contribution to this work is further evidenced in the copious quotations from his letters and works I have included.

Many others have offered assistance. Peter Tamony helped a great deal with the Glossary. Page Stegner shared with me his knowledge of Stackolee, as did Richard Buehler. D. K. Wilgus kindly sent me some toast texts out of his Kentucky archives. Richard M. Dorson sent me a number of kind letters on various subjects concerning Negro lore. Mack McCormick helped with discographical materials and shared with me his immense experience with Negro musicians in a tremendously helpful way. Bruce Jackson sent tape recordings and comments from his collections in Indiana prisons, and also shared many of his ideas. Neil Rosenberg sent some esoteric and important record references and transcriptions. Frank Hoffman, with his growing knowledge of bawdry, has helped on numerous matters. Charles Scott, at the time a graduate student in linguistics

viii

at the University of Texas, helped me with problems of style.

Professors MacEdward Leach and Tristram Coffin, who were responsible for the ease and dispatch with which my dissertation was effected, are in line for my special thanks. Characteristic of these men, it wasn't until years later that I heard about the big battle with the powers-that-be in their department over the nature of the material in the dissertation. Claire Rosenfield and Mary Edrich Redding both helped a great deal by their careful reading and editing of certain chapters. My sister, Marj Slavin, read a nearly complete manuscript and gave many helpful comments. Kenneth S. Goldstein has been of great assistance at every stage in this work, as a friend, commentator, folklorist, editor, and publisher.

I made many changes in this new edition because of astute readings of the first by reviewers and commentators—Nat Hentoff, Richard M. Dorson, Charles Keil, Alan Dundes, Ellen Stekert, Stephen Baratz, William A. Stewart, and especially John Szwed. I am indebted to remarks by black friends, especially Don Henderson, for emphasizing that I had only scratched the surface and for being willing to rap the whole thing out with me. To all of these people, my thanks.

Most of all, and apart from the rest, my thanks to my good wife, Mary, who has borne the brunt of the whole thing, listened and commented carefully, helped with annotation and bibliography, recalled important experiences, and best of all, got excited with me as pieces began to fit together.

Introduction to the Second Edition

ON DISCRETION, BETTER PARTS,
AND VALOR

Since the publication of *Deep Down* . . . in 1964, I have been hoping for the chance of this second say. I sensed from the beginning of the writing that I was not capturing the spirit of my experiences and the essentials of my observations and thus was unwillingly playing into the hands of racists. It wasn't until the era of black militancy (which began a year after its writing), however, that I was able to see how my *ex post facto* judgments had been conditioned by my reading of the scholarship on black life rather than by the life style I had observed and experienced. This introduction will serve as my belated apology to my neighbors and friends who unwittingly (indeed, unknowingly) were submitted to this minor indignity. I hope it will also serve as a testimony to their resilience and to their spirit for living in a situation that would have defeated less hardy and self-sufficient people.

This new edition permits me to revise a crucial orientation. My black neighbors were telling me about a way of life that calls for a constant consideration of the importance of the "me" element, and it was this very perspective that in my zeal to appear to be a scholar I eliminated from the first recounting of the experience. I eliminated myself from the proceedings, neglecting to build into the account the tremendous importance placed upon friendships and rivalries, loves

1

and animosities, all of which I was part of, at least in the lives of the few neighbors I came to know well. Gone from the account were the cultural gaffes I committed by which I learned so much. Missing were the experiences where taking my ethnocentric conceptions of trust and friendship into an encounter, I found to my dismay and disappointment that my values were not shared. All this crucial interpersonal data was hidden behind the curtain of objective description.

So the reader who knows this book from the earlier edition should be prepared for a change of orientation. I have redirected its focus, placing the people who were most deeply involved closer to the center. This alteration has had some side-effects. I have eliminated the introduction, which was directed mainly toward folklorists. The argument pursued there has developed into a whole pontification mode of folkloristic analysis (I call it a rhetorical theory of folklore); one thing I've learned in the interim is to segregate—to report in one place and to theorize in another.

Some readers will feel that the major change in the revision is the relegation of the "Mammy Family" argument to a lesser importance. In this, I am just following scholarly fashion, as any reader of the insightful *The Moynihan Report and the Politics of Controversy* by Lee Rainwater and William Yancey will know. I do so with great relief, since I feel this model of the pathological family was largely responsible for my misconstruing certain features of the life I encountered while living in South Philadelphia. In addition to the Rainwater and Yancey book, which I didn't see until quite recently, two books have had a decisive effect on my changing perspective. The first is the much read *Urban Blues* by Charles Keil; his revealing reading of my book made it clear to me that I had not made my major point as effectively as I had hoped, that there is an ultimate and fascinating relationship between social and psychological adversity and the black cultural mechanisms that promote emotional flexibility and creativity. The second book is the intriguing, straightforward account of a similar but somewhat older group of men in Washington, D. C., given by Elliot Liebow in *Tally's Corner*.

But once again I may be hiding behind my academic objectivity in saying that I emphasized the matrifocal family in the first edition because of the scholarly fashion of the time. As my dedication in the original (repeated here) indicates, this document was crucial in working out my own problems in relation to women. While I lived in the neighborhood, which is the locus for this study, I got married. This event created many of the same problems for me as it has for others. It is clear to me now that my personal situation at the time had a great influence on my interpretation of the life around me. This outcome was inevitable, and I make my *mea culpas* now only to make the record a little clearer. Objectivity in a field situation is only an ideal toward which we strive; but focus of interest will always be determined, at least in part, by personal problems.

Another limitation of the first writing was the insularity of the approach. I could not know then that the patterns of performance and their uses were not unique to Negro Philadelphia or to lower-class black Americans. I have found through field work in the British West Indies that the approach to words and word use and creative performance is shared throughout the two culture areas. Further, recent ethnographic works on Negro groups throughout Africa and the New World give indications that this attitude and pattern is an African cultural retention in its New World situations, subject to reinterpretation. Since a number of my recent articles (listed in the bibliography) treat this subject, I shall not rehearse the argument here.

There are other changes that should be noted, if only in passing. I have moved the appendices On Certain Obscenities and Toward the Discernment of Oikotype into the text proper. Both have undergone a "sea change." The latter has had a number of key changes made in terminology, the former has had most of the psychoanalytic baggage removed. This last change is characteristic of the revision as a whole. The imprint of Freud, Jung and Campbell, and Erikson as it led to certain ethnocentric judgments will not be so evident here; in the case of Jung and Campbell, the use of their ideas led me to a false evolutionism in regard to the changing concepts of heroes and heroism.

Many of the changes I would have made have become unnecessary since I have written another book on black culture, *Positively Black*—most notably, the consideration of songs that I would have added here. I thought of that work as a counterpart to *Deep Down* . . . since they cover much of the same kind of material (indeed, I reprint a few of the same texts)— but *Positively Black* covers the black experience from a larger and more sociological perspective. Here I am more involved with the function of traditional oral performances in one group of men; there I am more concerned with analyzing the content and style of key words, jokes, and toasts in relation to the changing attitudes and perspectives of lower-class black life.

There have been many crucial changes in the neighborhood I describe here; most notably it has now become all white. This shift created a small crisis in the revision because in the first edition I adopted the present tense throughout, as if the experiences were ongoing. I have kept to this technique because I don't think conditions have changed that much for the men from whom I collected, and because it permits a much more active style of description and narration.

THE NEIGHBORHOOD AND THE NOT-SO-SILENT OBSERVER

I want to begin with Camingerly, the neighborhood, and the people who lived there when I did in 1958 and 1959. Camingerly was really just us white folks' name for what the men called the Twelfth Street neighborhood, the place the old Twelfth Street gang used to rule until they got old enough to have jobs, "old ladies," and to get thrown down by circumstance. "Camingerly" was our abbreviation of Camac, Iseminger, and Waverly, the three small streets that come together between Twelfth and Thirteenth, Pine and Lombard. On it are the old row houses built as servants' quarters as satellites to the square and townhouses on the larger thoroughfares. We called them "Father-Son-and-Holy-Ghost Houses," as did some of our neighbors, because they each had three rooms, one on top of the other. Some of them, in fact most of them, had a lean to kitchen appended to the first floor; and some of them had indoor plumbing. All the houses on our street were electrified, but not those two blocks south of us. The local hardware stores carry the stock of the country store, because in many ways the city life style hadn't reached these parts completely.

This was not the heart of black Philadelphia, though it was only a block from one of its main centers of activity, South Street. It was a little too far north, too close to the high-priced townhouses and stores. It *was* pimp country, Alice's Playhouse, barbecued-chicken-on-the-corner country; but just one block north was Pine Street with all its antique stores and its police station (run by Frank Rizzo, the tough Italian cop who now heads the whole show in Philly). And Camingerly already had a number of invaders from Center City. Miss Haines had lived there for years, a Quaker nurse of great sensibility who was at home wherever she found herself. And there were four or five others, more recently come, attracted by the closeness to downtown Philly.

But in '58 the place was unmistakably black. This was when I lived there.

For me, moving into Camingerly was an adventure, but not the sort one might imagine. I didn't move into a ghetto because I was interested in those modern primitives, lower-class blacks; rather I wanted to live in an exciting and old house. I was a graduate student in folklore at the University of Pennsylvania and I needed quarters close to transportation to Penn. Most important, I had a friend, a roommate from college, living just a block away, and he was willing to take me to his landlord and to help me strike the same kind of bargain he had been able to make—reduced rent if improvements were made by the tenant. (This was the landlord who later made the local headlines when he had garbage dumped on his suburban front lawn.) So I moved to 421 S. Iseminger and began the never ending job of fixing the place up.

One of the reasons why moving into the area was exciting was that a couple of years before, my wife-to-be and I had been driving through the area and had seen an old man sitting on a doorstep playing his five-string banjo. I was a folksinger then, just beginning to collect songs and singers, and so we leapt out of the car and had a delightful hour with "Old Banjo," as he called himself. So in moving to Camingerly I had hopes of collecting oldtime songs, survivals of the trip north by immigrant singers. However, after I moved I soon found that "Old Banjo" had been dead a year and that not only were there no old bluesmen in the area, but that kind of "down-home" music was scorned by my neighbors. So I quickly gave up hope of finding a store of folkloric material.

But here, as in so many other things, I was to learn from my neighbors; for when I looked about I saw those vestiges of an agrarian way of life that a folklorist commonly tunes in on. My first clue came when I saw that the children were still playing the kinds of ring games I had only read about in regional collections. Here was "Little Sally Waters" and "Sally Go Round the Sun" being played nearly every autumn day, plus similar inventions like "Here Comes Uncle Jessie" and "Here We Go Zootie-O" and "There's a Red Bird in the Ring" which I had never before encountered.

Ultimately it was not vestiges of the past traditions that exploded in my folkloristic imagination, but the oral traditions that were largely the product of the urban experience—the performances of "sounds," the openly heroic, wildly imaginative, coercive, often violent stories and epic poems manufactured and performed by the young men. This ingroup material did not come to my notice until I had lived in the neighborhood for many months.

My first and closest friend in Camingerly was Bobby Lewis. As I was tearing down walls, exposing fireplaces and Dutch ovens, generally fixing the house up, Bobby would come by and help. We would work and talk and share a meal hurriedly bought at Sam's shop across the street. (Bobby told me not to buy pickles there because Sam, who couldn't stand Negroes and told his customers so twenty times a day, pissed in the brine.) We talked a good deal about singers and songs, since that was one of my main interests, and he introduced me to Chuck Berry, B. B. King, Bobby "Blue" Bland, Bo Diddley, and Jimmy Reed. And I played some of my country records for him (he couldn't understand why anybody wanted to listen to that kind of music).

One day Bobby asked me, since I was a performer, whether I knew the one about "Shine." I didn't, and he just laughed. I asked him to sing it for me and he laughed some more. Taking this for shyness or inability I let the subject drop. I kidded him about it a few times, since he was always singing while we worked, and I always was answered by the same chuckle. Then one day, for no reason, he began to perform his version of "Shine," and his recitation really lit my light. I got out my tape recorder and had him perform into the microphone (which gave him great delight).

> The eighth of May was a hell of a day
> When the *Titanic* was sinking away.
> Yeah, what a hell of a day, when the news reached the
>   seaport town
> The *Titanic* was sinking down.
> Shine went below deck, eating his peas
> Till the water come up to his knees.
> Shine went up on deck, said, "Captain, I was downstairs
>   eating my peas
> Till the water come up to my knees."
> Captain said, "Shine, Shine, sit your black ass down.
> I got ninety-nine pumps to pump the water down."
> Shine went back down below deck, looking through space
> Till the water came up to his waist.
> Shine went up on deck, said, "Captain, I was downstairs
>   looking through space
> Till the water came up to my waist."
> Captain said, "Shine, Shine, sit your ass down.
> Got ninety-nine pumps to pump the water down."
> Shine went down below deck eating his bread
> Till the water came up to his head.
> Shine went up on deck, said, "Captain, I was downstairs
>   eating my bread
> Till the water came up to my head."
> He said, "Shine, Shine, sit your ass down.
> Got ninety-nine pumps to pump the water down."
> Shine took off his shirt and started to take a dive.
> Captain's daughter came over to Shine.

Said, "Shine, Shine, save poor me.
Give you all the pussy eyes ever did see."
Shine said, "Pussy ain't nothing but meat on the bone,
You can fuck it, you can suck it, you can leave it alone."
Shine jumped in the water and met up with a shark.
Shine said, "You may be king of the ocean, king of the sea,
You got to be a swimming motherfucker to outswim me."
And Shine swim on.

This brief recording session was important for two reasons. First, when Bobby found to his great amusement that this "toast" appealed to me, he invited me to go with him to the local poolhall where all the best talkers hung out. There I met "Kid" and Arthur and later they became constant visitors to my house. There, too, I heard a lot of jiving and a few toast sessions, though I was never able to even discuss the possibility of having tape sessions at the poolhall; there was far too much other activity, and I was the only white person there anyhow. Most of the material in this work was taped in my own home. And I had to wait some five months after first hearing "Shine" before I made the next recording.

The second development was that Bobby immediately wanted to learn how to use the recorder, a feat accomplished in five minutes. After that, he would stop by about once a week to borrow the machine for what he promised would be some recordings of jokes for me—but what almost always proved to be tapings of one girl or another who he felt might be impressed with his having the recorder. But every once in a while he did come by the house with one or another of our good-talking friends when I was not there, and at such times he recorded some of the texts I include here.

Fortunately for me, a number of the good performers from the neighborhood liked the idea of getting their entire repertoire down on tape (and listening to it played back). Sometimes, they would come by expressly to be recorded—so that for those few talkers these texts represent their best performances. However, it must be noted that they generally came by individually, so that an important dimension of the accustomed context of these performances was missing—the presence of an approving, reacting audience, including other performers. Consequently, the texts here tend to be somewhat shorter and less hyperbolic than those I heard at the poolhall or at Alice's Playhouse, the local saloon and pimp's showplace.

John H. "Kid" Mike was the first of the great talkers to come by, and he soon agreed to tell me his stories and toasts. He recorded a few of them—"Shine," "Stackolee" and one of the "Signifying Monkey" toasts—and I immediately made transcriptions. Being a graduate student in folklore, I brought the texts to my professors, MacEdward Leach and Tristram Coffin. They both became excited about the stories and their performance and encouraged me to write about them in a term paper. By now I was constantly getting new material, and it became clear that there was more than could be covered in such a paper. Still, I began collecting from my neighbors on a full-time basis.

The neighbors never had any problem understanding what I was searching for. I explained that I was writing a book about life in the neighborhood, with special emphasis on the ways in which people enjoyed themselves there. My greatest initial successes were with the children. In fact, the success was on some days too great, because every child in Camingerly wanted to hear his own voice on the recorder and to have his name put in my book. Since I was trying very hard to make myself into a folklorist at the time, I carefully instructed the children that I did not want to record anything learned from a teacher or T.V. or radio, though I now realize that such material is as valuable and culturally relevant as the word-of-mouth traditions.

Hardly a day passed without some small eyes peeking through the mail slot in the door and yelling in, "You havin' any company?" Most of the time the children would come and help my wife cook dinner or look at some of our picture books or listen to themselves on the recorder; then they could vie to see who could remember the most singing games or jump-rope rhymes. This material was included in the dissertation but not in the book.

Success with the youths and men was much slower in coming, and never occurred with the women. Because the material

I was recording was often obscene, the men felt that I was going to make a lot of money on the book and they didn't know if they wanted to contribute to my future. Here, Bobby Lewis helped immeasurably. Not only did he take me around to the hangouts for the young men, but he also spread the word about both my tape recorder and my interests. I had become an important part of his friendship network, his "cutting man" or "ace" (friend), and this was a fact to be advertised by him.

One of the most important informal organizations among the young men was quartets who sang songs learned from the popular rhythm-and-blues groups of the time or, less commonly, songs of their own composition. No matter where they derived their repertoire, each group originated most of its own arrangements. There were many of these groups and each dreamed of the great riches that lay around the corner if only they could be heard. So when some of them learned that I had a recorder, they were anxious to hear themselves on a medium that resembled radio or disc records. A couple of the groups from Camingerly began to come to the house about once a week, and in this way I became acquainted with a number of men who jived a good deal and who told jokes but who were not regarded as really good talkers. Through them I learned about "sounding" and "playing the dozens," and through their performances I was able to see how the group itself judged whether a talker was good. It was in one of these singing sessions that I met Charley Williams, one of the best talkers I have ever encountered.

In all of this, I was fortunate in having a very patient wife who understood exactly what I was trying to do. Because of her hospitality and good humor I was able to establish the house as a center where anyone could drop by and find welcome. Many evenings five or six came to talk, and as often as not, no recording would be done that night. Sometimes, however, someone would arrive announcing he had learned a new toast or joke and out the recorder would come.

One evening I was not at home when Bobby and two others came over. My wife ushered them in, showed Bobby where the tape recorder was, delivered the refreshments (as these were adults, a bottle of vodka), and politely retired. When she came back later, she found the men rather inebriated. They realized it too, and decorously left. Needless to say, that kind of evening was never repeated, but the tape they left behind contained some of the best material in this collection.

As in any collecting experience, forays into the field were not always successful. Perhaps my most prominent failure was with James Douglas, a man who worked across the street at the Morris Animal Home. Douglas (as all called him) was a well-spoken man, extremely intelligent, proud of his education (he had completed high school and had a profession as mechanic), and was a veritable storehouse of folklore. The very first time I explained to him what I was attempting to do, he understood completely. But he decided he was going to have some fun with the whole affair. He would think up the most tempting bit of lore and whenever he would see me without my notebook, he would casually walk over to me and rattle it off. Yet when he saw me with my notebook, he would run off cackling. Not even the ruse of carrying a small notebook concealed in a pocket would work, because when he saw me start to get it out, he would rattle off so many things so quickly that I would be unable to get most of them down. This was a grand kind of joke and gave the other denizens of the street a big laugh at my expense; as they sat around in their customary seats, their portable chairs in front of the Animal Home.

"Blood," one of the finest toast tellers, would do the same thing. He knew that I had been actively searching for someone who knew the toast about the James brothers. One evening at Alice's Playhouse he sauntered over, took a deep breath, delivered a marvelously full text that lasted for fully fifteen minutes, tipped his hat, and danced down the street. He knew at least ten others and he told them well, but he never recorded for me. I heard that if I would pay him five dollars (he had heard wrongly that I had paid one of my informants) he would record for me.

I found out early that when I went more than two blocks away from the area in which I was known, I ran into a stone wall. To many Negroes in this section of Philadelphia, a white man is either a policeman, a landlord, or a bill collector. Thus most of this collection was gathered from within two city blocks of the house on Iseminger Street. I never went farther east than Twelfth Street, farther north than Pine, farther south than South Street, and farther west than Juniper. I frequently was able to collect from some who lived farther away, but only when they were with people I already knew and had collected from. I did not make great efforts to become known outside Camingerly because I found a wealth of material right there, and because going elsewhere was too often unpleasant and threatening.

Since I had had little field experience at the time and that primarily in search of ballads I had neither learned nor evolved a set technique for collecting. My song-hunting trips and my ongoing training as a folklorist in the late fifties made me very text-oriented. I felt that my major job of collecting was to get the performances down in whatever way I could.

When I transcribed a tape or looked at what I had recorded in my notebooks, I sensed that too much was lost in the transcription. There was probably no more loss in this than in writing down songs' texts and tunes, but for the latter there was a long tradition of book-renderings, while there wasn't for these materials. At that time in university seminar we were beginning to talk about the importance of recording the cultural context of collectanea. Dr. Leach had been evolving his ideas on the subject and Kenneth Goldstein, then a fellow grad student, had begun to work out the methodology eventually formalized in his *Guide for Field Workers in Folklore*. This new perspective made me ask some questions I otherwise would have neglected, and resulted in the sections of this work on verbal contest and on formulaic composition. But looking back, I remember many important neighborhood conversations concerning the whole process of talk and performance on which I never took a note—indeed, in which I never saw any significance. Furthermore, there were numerous discussions about friendship and filial obligations, or how to live with style, which I similarly ignored, much to the detriment of the presentation of my data.

In a certain sense, my sights were too wide at the time. Though the material in the young men's performances was most exciting to me, I persisted in trying to collect from the older members of the community, especially the women. In this I failed for the most part, and for reasons I only figured out after the experience was over. If I had followed the advice of my co-adviser, Tris Coffin, to center on the lore of the men (as this book does), I might have been able to give a feeling for the neighborhood setting more successfully. But I make these remarks after spending a number of years in the field in the British West Indies—time that allowed me to see this material in cross-cultural perspective and to work out a more methodical and economical technique of collecting.

This book, then, is the record of an experience, a prolonged encounter which has shaped so much of my life since. I realize now that my major problem in analyzing the lore was that I didn't know enough about Afro-Americans elsewhere. I have since done work in Texas and the British West Indies that in many ways is a follow-up on the Camingerly work and in other ways a development of some of the perceptions I made there. In this revision I have incorporated some of the perspectives derived from my subsequent work, especially in regard to the importance of friendship networks and of creativity as a device for social approval.

Section **1: the tellers**

1 Neighbors and Relations

for residents in Camingerly, life is a series of oppositions, combats, polarities. Life is suffused with a constant need to compete in order to cope, for the Negro residents are confronted with the ever present black-white polarity in which they find themselves in a socially subordinated and economically deprived position. But this is not the only polarity operating in their lives. In fact, the strong division that exists between the men and the women is more constantly experienced in their day-to-day lives. Interpersonal rivalries and contests between members of the same sex are legion. Out of such an environment emerges a view of life in which contest or coercion is expected in any interpersonal encounter.

However, existence in Camingerly is not unstable and totally divisive. Once the coercion model of life is adopted, all manner of techniques are devised by which cooperation and concord become possible. Furthermore, a contest orientation is not necessarily a constantly hostile one. Under the most anxious conditions, to be sure, fights and even street battles arise out of these tensions. But on a day-to-day basis, contest becomes an effective launching ground for creative as well as cooperative activities. In spite of the pervasive white attitude imposing the label of instability on the Negro family and the black ghetto community, many stable (and stabilizing) features are to be observed there.

16

To understand the quality of the interpersonal lives of the Camingerly residents it is necessary to recognize the tremendous number of potentially meaningful relationships a person may have. Whites tend to see the Negro family in pathological terms because the relationships on which the middle-class notion of stability (between parents of both sexes and their children) is predicated is either noticeably absent or an apparent failure. Whites tend to see emotional stability arising from feelings of trust and its concomitant communication as they are established between parents and their offspring. Furthermore, it is assumed that through this kind of constant relationship, a successful ego identity is established. Therefore, it seems to observing whites that blacks, and especially black men, have male identity problems because there is commonly no male parent in the home on any constant basis, and hence no image-producing older figure with whom boys may identify. This point of view ignores a great many salient features of urban black life.

There is no doubt that the most stable element in the interpersonal lives of Negro children is the maternal figure in the home. Because she has been so strong a center of gravity for most young people in Camingerly, the maternal figure remains the major personage in the important relationships, and this maternal focus is strongly reflected in their traditional expressions. On the other hand, many other individuals take an important place in the lives of the young and contribute to the sense of stability. For boys, many older males in the community—if not in the home—provide a strong male image and patterns of life the boys are able to emulate, thereby developing their masculine identities. Since so much of the life of the young, especially the male children, is spent playing and talking and running errands on the streets, the absence of a permanent man in the house does not create the emotional deprivation so often imputed to their lives.

Middle-class America predicates adequate emotional strength on the ability to develop depth relationships that grow out of the model parent-child involvement. Lower-class Afro-American culture offers an alternative that approaches the ideals and attitudes of the extended family (and is therefore perhaps a legacy of a rural Southern background). While the white middle class seeks to keep its children off the streets and in the homes, playing with a limited number of other children and developing some meaningful and continuing play relationship (which develop into the early dating and "going steady" pattern), black mothers teach their children to get out of the home and onto the streets. There they learn to develop relationships of a conventional nature with a potentially large number of their peers. The breadth of relationships is thus more important than the depth.

This breadth approach is engineered through many people, members of the family or friends, who may take care of the smaller children. Older women are, of course, the usual resource in such a situation, but frequently they have developed satellite arrangements by which a young person (usually but by no means always a girl) who knows the rules of street life will keep an eye on the younger children. The importance of this figure cannot be overstressed, for these older children not only assure the safety of the younger ones but they also teach and lead them in games and imaginative play activities. These "little mamas" are thus given an early introduction to responsibility, which serves in part as an initiation into the self-sufficient female role.

At about the same age as these girls receive responsibility, the boys are assumed to have enough sense to make their way around the neighborhood successfully and to keep out of trouble. There are many older boys and young men in the neighborhood who provide the model on which the boy begins to fashion his life. One of the crucial figures in the role-formation process is the gang leader, for the primary grouping of the boys is gang like—that is, their play activities tend toward group endeavors and side-taking games. Other male figures of equal importance are the pimp or hustler, who lives with great style and appears to have totally defeated the problems of living on the streets through the exercise of his wits, and the bully, who seems to persist because of his strength and fighting abilities. One of the features of the pimp type, the sharp dresser who does everything with spirit and style, is his ability with words. In this regard he is the model of the good talker, whose role we shall investigate at some length in this work.

All these features of life emphasize the importance of resilience in the face of the constant possibility of change. The individual, child or adult, finds for many reasons that he must remain mobile. Because of the uncertainty of life, especially economically, a person learns to make as many friends as he can so that he has many people on whom he may rely during tight periods.

However, the countervailing force to this interpersonal arrangement is the assumption that everyone in your network, friends or lovers or family, is almost always trying to manipulate, coerce, or use you. Consequently, life is seen as a constant hustle, and the one who does best is the one who manipulates most and is manipulated least. This is why, to a large number of young men, the pimp is regarded as a culture hero.

This emphasis upon the number of friends one has often leads to acts that publicly advertise cooperation; everyone involved stands to gain by it since you are regarded highly if you can demonstrate your many friends. On the other hand, this friendship arrangement calls for the building of respect and status on the basis of how many people one can refer to as one's friends. This situation leads to a great deal of talk involving the names and activities of others. Gossip may, of course, be a divisive force in the community, especially when its subject is regarded negatively.

There were many ways in which my wife and I became involved in these important friendship networks, often unknowingly. Bobby, of course, relied on us heavily as friends and as resources to enhance his image and broaden his own network. This dependence meant loaning him clothing (Ivy League was the style at that time) and money, as well as the tape recorder. He always referred to me (at least while I was around) as "my cutting man" or "cutty." On one occasion he used his access to our home to take a sheet to an arthritic friend who needed one, neglecting to tell us about the action. With other neighbor-friends we were asked to provide transportation at a couple of weddings in the neighborhood, and, more dramatically, for hospital-bound pregnant women. Further, our house became something of a center of operations for the family next door.

All such involvements were welcome as they were evidence of fulfilling relationships for us. But certain encounters were somewhat less welcome. One of our young friends, Bobby's eighteen-year-old aunt, Sissy, came to my wife one day with a story about friends of ours, a white couple recently moved to the neighborhood. She said that while she had been visiting at their home the woman had begun crying and had run upstairs, thrown herself on the bed in front of her husband, sobbing and claiming that he didn't love her any more. We never figured out what Sissy's objective or expectations were (other than being able to show that she was privy to what was going on in that household), but we were amused and a little frightened to find that she had told the other couple exactly the same story about us. Maintaining such friendships was often a delicate matter.

One of the results of the ambivalent attitudes toward friends and family is that on certain occasions fear of exploitation overcomes need for friends. This attitude often rules man-woman relationships and has resulted in a high degree of active distrust between the sexes. Because of this, but unrecognized by me at the time, my relations with the women in the neighborhood (especially the older ones) were usually very restrained and respectful. The image the older women had of themselves demanded respect; but more than that, they betrayed a real wariness of me and my questions and observations, an attitude undoubtedly due to my sex and the pigmentation of my skin. Consequently, my understanding of the social structure of the community is strongly biased by the view of life of the young men whom I came to know best and in whose friendship networks I was most fully included.

Nevertheless, any study of the neighborhood must take into account the tremendous psychological and economic importance of the maternal figure. Though the young people have a great number of influences outside the home, the dominant mother type and the accompanying matrifocal family orientation remain a matter of emotional and attitudinal significance throughout the lives of everyone, even long after they are no longer a functional member of this type of mother-centered household. Thus it is necessary to discuss at some length the role of women in Camingerly.

A large majority of the women in the neighborhood are either not married or not living with a man on a continuing basis. The women not only assume all of the usual motherly roles of cooking, keeping house, and providing a sense of order of the family, but also those usually associated with the father: providing discipline and income. Even in homes where a man lives with a woman, the woman seems to assume most of these roles.

This is not an unusual situation among Negroes in the United States. Similar family units have been noted by virtually every sociological study made of lower-class black communities. However, the tendency to focus on this family structure as the pathological source of the Negro situation, brought to a head in the Moynihan Report,[1] has recently come under fire, especially by militant blacks. Illustrative of this reaction is the study *Black Families in White America* by Andrew Billingsley. He notes:

> This system has existed since early slavery, and because of modern hiring practices, social attitudes, and methods of obtaining relief from the state, will remain. The Negro woman is capable of earning a more regular income than is the man. They can get domestic work any time they wish. If they take commercial training in high school there is no difficulty in getting a secretarial job upon graduation. Even with only a partial high school education some companies will take Negro girls as clerks. If a girl has a child, custom provides that she can always find someone to care for it, her mother or some other older woman, if she cares to continue to work. If she doesn't the state will pay her a subsistence allowance for herself and each child; that is, if she has no one "living" with her, or providing visible, adequate support for the children. Thus, the

1. Rainwater and Yancey, *The Moynihan Report and the Politics of Controversy.*

women of the community can regard themselves as financially independent in one way or another.

It is not surprising then that under such a system a woman hesitates to marry, except where she can be sure, in some way, that the man she marries will be able to provide for her (and himself) better than she herself can. Furthermore, because of a natural bias (perhaps inherited from farm life) that having children is beneficial (to provide in old age is the rationale often given) plus the incentive provided by state relief laws, most of the children in the neighborhood are born out of wedlock. (p. 31)

Just how this situation came into being has been the subject of some controversy. Melville J. Herskovits in his search for Africanisms saw the family structure as a reinterpretation of certain African patterns.[2] But this theory was heatedly (and successfully) disputed by E. Franklin Frazier in his *The Negro Family in the United States.* He relates the situation to the effects of the slave system upon the Negro family. Women were more highly valued on a plantation, he tells us, because of their breeding capacities and their ability to perform most of the same jobs as the men (especially during harvest). The Negro, further, could not marry legally because this would have given him legal rights. As the production of more slaves was desirable, the slave owners encouraged free sexual habits among their chattels while denying them the benefit of marriage vows. They were even known to increase the Negro population by the addition of their own seed (though this practice is perhaps overstressed by critics of the "old order").

As Frazier brings out, nothing since the liberation of the slaves has militated to change the social system formulated under it. As a matter of fact, much of the father-dominated family life that was fostered then was eliminated by social forces after the Civil War. Suddenly the Negroes found themselves freed, but without any means of livelihood. Many were able to sharecrop or buy or rent land. This group, though to some extent mother-oriented, has more of the basic pattern of European family life.

2. Most notably in his *Myth of the Negro Past,* especially pp. 173 ff.

On the other hand, for a large group, "as the old order crumbled, thousands of Negro men and women began to wander aimlessly about the country or in search of adventure and work in army camps and cities" (Frazier, p. 209). This group grew each time some disaster, such as drought or depression, drove the agricultural Negro from his land, especially after the depressions of 1879 and 1929. When new factories opened during the industrial expansion in the north in the early twentieth century many Negroes came north in search of employment. The manpower shortage of World War II opened up jobs and opportunities that had never existed before for Negroes and intensified the northward movement. During less crucial periods, this migratory group usually went from farm to lumber to turpentine camps, or from railroad gangs to the towns or cities. There was a large dispossessed class of people who wandered about the country looking for whatever work they could find. Idleness, poverty, and the tensions resulting from these problems prevailed. The dispossessed, developing upon certain features of the mother-oriented family (functional in the earlier slave society), formed new attitudes in relations with each other, especially in regard to sex and crime and violence. The anonymity afforded by the migrant nature of their lives gave them almost complete freedom from social controls within their own ranks.

This freedom is not unusual among lower-class Negroes living in urban areas. It is but one result of the seething drama of the Negro under slavery and since; a story of their transportation to the United States as slaves, of their subjugation, their freedom, and of an uprooted people exposed to new social situations without understanding them, and the subsequent migrations around the country looking for ways to earn a living.

The older members of the Camingerly neighborhood were actors in this great social drama; the younger members were born of it. Many of the younger members, as well as the older, were born on farms in the South. Some, such as Sam Stogie, had experienced much during their long lives. Sam had been born on a farm and had worked there off and on for many years. He had worked in lumber camps, turpentine camps, as a stevedore, a railroad worker. Others told the same story.

The women came when the men sent for them. Eula came from North Carolina with her first child. Eugenia came with her husband, Charlie, a blind street singer, playing the streets from Georgia to Chicago and finally settling in Philadelphia. Gladys came with her father when she was ten. He had been a farmer in Virginia and had come north to find work when he lost the farm. With them came their attitude toward the family.

Because the woman has the greater financial independence, she tends to develop a personality that is positive, forthright, aware of her more flexible position. She knows that she is in many ways in command of the male, and she often expresses it by alternating attitudes of enticement and disdain. As a woman gets older, much of this dominating attitude is transferred to the raising of her children. Before she is ready, however, to resign sexual byplay, she may have many children. As children tend to restrict her activities, she often will turn them over to her own mother or some other older relative experienced in childrearing.

This older woman has often been designated as the center of the Negro concept of the family.

> The Negro grandmother's importance is due to the fact not only that she has been the "oldest head in a maternal family organization but also her position as 'granny' or midwife among a simple peasant folk." As the repository of folk-wisdom concerning the inscrutable ways of nature, the grandmother has been depended upon by mothers to ease the pains of childbirth and ward off the dangers of ill luck (Frazier, p. 153).

This is especially true in rural society. It is a situation that probably stems from the slavery system, for it was the "granny" who raised not only her own children but often many of the young, those who were needed in the fields or in the house, or who were the children of her owners.

Eula, who was the most dramatic of these "mammy" figures in our neighborhood, had thirteen children; many of them, after moving to places of their own, had sent some of their children to be raised by her. She had living with her at the time

of this study three of her own children, two children of another daughter, plus numerous others who would come for
a short stay. Her household was in constant flux. The boys she
had raised often came to see her, to bring her presents and to
help keep her house in good repair (something in which she
took great pride). Even with those of her children not living
with her, she regarded it within her province to teach them
manners and good habits, and generally to "keep them in line."
Once she publicly "broomed" one of her daughters who lived
close by for not keeping a clean house. She was looked to by
many of her female neighbors as a great help in controlling
their children and as the person to consult in case of sickness
or emergency. In any questionable decision, however, she
tried not to "meddle in other people's business." (Because of
crowded housing, privacy is much wished for but seldom ob-
tained. It is only the older women who don't seem to care for
gossip as much as they value maintaining their own privacy.)

Eula is an extremely forthright, positive woman, having
channeled her energies into her dominant relationship with her
family and neighbors. Naturally, women in the neighborhood
who are in an equally dominant role react to her negatively.
Foremost of these is Eugenia, a "granny" herself in many
respects.

Eugenia had lived two doors from Eula but had moved further down the street before I moved into the area. She is the
mother and grandmother of many children. She is obviously
an extremely strong family woman from the stories she tells
and from the letters and support she receives from her children. They are living in different parts of the world (one son
in the army, another in the navy). She finds full expression of
her expansive feelings through her activities in the church, at
which she serves sometimes as preacher, sometimes as song
leader, and always as spiritual healer. People from all over the
East come to consult her on the problems of illness, physical
and spiritual. Both are regarded by her as curable by the same
method—prayer. Her "family," then, is large and constantly
fluctuating, people coming to her for the wisdom of the ages
(or the aged, as it were). Eula seems to resent her power (and
perhaps her income) and has called her a "witch woman." Eu-

genia in turn envies Eula in having her own family around her. She indicated this when she tried to adopt foster children, but she couldn't at that time because she was not married, her husband having died some years earlier. I have seen such rivalries result in violence (though not as often of course as among younger women), but in this case the only expression was slur and disdain.

Eugenia married a man who had been boarding with her and who took to sleeping overnight. She said that she would not allow any man to stay with her without getting married. In this she does not echo the attitudes of most of the women in the neighborhood. There are, to be sure, many marriages among its members, but for different reasons. There does not seem to be much relationship between sex or even having a family and the legal sanction. Marriage is generally regarded as an act of love, in which one vows to live with another for life (even though in practice this does not usually work out).

Margaret, eighteen, and Petey, sixteen, were married after Margaret had already borne him one child and conceived another. At their wedding, Margaret's mother marched down the aisle holding their baby girl and they stood at the altar proudly watching the ceremony. It seemed to be regarded as an announcement to their friends that they were solemnizing their union, and that they were doing it properly (especially from the white point of view). They had all the trappings of a traditional wedding, the flowing white dress, the veil, the descent down the church steps, the throwing of rice, the horn-tooting ride to the reception, the cutting of the wedding cake. The reception was held in the same building as the wedding, so after the ceremony the happy couple exited to the front steps, had rice thrown at them, got into cars, drove around the neighborhood in a wide circle with appropriate sound effects, and returned to continue the festivities.

Some of the other young people, as much through envy as conviction, followed suit. Yet in no way can it be considered a movement away from the basically mother-oriented family organization, or the very free attitude toward sexual relations and the conception of children. In families where the man has been able to provide a steady income, family life more nearly conforms to the European middle-class pattern. Yet even those families don't seem to attach any stigma to others having sexual relations apart from marriage.

Having children, whether in or out of wedlock, is considered the highest good. The more children one can take credit for, the more pride one has in one's capacities. This attitude may be a further residuum of slavery days when the Negro woman was encouraged to breed as often as possible. On the other hand, the attitude is characteristic of many agricultural societies.

No matter what the historical source, both men and women are unwilling to use contraceptives. As in rural society, children in the city are looked upon as possible economic assets to help the mother in old age, if not before. (However, this seldom works out, as it is difficult enough for each to provide for himself. The state must consequently assume the burden of providing for the aged.) The functional reason for the large family has passed, yet all its trappings remain.

There is still a great stigma attached to birth control, too, because both men and women see the essence of their sexual identities in the ability to produce children. Eula's daughter Constance is very defensive about the fact that Bobby is her only child. Those with no children at all seem to feel like pariahs. Sissy, Constance's sister, though she is only eighteen, is quite conscious of not having a child (most of her contemporaries have at least one by this time). For a long time she went about saying that she had been sick and in the hospital and had one breast amputated and that was why she hadn't yet had a baby. She later told everyone that she was pregnant. All of these stories were denied by Eula. My wife and Sissy had many conversations on the subject of children and Sissy could never understand why my wife did not want any yet.

The women see men as inconstant and weak, "no good." This naturally has an effect upon rearing attitudes. Boys will grow up to be men and must consequently be placed at an emotional distance. Girls have to be taught about the treachery of men. Boys will have to leave the home eventually, or submit to the emasculating influence of their mothers; girls are potentially permanent and loyal members of the household, and they get the greater part of mother's attention and affection.

In a psychosocial study of New Orleans Negroes, *The Eighth Generation,* by Rohrer and Edmondson this situation is revealingly commented upon:

> It does not appear that they [the boys] get markedly different maternal treatment from that accorded to little girls, but it seems clear that vesting all parental authority in a woman would have rather different consequences for boys and girls, and the spirit of rebellion against authority so prominent in the gang is mainly derived from this source. The matriarchs make no bones about their preference for little girls, and while they manifest real affection for their boy children, they are clearly convinced that all little boys must inexorably and deplorably become men, with all the pathologies of that sex. (p. 158)

Women in Camingerly, before they achieve full matrifocal status, are not in absolute agreement on this last point. It is perhaps an important rationale for the strong emotional position of the older women. The women in the neighborhood tend to cling together, except when a clash between matriarchs occurs. The women visit back and forth, and there seems to be a depth of affection in their relations with each other that I never perceived between the men. The command of the younger women by the older women begins at childhood, often remains throughout the life of the mother, and may be fanatically observed by both mothers and daughters. This close relationship does not include men. They are outsiders except as they conform to the demands of subservience by the matriarch, thus producing the passive, masochistic, subservient Negro common during slavery days but becoming less so now.

Men are regarded by the women as untrustworthy for the most part. An active division of sexes is thus created which is brooked only by temporary alliances. Even then, the women sense their superior position and seem to enter the situation for the sensual pleasure involved more than to build any sort of relationship. The state of Pennsylvania, though guided by humanitarian aims, has provided laws that unfortunately encourage these sensually oriented, temporary relationships. Welfare has not only made the woman with children financially independent, but it has insisted that in order to get money, a man should not be living with her. The law then seems to foster the male-female dichotomy.

This family structure continues in great part because the Negro man cannot find employment that pays sufficient wages to support his woman and children in the manner in which they can provide for themselves. Even though factory work has opened up new jobs for unskilled Negro males, it is still very difficult for the average man to get a steady job without some kind of special training. Often when skills are developed through vocational schools, they are useless because of a color line drawn by many factories and some unions. Most of the men in the neighborhood do odd jobs for subsistence. The younger men often are able to get seasonal jobs, such as working for four or five months in the spring at a factory in Camden assembling outdoor summer furniture. Both men and women during harvest season take farm buses into the New Jersey countryside to pick crops, which, though paying poorly, has the advantage of the "kindness" of the farmers who parcel out damaged, unmarketable produce to the pickers, which they in turn sell to their neighbors.

The men, because of the economic and psychological pressures they have felt since slavery, are still leading a mobile existence. Even the young men have long histories of wandering, sometimes to find work, sometimes just for adventure. Bobby and Charley, two of my finest informants, had gone to Florida together. Victor, a member of one of the many quartets that used to come to our house, went down to Richmond, Virginia, on a lark, got into a crap game, killed a man in a fight, and is now in jail in that state. Arthur also went to Virginia to go into the tonsorial business, but returned after "having some fun."

This ability to be mobile makes the Negro male very adaptable to army life. Since the armed services have become integrated, they offer the men one of the best possibilities for consistent employment and even advancement. Many of the boys who formerly lived in the neighborhood are in the services as a career. Bobby attempted to enlist on a number of occasions but always failed the examinations. There are a number of other reasons why the services continue to attract the men. Many of the adolescents regard the uniform as having "style." But the major reason is that the armed services are strangely in tune with the essentially heroic world view the men have, a view which results in the men's creation of a totally male world outside the home—in poolhalls and barbershops, in saloons and on street corners.

The lower-class Negro man is confronted with a number of social and psychological impediments in establishing a firm sense of his own masculine and cultural identity. As mentioned, his situation as a black man in a white man's world tends to aggravate whatever feelings of insufficiency he may have. These insecurities are also activated in most of his contacts with the opposite sex. Even his relationship with the woman or women who have raised him is suffused with the problems of psychological domination and at least a latent sense of rejection stemming from his being an unreliable male. Distrust between the sexes runs very deep in lower-class black culture. Young girls are taught early and often that men are not to be trusted—and the lesson is carefully explained in the presence of the boy children. As soon as the boys become denizens of the street they begin to hear the contrary story from older boys, and the seeds of the lesson usually take root. The boys thus learn quite early that they are not as welcome in the home as the girls, and they begin to spend much of their time away from the home. This development is one of those self-fulfilling prophecies, for the maternal figure expects it but in many ways also sees it as a betrayal.

As the black man grows up, he is progressively rejective as a man by the women in the matriarchy, producing intense feelings of anxiety and rootlessness around the beginning of adolescence, which often lead to a self-destructive attitude and an open resorting to the totally male security of the gang. In the gang the adolescent can find both a meaningful model for masculine activity and an environment in which he can test his emerging feelings. The gangs, in spite of their bad publicity, do provide adolescent boys with a place of their own and permit the trying-on of the male mask and enactment of male motives.

The adolescent engages in gang activities knowing they are condemned, not only by white man's laws but also by the women in his house. Seeking this kind of heroic male environment is in part a reaction to the emotional dominance of the mother or grandmother. The adolescent male learns that women, while untrustworthy, are useful and usable objects. They can make money for you, and they can enhance your stylish image, especially if you are seen in the company of a stylish woman. And they can make babies for you. But they *are* untrustworthy, always trying to outhustle you, and so you must learn to dominate and scorn them, not to rely on them too heavily and to move on to another when the need arises. In a very real sense this is a part of the mother figure's self-fulfilling prophecy, for it means that in the life of the men there will be many women but only one mama—that his ultimate allegiance to her will remain. Consequently, the acts that men see as getting back at women by coercing and manipulating them actually demonstrate, at least in part, the continuing emotional dominance of mama.

The totally male world of the gang, which soon passes, is continued in the pattern of life that leads away from the heterosexual environment to the social round of poolhall and barbershop (the latter is often the center of male talking activity). This must be regarded, at least in part, as a rejection of female dominance in the home—but its existence means that there is a alternative male image which is observable to growing boys. In male company there is the opportunity for one to express virility, through both talk and action. What Rohrer and Edmondson say of gangs and gang values is really true of all the male social arrangements, organized and *ad hoc*, in which the young men become involved:

> Thus an organizational form that springs from the little boy's search for a masculinity he cannot find at home becomes first a protest against femininity and then an assertion of hypervirility. On the way it acquires a structuring

in which the aspirations and goals of the matriarchy or the middle class are seen as soft, effeminate, and despicable. The gang ideology of masculine independence is formed from these perceptions, and the gang then sees its common enemy not as a class, nor even perhaps as a sex, but as the "feminine principle" in society.[3]

The most common expression of this antifeminine attitude is in the rough talk which naturally goes on in adolescent and postadolescent male groups. Obscene references are forbidden in the matrifocal home. Consequently, one of the important dimensions of cursing is the rejection of the "feminine principle." This is made plain by the content of the word-play ritual called "playing the dozens," through which adolescent males learn to express dirision wittily. "Playing," which will be described at greater length in Chapter 3, is a series of ritual insults, usually obscene, generally directed by one against the mother of another in the group.

This rejection of the feminine is even clearer in the most common obscenity of the men: "motherfucker." In this word one can see in telescoped form the great depth of ambivalence associated by the men with motherhood and their own mothers. As noted, the system calls for a rejection of the feminine by the men and a concomitant mistrust of all women. But there is an often voiced and continuing respect for whoever is called Mama, a feeling strongly encouraged by the older women in the group. This, however, also carries a certain amount of ambivalence with it, for though an attitude of love and respect remains, Mama has often been the source of the first feelings of rejection. Therefore she is implicated as contributing to the feminine principle and so her boy carries this strong ambivalence into every encounter with her, even when he is 35 or 45 years old. That this ambivalence remains a psychological problem all through a man's life is strongly implied by the continuing focus on the ambivalent term motherfucker (ambivalent in that it may be either a praising or damning term depending on its context of usage) and on the explosive nature

3. Rohrer and Edmondson, *The Eighth Generation*, p. 163.

of someone who begins to play the dozens in the postadolescent years.[4]

But the problem for the young men seems to be not so much that they are caught in ambivalence toward women but that their economic situation makes it very difficult for them to aggress against women (or the world in general) in many creative ways. Thus, anxieties which arise out of their unresolved status too often drive them to destructive activities that result in further rejection by women or by society in general—in the latter case, often through police harassment and incarceration.

I do not mean to argue that there is nothing fulfilling in the lives of the young men. A life pattern develops which, in spite of limited economic opportunities, involves a great many meaningful interpersonal experiences. Life, seen as a perpetual adventure, has to be viewed in "hustle" terms. Viewing life in terms of manipulation can lead to visions of infinite personal creativity, for the world may be shaped to one's own beautiful image, even if this usually occurs only in dreams. Each encounter is potentially a manipulative act, and where one expects this kind of game of others and feels it is expected of him, life becomes in a sense a constant performance. In certain cases this approach defeats a person because the state of heightened sensitivity to the presence of others makes him too self-conscious of his inabilities. On the other hand, those who excel at such performances must be regarded as tremendously talented and creative individuals, especially in view of the demands of their audience. This point is made repeatedly in the stories concerning the heroes of the group, for they are figures who contend successfully in a coercive world. But it is also made in regard to who the boys look up to, both within the community and outside of it.

4. It should be noted that a certain amount of male ambivalence, especially of the love-hate sort, is regarded as essential to the use of obscenities throughout Western culture. Dirty words are commonly conceived of as aggressions against mother, as taking of words which when first produced by the child were viewed as a gift to her, and perverting their direction, thus in a sense "Indian-giving." Obscenities in such a case call attention to the mother-child situation, saying, "Look what you've done to me by rejecting me—but look what I can do to you in return." For more on this line of reasoning see Edmund Bergler, "Obscene Words," *Psychoanalytic Quarterly*, V (1936), pp. 236 ff.

The heroes of the young men are "bad men" like the bully Stackolee, or Jesse James, or are tricksters like Shine and the Signifying Monkey. Both of these hero types flaunt the rules of established order to demonstrate their ability to cope in the most adverse circumstances. They often embody rebellious (indeed diabolic) motives in their rejection of rules. By rejecting society in general, especially white men's rules, they obviously provide a model of behavior observable in many gang activities. We cannot doubt that such criteria operate in the imaginations of many young men when one hears them talk animatedly about pleasures and hazards of gang activity. But the heroes of their stories are not admired so much for their antiauthoritarian actions as for their ability to persist and manipulate others, and through these efforts, to live with style.

Gangs offer an organization through which these motives can be acted upon sometimes (and talked about a great deal). Given this heroic orientation, what becomes most highly valued is the adventurer, the fighter, and the artful talker, individuals who are able to contend in a coercive world. Gang members often act directly in terms of these values. Thus, in gang activity (and later in other unlawful acts) the Negro is striking out against an almost impersonal foe, and he is able to come off fairly undamaged in the eyes of his group even if he loses. Being put in jail or getting "sliced up" by a group you don't know personally is just as manly as winning. Physical violence is preferred to cowardice. But all this contention would not be worth it if the individual boy did not feel the gang's protection in the neighborhood.

The gang never has been a highly organized machine, however. It is a loosely formed grouping with leaders who are acknowledged and, in hostile situations, acclaimed. But the gang does function as more than just protection under the threat of aggression from other such groups. It also gives boys in the area a sense of place and a constant set of friends upon whom they can rely. The gang, like many other totally male groups, promotes a kind of expressive interaction in which masculinity is in constant question and therefore must constantly be proven by word or deed.

The heroic vision of life fostered within the gang continues

long after gang membership dissolves. One encounters the
same heroes having their praises sung and in the same obscene
and boastful form, and this from men who have grown too old
(by their own admission) for gang membership. However,
though a young man no longer belongs to a gang, often little
else in his daily life has changed. Though he may have developed a regular relationship with his "old lady" or though he
may have occasional employment, when he is in the neighborhood he still keeps company primarily with his male
friends.

Furthermore, nothing has been introduced into the lives of
the young men to change their view of the coercive nature of
interpersonal life, and therefore the heroic-contest method
of meeting situations remains functional. Encounters with
women on a sociosexual basis reinforce the idea of a coercive
world, for they too share this coercive view of life and see
man-woman relationships in contest terms. Since the women
often carry into such relationships an understanding of their
superior ability to provide money, they often look for something other than security from men; it may be a good time, or
sexual satisfaction, but it must be achieved through a coercive
use of womanly guile or wits. This is understood by the men
and is a subject of much talk among themselves. But in the
male environment, this sort of talk often becomes imbued
with the all-male, supermasculine approach.

It is hardly surprising that so many stories, jokes, and toasts
are concerned with the sexual feats of the men. One informant,
"Kid," who has had his share of bad experiences with women's
fickleness and demands, says only half kiddingly:

> Yeah, I'm fast. I'm so fast, a girl told me one time, she said,
> "Kid, now if you can get some cock 'fore my mother get
> back home, and she's coming 'round the corner right now,
> you can have it." So I said, "Lay down." She laid down, I
> pushed the light switch, got undressed, jumped in bed,
> busted two nuts, got dressed, and got outside the room
> before that room got dark.

Though this kind of boasting is rarely done in front of the
women, an equally overt but not quite so raw verbal byplay

has developed. The male makes some kind of "smart" overture to a woman that is either ignored or answered in equally "smart" but negative terms. Cleverness and strength of language become ends in themselves because the woman is asking the man to prove his masculinity and he can do so by words as well as by actions.

Bobby, from time to time concerned with my apparent ineptness with the opposite sex, would give me long lectures on how one had to "deal rough" with women. He would say, "Lookahere, bitch, when I say jump you jump, 'cause I didn't come here to fool around. I come for business," or something of that tone. Although Bobby's words were almost always much bigger than his deeds, in many other cases actual physical violence is the only way the man can finally subdue the woman, "put her in her place."

The men's attitude toward virility is shown clearly by the fact that they are so proud when they make a girl pregnant. Even in cases where they cannot be sure that they are the father (how could they be when they argue that you can't trust any woman in matters of this sort?), they will claim to be so and be proud of it.

Similarly, choices of professions and real-life heroes are dictated by the manliness of the activity. Of the fields open to Negro men, the ones they have chosen and excelled in are the ones in which performance is emphasized. The heroes of the Negro are the ones who pioneer and excel, and who exhibit their control in the "classiest" way. Athletics is the most obvious activity calling for performance, and the greatest heroes of the neighborhood are Willie Mays and Hank Aaron and other baseball players who have made a name for themselves. Boxing was one of the sports in which Negroes were able to excel earliest, and Sugar Ray Robinson still excites great admiration, because of both his athletic ability and his style of life.

The profession in which Negroes made their earliest gains is entertainment. Many fixed conceptions about the Negro concern their entertainment abilities, their musical sense, their ability to hold a tune, their rhythmic sense. Naturally, these are just as false as fixed conceptions about any group, but the fact that the white world has this view of the Negro has made it possible for certain Negroes to make a success in the entertainment field—and has created a desire on the part of an unnaturally large number of Negroes to make a success on the stage. Nearly every boy who can sing belongs to a quartet, and every quartet dreams of professional success, which many of them are getting through rock-and-roll recordings. Kid features himself a professional comedian. Singers, song writers, dancers are to be found everywhere in the Camingerly area. The fact that Charley had been in a group (The Turbans) that made a record made him the object of much respect in the neighborhood.

Exhibitionism for purposes of attraction is manifested in many aspects of Camingerly life from gang activity to the style of playing cards, pool, baseball, or any contest activity. Style of living is more important than life itself. Men say in their boasts and toasts, "I'm a mean motherfucker and I don't mind dying," and one cannot doubt that there is a good deal of truth to their words. It *is* more important for many of them to feel mean or tough (anything good is "tough," as "that was a tough movie") than for them to go on living.

Most noticeable to outsiders is the individual's manner of dress and way of walking. His cock-of-the-walk attitude is echoed in his clothes; he reflects the trends in men's fashions (indeed, he has sometimes dictated these trends); but he dresses in brighter colors in more daring combinations than whites generally do. As is clear from the toasts, he is very conscious of the sharp dresser. The Signifying Monkey's clothes are described in detail:

> Now a few stalks shook and a few leaves fell,
> Up popped the monkey one day, 'bout sharp as hell.
> Had on a one-button roll, two-button satch.
> You know, one of them boolhipper coats with a belt in the
> back.

The baboon, too, gets a once-over:

> The baboon stood with a crazy rim.
> Charcoal gray vine with a stingy brim.

Handful of dimes, pocket full of herbs.
Eldorado Cadillac parked at the curb.

Consciousness of dress is further expressed in emphasis on hair style. Negro women for some time have attempted to have their hair straightened so they could wear the same styles as white women. This is still true, but (purportedly because of the influence of boxer Sugar Ray Robinson) the men have taken to having their hair straightened in a pompadour style, called a "process," and more recently the "Afro" or "natural" has come into popularity. Hair is very important in establishing one's sexual identity, whether male or female. It is the very essence of style, even more important than proper clothing.

The idea of living in a contest world thus suffuses the life of young black men. If one viewed the contest solely from the perspective of results it would seem meaningless, since victories in the world are Pyrrhic and short-lived, and therefore provide such small ego gains for men who seem to need such big and permanent ones. But looking at life in such terms would ignore the vital spirit that invests their lives: wanting to try and improvising in a continuing effort to contend effectively. Though the men are often defeated, especially in their encounter with the white world and with their women, their defeats have not taken away their place in the male world; and they have thus persisted in conceiving themselves, at least in some dimension, in contest and performance terms. It is these verbal contests and performances that make up the major portion of this book.

2 Verbal Contest and Creativity

One of the major cultural differences between the white middle class and ghettoized Afro-Americans is that the latter have preserved an oral-aural world view while the former have invested their creative energies and imaginations heavily in books, in the typographic-chirographic world. As we know from many recent works on media, this difference is of much greater importance than simply illustrating the ability or inability to read. In point of fact, there wasn't one Camingerly resident who could not read, but reading simply did not enter their lives very often.

Many ethnocentric judgments about blacks stem from the white man's inability to understand or appreciate the creative aspects of living in an oral atmosphere. He neither understands nor remembers the ways in which an effective talker-performer may strongly influence our attitudes. He does not value words effectively used in speaking events enough to confer high social status on the effective speaker. Good talking capable of totally enlisting the attention and support of an audience is something he regards as dangerous at its worst (associated with demagoguery and dictatorship) or as insincerity at best. Consequently, a good talker as judged by ghetto Negroes is often regarded by whites as hostile and arrogant.

To understand the quality of male life in Camingerly, it is crucial to comprehend the importance and nature of good talk in interpersonal encounters. For it is in this realm that much of the creative life (probably characteristic of many oral-aural cultures) arises and is pursued. Since this is a folkloric phenomenon, it seems necessary to analyze briefly how such traditions operate in any group as part of the process of growth and increased control over the social and natural environments.

Form, order, structure—these are important in creating the psychological situation where instincts otherwise repressed can be exercised on the unreal, yet lifelike, playground of folklore. By creating or utilizing previously created formal unities the individual is able to dupe society into allowing the expression of certain aggressive attitudes that otherwise might remain unuttered or unenacted. No group will allow unchanneled aggression. In one way or another, methods will be developed that will allow a free play of the agonistic impulses of the individual. A balance will be struck between the needs of the community and the needs of the individual, though in many cases that balance will be a precarious one.

Aggression is usually allowed in a play or contest situation. Most of what we call folklore is play in its broadest sense. Such traditions involve us in some dimension in the play world of the game or in the play world of the fictive experience. It then offers us two ways of playing out our aggressions: through the symbolic movements of games and players or through the vicarious dramatic expression of the narrative world. Either play world has restrictive conventions (rules and boundaries and both involve symbolic role playing (mimesis). Both are intimately related to the real world and yet are substantially removed from it by the psychic distance provided by these conventions. The elements of society in our psyches and in our group existence allow this kind of aggressive expression as long as it does not exceed the bounds of the rules. When it does, as in such playlike contest situations as stone throwing among children and gangsterism in adult life, society must step in and end it.

As we grow older, our competitive motives become more complicated and rechanneled. Our playgrounds change from the child's play world to the athletic field, the law courts, and the stock market. These motives remain the same, our strategies and expressions become more diffuse and our motivations more complex as we begin to realize the existence of the intentions. Our symbolic actions become more and more removed from their immediate objective; we increasingly use the more vicarious expressions, viewing the battle and identifying with the contestants rather than engaging in it ourselves.

This growth in strategy and complexity is important for our psychic development. Contest does not exist for itself; it is a mechanism for the dramatic dialectic expression of specific psychic problems, generally brought about by the inherent conflict of the individual living (or trying to live) in society. This conflict has many facets, and the individual's psychic and somatic growth causes these facets to be progressively (rather than simultaneously) developed. Furthermore, "all . . . developmental periods are intimately interrelated and defective development of one phase will serve to make the successful negotiation of a subsequent phase more difficult." [1]

We encounter at a specific period a problem of psychic growth, paralleling a somatic development. This growth and development involves a struggle between opposing forces. We must expect an effective synthesis to come from this struggle. In a fixated state none emerges, and if the synthesis is only partially successful, the next conflict will be harder to fight, and the less chance remains that further syntheses will be effective. We encounter, in situations of this sort, noncommittal syntheses, resolutions that are at best temporary.

Of all of these conflicts, the ones brought on by adolescence are the most crucial and the most difficult because of a tremendous somatic change, a change which insists on an equally radical psychic reorientation. It is this situation that results in initiation ceremonies in many cultures. The problem in Camingerly is that adolescents develop important mechanisms to channel their conflicts in successfully creative albeit heroic directions; but because of social circumstances, postadolescents find it necessary to fall back on certain elements of the adolescent mechanisms, and in many respects the devices are inadequate to help the men find their place in the com-

1. Rohrer and Edmondson, *The Eighth Generation*, p. 87.

munity as men. In regard to the oral dimension of their expressive culture, they find no new areas in which they may utilize the techniques they have developed highly in late adolescence and early adulthood. (This situation has changed somewhat since I collected my data with the growth of black militancy among the ghetto men. Their rhetorical skills have become extremely useful in the developing confrontation with the power structure of the white world. Thus, some of the frustration of the good talkers that I observed in the late fifties has found a creative outlet, though it is not always recognized as such by whites.) In contrast to oral cultures, in our society there are few high-status positions open to the men who have developed high verbal skills (this is one reason why the Negro entertainer is so idealized).

By looking at the wide range of speech activities in Camingerly, it is possible, in part, to see how the good talker develops his skills. One of the first and most anxious situations with which any child finds himself confronted is the inability to control his motor responses. Folklore, especially in the form of rhymes and songs, provides him a controlled context within which he can practice safely with words (one of his major motor problems) to gain some feeling of mastery. When control of the limited word units is achieved, the child, released from the previous anxious situation, experiences pleasure. The formal unit is important in the attainment of this control, as it has provided oral cues which have helped the child remember (rhyme, repetition, meter). Furthermore, the pleasure the control initially gives is relived constantly by recitals of the same piece. We all play over our conquests, children perhaps more than others because their anxieties are greater.

The child's tacit recognition of the importance of words as controlling agents remains a subconscious resource the rest of his life. Words are power, the child learns. The capacity to name and describe gives us the secure feeling of control, even before we learn the power of words strategically used. Our physical growth is paralleled closely by our growing power with words; both are sources of control.

When we subsequently run into other anxiety-producing situations, we tend to use devices that have been successful in the past to conquer them. One of the early victories we keep returning to is our first efforts at power through word control. We constantly use rhymes and other forms of childish wit to channel, control and therefore combat, our otherwise most recurrent anxieties. Especially when we reach adolescence, we revert to childhood expressions to try to control the new social situation brought about by interest in the opposite sex. The subjects of the witticisms are different, but the technique is the same. This is why we tell jokes and make quips about things we otherwise can't talk about.

We use folklore, then, as a familiar weapon for fighting a new battle. Songs, rhymes, and taunts change subject matter, but they retain the forms and formulas of childhood expression. To return to these devices is, in a large sense, regressive.

The Camingerly Negro not only goes through this regressive process when he reaches adolescence, but, because of the necessity of remaining in a male world, he must continue to fight for a sense of control with essentially the same devices he learned in adolescence. This is amply illustrated by the large part rhyming plays in the life of the man of words. He not only uses traditional rhymes as part of his entertainment repertoire, but uses his abilities to insert rhymes that may entertain into any social situation. Such devices as "See you later, alligator" and "After 'while, crocodile" (which I am certain are Negro in origin) are found in much of the public discourse of these men. One day, for instance, while Kid and others were sitting around telling jokes, he said:

> We can sit here and shuck and shive.
> We can sit here and do the split.
> We can sit here and do this.
> We can sit here and shit.

Almost any cliché is stated in rhyme form. Here is a common dialogue routine illustrating this:

> What you mean, jelly bean?
> What I said, cabbage head.

Similar rhyming situations emerge with other expressions:

Me and you, Fu Manchu.
Tell the truth, Snag-a-tooth.
'Nough said, Ted.

This propensity to rhyme found wide use in the days of be-bop (late 1940's and into the 1950's) by disc jockeys. Even to-day, Negro disc jockeys use rhyme to introduce their records, but the technique is not nearly as widespread as it used to be. "Jocko" was a favorite Philadelphia bebop disc jockey, and the rhymed introduction he used for his show remains a part of the lore of Camingerly in a hand-clapping version of "Who Stole the Cardinal's Hat?" ("Who, sir? Me, sir?"):

Be, bebop
This is your Jock
Back on the scene
With a record machine.
Saying "Hoo-popsie-doo,
How do you do?"
When you up, you up,
And when you down, you down,
And when you mess with Jock
You upside down.

The conscious manipulation of words in rhyme for exhibi-tion of masculinity is nowhere clearer than here. Jock is not a man to be "messed with" because he will turn you upside down, put you under his control. Because of a constant need for such expression, the man of words, the good talker, has an important place in the social structure of the group, not only in adolescence but throughout most of his life.

Words are power to him in a very real way. They function powerfully in the sexual battle which is typical of adolescent life. The sexual power of words is, of course, patent. One need only see a popular singer or an effective speaker at work and watch the effect of such language upon women.[2]

2. Puckett, *Folk Beliefs of the Southern Negro*, p. 30, has pointed out that the Negroes of the South were instructed by an older man who was "experienced in the words and ways of courtship, [who could teach] young gallants . . . the way in which they should go in the delicate matter of winning the girl of their choice." This tacit acceptance of the

The men of Camingerly use this inherent power in their most important battles, their verbal contests.

Verbal contest accounts for a large portion of the talk between members of this group. Proverbs, turns of phrase, jokes, almost any manner of discourse is used, not for purposes of discursive communication but as weapons in verbal battle. Any gathering of the men customarily turns into "sounding," a teasing or boasting session. Here for instance is a description by Kid of the kind of talk often heard in poolhalls or barbershops, wherever the men have established their headquarters:

> Just like mounting on the wrong guys down at the poolroom. Cats be coming in there, gambling. Suddenly one of them says, "Suck my ass." He say, "You suck my ass and the box, that way you can't miss my asshole." Cat says, "Sucking ass is out of style, button your lipper, suck my dick awhile." He said, "Sucking dicks ain't no trick. Button your motherfucking mouth up my asshole, nuts and dick." Anything. Just one's trying to get above another one, each time they say something, you know.
>
> "Now you suck my ass." "Ain't nobody fucking with you." "You fuck with me and I'll bust your motherfucking mouth." You might say to him, "Well, you'd be better locked up in a phone booth sandpapering a lion's ass (and that's close contact) than fucking with me." "You'd do better jump in a fire with a gasoline suit on than be jumping on my chest." They say like, "You'd be better in a lion's den with a motherfucking side of beef on your shoulder, than do any fucking with me." Might tell a guy something like, "Don't you know I ain't worrying about you 'cause I'll run up your motherfucking throat, jump down your motherfucking lungs, tap dance on your kidneys, remove your motherfucking appendicizes, move out your goddamn intestines, kill your dick and die, your heart

---

relationship of words and sexual attraction is found in many parts of the world. The whole idea of love letters is anchored here, as is the strategy of the love poem and song. As Legman says: "This is a phenomenon observable not only among other mammals, but throughout animal nature (with the exception of fish, which are mute) . . ."

stop beating." It's just passing speech. Guys don't mean no harm; they just saying it. If people walked past and didn't know you, they'd swear there'd be blows coming. You get used to it. And when somebody say something, just say something back. People that don't know you would figure you're just getting ready to fight. Just passing speech.

"I'ma put something on your ass." You know, just passing speech. Words that just comes naturally, you heard, and heard, and you repeat 'em and repeat 'em. After a guy gets to hanging around so long, he learns them. You find a guy coming in who never cursed in his life, after a month or two, same thing. He come in, say "What you doing, man?" "Fuck my ass." You know, before he came in never cursed in his life. Now every third word he's going to curse. Rabbit's cattin' pool, every second word is "motherfucker." Just passing speech.

With some modification this kind of talk is found in practically every area of social intercourse, both in male groups and between males and females. The terms in which the arguments are waged indicate that the word battles derive their impetus from sexual matters. A verbal attack is called "mounting" or "getting above"; that is, placing the other in the female position. Getting the best of someone is called "putting him down," a similar sexual slur. Winning such a battle not only proves the masculinity of the victor; it conclusively feminizes the other.

The verbal contest exists among the Camingerly children. Taunts, jokes, riddles, all give the child an opportunity to indicate his abilities through the control of words. "Catches" (a form in which a tricker, by means of questions or leading statements or by establishing patterns, leads the answerer into an indefensible position which results in a penalty) illustrate this element most clearly:

> Look up [*other does*].
> Look down [*other does*].
> See my thumb [*holds his thumb up*]?
> Gee, you're dumb.

Could you read?
Yes.
Could you write?
Yes.
Could you smoke your daddy's pipe?

Say "washing machine."
"Washing machine."
I'll bet you five dollars your drawers ain't clean.

The impulse to verbally best someone, coupled with a growing awareness of sex and the complex of emotions that sur-
round it, results among youths in "playing the dozens" in
rhyme. Because this verbal game is an important aspect of
Camingerly agonistic expression and an integral part in the
growth of verbal dexerity, it will be described in some detail.
A discussion seems even more important since the "dozens"
has excited critical attention, some of which has been unin-
formed and misguided. Variously called "playing the dozens,"
"playing," "sounding," and "woofing," this game helps the
young male Negro adapt to his changing world and trains him
for the similar but more complex verbal endeavors of manhood.[3] The terms indicate the procedure involved; "playing"
illustrates that a game or contest is being waged, "sounding"
shows that the game is vocal, and "wolfing" or "woofing" points
out the similarity of the procedure to a dog's bark.

Sounding occurs only in crowds of boys.[4] One insults a
member of another's family; others in the group make disap-
proving sounds to spur on the coming exchange. The one who
has been insulted feels that he must reply with a slur on the
protagonist's family clever enough to defend his honor (and

3. For a consideration of the derivation of this term (along with many
other special slang words found in Camingerly), see the Glossary.
4. One will occasionally find girls making "dozens" remarks, but for the
most part not in the organized fashion of the boys. The boys do not generally play in front of girls, except where one boy is trying to put another
down. In this case the game can lead to a physical fight. Dollard, in an
important article discussed in the Glossary under "Dozens," seems to have
encountered more female players than I have. Sounding certainly could not
perform any similar psychosocial function among females as it does among
males, but the mechanism does exist as an expression of hostility by either
sex.

that of his family). This, of course, leads the other (once again, more because of pressure from the crowd than actual insult) to make further jibes. This proceeds until everyone is bored with the whole affair, until one hits the other (fairly rare), or until some other subject interrupts the proceedings (the usual outcome).

When the combatants are quite young (just entering puberty), they are obviously trying out some of the words and concepts they have overheard and are just beginning to understand. Thus, their contest is liable to be short and uncomplicated, but the pattern is established:

> I hear your mother plays third base for the Phillies.
> Your mother is a bricklayer, and stronger than your father.
> Your mother eats shit.
> Your mother eats shit and mustard.

As sexual awareness grows, the vilification of the mother is changed to sexual matters, the contests become more heated and the insults more noteworthy. Many of them take the form of rhymes or puns, signaling the budding of verbal dexterity which blooms later in the long narrative poem called the "toast" and indicating the necessity of applying strict formal structure to highly volatile matters. A sample of a fracas involving two fourteen- or fifteen-year-olds might run as follows: Someone mentions the name of someone else's mother in the course of a joking conversation—"Constance," for instance. At this point someone in the crowd says, "Yeah, Constance was real good to me last Thursday." Then Constance's son has to reply in kind, "I heard Virginia [the other's mother] lost her titty in a poker game." "Least my mother ain't no cake; everybody get a piece." The other might reply:

> I hate to talk about your mother,
> She's a good old soul.
> She's got a ten-ton pussy
> And a rubber asshole.
> She got hair on her pussy
> That sweep the floor.
> She got knobs on her titties
> That open the door.

And this in turn elicits any of the numerous retorts printed in the following pages. Eventually the boys' verbal dexterity increases to the point where they can achieve more through subtlety and innuendo than through rhymes and obvious puns.

Somewhere between the ages of sixteen and twenty-six playing begins to lose its effect and passes out of frequent use. When someone indicates that he wants to start, the one who is supposed to be insulted may reply, "Oh man, don't play with me." If he needs a more clever retort, he may rely on the proverb, "I laugh, joke, and smoke, but I don't play." Yet the game is never really forgotten. While the boys are still running in groups of their own sex, any argument can be complicated and enlivened by some fleeting derogatory reference to a member of the other's family. It has been reported to me many times that the dozens is often invoked by Negroes in the army, under its restrictive conditions of regimentation. When the dozens is used under such circumstances, it almost invariably leads to a fight. Similarly, when used by older males as a verbal battle in such places as a bar or a poolroom, it also often ends in blows.

Playing functions quite differently among men than among adolescents. Among the older males references to the family of another are fleeting and not necessarily directed against anything specific. Among adolescents, especially the younger ones, the insults are much more rigidly constructed and are directed toward or against certain things. Most prominently, they are concerned with sexual matters. Usually both the rhymes and the taunts are directed against another's mother, alleging sexual wantonness:

> I fucked your mother on an electric wire.
> I made her pussy rise higher and higher.
>
> I fucked your mother between two cans.
> Up jumped a baby and hollered, "Superman."
>
> At least my mother ain't no doorknob, everybody gets a turn.

Sometimes the rhymes just place the other's mother in an embarrassing position:

I saw your mother flying through the air.
I hit her on the ass with a rotten pear.

Another common subject is the effeminacy or homosexuality of father or brother:

Least my father ain't pregnant in the stomach.
Least my brother ain't no store; he take meat in the back.

Whether the game involves rhymes or not, it involves language different from the everyday language of the contestants. Such linguistic (or paralinguistic) elements as changes in pitch, stress, and sometimes syntax, provide the signals of contest. Just as counting-out introduces a children's game, with its suspension of reality, or the phrase "Have you heard the one about . . . ?" leads us into the permissive world of the joke, so when someone makes a dozens type of preliminary remark, he is about to construct a hypothetical playing field on which a verbal contest is to be played.

The linguistic features of the dozens outline the rules of the verbal battle. The rules seem to say, "You can insult my family, but don't exceed the rules because we are dealing with something perilously close to real life." The most prominent linguistic features are (1) the reliance upon formulaic patterns, (2) the use of rhyme within these patterns, and (3) the change of speech rhythms from natural ones to ones that conform to the demands of the formula. These are the strictest boundaries imposed by this game. As the youths learn to use words, any contrived witticism will supply the needed formulaic requirement. Until then, it is psychologically safer to be clever within the confines of the appointed rhyme form.

This point is made convincingly by Martha Wolfenstein in considering the strategy of children's rhyming habits, specifically in regard to the ancestor of the dozens rhyme, the taunt:

What is the function of rhymes in these joking attacks? I would suggest that the first rhyming word has the effect of compelling the utterance of the second, thus reducing the speaker's responsibility. . . . There is a further reduction of responsibility in the use of a rhymed formula: the words are not my own. Moreover the rhyme is apt to induce other children to take it up; the attacker will cease to be alone. It should be added that rhymes are often in themselves funny to young children. Children of three, for instance, may laugh simply at finding two words that rhyme or a word that rhymes with a name. Thus the rhyme affords a façade of harmless joking to facilitate the expression of hostility in the rhymed insult.[5]

The relationship between the taunt and the dozens is an important one, for it points up the fact that the dozens utilizes many devices of the controlled aggression of children. The technique, length, rhyme, meter, and restriction of form are a regression to children's forms; in subject they are wholly adolescent:

> Roses are red,
> Violets are blue.
> I fucked your mama,
> And now it's for you.

The rhyme

> I fucked your mother between two tracks.
> It stung so hard, the train fell back.

is very similar to these lines from a children's rhyme:

> Just before your mother died
> She called you to her side.
> She gave you a pair of drawers.
> Before your father died.
> She put 'em in the sink.
> The sink begin to stink.
> She put 'em on the track.
> The train backed back.
> She put 'em on the fence.
> Ain't seen 'em since.

A device which links the dozens to childhood behavior is that of "signifying." Signifying seems to be a Negro term, in use if not in origin. It can mean any of a number of things; in the

5. Wolfenstein, *Children's Humor*, p. 182.

case of the toast about the signifying monkey, it certainly refers to the trickster's ability to talk with great innuendo, to carp, cajole, needle, and lie. It can mean in other instances the propensity to talk around a subject, never quite coming to the point. It can mean making fun of a person or situation. Also it can denote speaking with the hands and eyes, and in this respect encompasses a whole complex of expressions and gestures. Thus it is signifying to stir up a fight between neighbors by telling stories; it is signifying to make fun of a policeman by parodying his motions behind his back; it is signifying to ask for a piece of cake by saying, "My brother needs a piece of cake." (See Glossary for further discussion of signifying.)

This technique of indirect argument or persuasion which underlies many of the strategies of children is utilized more subtly in the dozens. The same approaches of signifying and the dozens is illustrated in a toast from an older age group, called "The Signifying Monkey and the Lion." This verse narrative is a dialogue between a malicious, childlike monkey and a headstrong lion, in which the monkey is trying to get the lion involved in a fight with the elephant. The monkey is a "signifier," and one of the methods he uses for inflaming the lion is to indicate that the elephant has been sounding on the lion.

> Now the lion came through the jungle one peaceful day,
> When the signifying monkey stopped him, and this is what
>   he started to say:
> He said, "Mr. Lion," he said, "a bad-assed motherfucker
>   down your way."
> He said, "Yeah. The way he talks about your folks is a cer-
>   tain shame.
> I even heard him curse when he mentioned your grand-
>   mother's name."
> The lion's tail shot back like a forty-four
> When he went down that jungle in all uproar.

It is significant that the monkey is childlike and that for his signifying he gets killed in many endings to this toast. Signifying is regarded as a children's device, and in many cases is scorned by adults. They may say at such times, "Signifying is worse than dying," at the same time recognizing that they themselves easily fall into the same pattern, by saying "Signification is the nigger's occupation."

The dozens uses many of the techniques of childhood discourse but places them in a context that leads directly to adult modes of expression. Both the reliance on rhyme and wit and the use of signifying remain as major parts of adult male expression, but in considerably altered form. The dozens signals this mutation.

Many have commented on the institution of playing the dozens, but few have discussed its function in the life of the young Negro. John Dollard's article, "The Dozens: The Dialect of Insult,"[6] perceptively points out that the game acts as a release mechanism for the anxieties of Negro youths. But Dollard's uncertainty as to the manner of release and a misunderstanding of the exact nature of its psychosocial importance leads me to make further remarks on the way in which the dozens function. Specifically, Dollard does not seem to differentiate between the dozens as played by youths and by adults. Further, he sees the game as a displaced aggression against

6. *American Imago*, I (1939), pp. 3–24. See also R. F. Berdie, *Journal of Abnormal and Social Psychology*, XLII (1947), pp. 120–21, who describes the game accurately in a note. William Elton in two notes, *American Speech*, XXV (1950), pp. 148–49, 230–33, indicates a number of places the term is encountered in contexts literary and scholarly. He ties the practice to the "joking relationship," especially among the Dahomeans and the Ashanti, the two phenomena being similar only in the socially permissive and initiatory functions. But "joking relationships" develop their permissiveness out of a familistic structure, and the dozens do not.

Samuel J. Sperling discusses the procedure quite cogently in relation to teasing in general in "On the Psychodynamics of Teasing," *Journal of the American Psychoanalytic Association*, I (1953), p. 470. C. L. Golightly and I. Sheffler have a once-over at the literature on the subject in a note bringing Berdie up to date, in *Journal of Abnormal and Social Psychology*, XLIII (1948), pp. 104–105. They conclude: "These youths are blocked off from most of the avenues of approved self-expression. They live in a limited cultural world with patterns for emulation and stimulation. In their play groups they frequently use sex experience and prowess as a means of attaining status."

See also Davis and Dollard, *Children of Bondage*, pp. 82–83; *American Notes and Queries*, I (December, 1941), p. 133; Robert C. Elliott, *The Power of Satire*, pp. 73–74; Dollard, "Dialect"; Johnson, *Growing Up in the Black Belt*. For all the texts I collected in Philadelphia, see the *Journal of American Folklore*, LXXV (1962), pp. 216–19.

the Negro's own group instead of against the real enemy, the whites. Dollard's arguments are suggestive but lead to a kind of circular argument, since almost any aggression committed by the underprivileged group within a society can be seen as a substitute aggression, a principle similar to sublimation.

Samuel J. Sperling seems to drive at somewhat the same point as Dollard.

> This teasing game promotes the toughening of emotional sensitivity, and the inhibiting of impulses toward physical aggression. Frustrated outgroup aggression is safely channeled into the ingroup. In this way the formalized game of "The Dozens" has social value to a group subjected to suppression, discrimination and humiliation.[7]

The social values exist, I would argue, not just because this is a group suppressed and discriminated against, but because black males find themselves in a totally male environment in which the necessity to prove one's masculinity (and to reject the feminine principle) recurs constantly.

Certainly these rhymes express the growing awareness of the adolescent performers, especially of matters of sex; the dozens is an expression of boys in transition to manhood. In fact, sounding is one of the major ways boys are able to enunciate their growing sense of masculine power and sexual differentiation.

As described in Chapter 2, a boy learns early to orient himself to living in peer groups away from the home. This does not mean that he ever loses his emotional allegiance to the maternal figure in his life. But because he recognizes that as far as his mother or grandmother is concerned he is a member of an untrustworthy sex, he is caught in a psychological dilemma. Existence away from the home with the other boys is expected and in certain ways encouraged, but in other ways (and in the same breath) condemned. Further, he finds himself at odds with his mother's constraining influence at this time. His problems of adolescent initiative in the face of these

---

7. Sperling, "On the Psychodynamics of Teasing" (n. 6), p. 470.

familistic forces tend to focus on his mother as the most familiar image of the feminine which he is learning to distrust (the
seeds of distrust are often already there because of feelings of
rejection engendered when other children displaced him as
the center of this maternal figure's attention).

At the beginning of adolescence the boy cannot openly attack his own mother and her values either to himself or to his
peers. His emotional stability will not allow him to do this, because of the oedipal attraction of his mother. Yet he must
reverse his attitude, for not to do so would be to place himself in a vulnerable position with his peers and with the older
males. So he must in some way exorcize her influence. He
therefore creates a play situation which enables him to attack
some other person's mother, knowing that that person must
come back and insult his own. Thus someone else is doing the
job for him, and between them they are castigating all that is
feminine, frail, unmanly. (This is why the implications of
homosexuality are also invoked.) By such a ritualizing of the
exorcism procedure, the combatants are also beginning to
build their own image of sexual ability; for these rhymes and
taunts not only free otherwise repressed aggressions against
feminine values, but they also affirm the speaker's own masculine characteristics. To say "I fucked your mother" is not only
to say that women are unreliable and weak, but that the
speaker has capitalized upon this weakness sexually. At the
same time he has prepared a defense for himself against in-
cest or any other forbidden sexual motive. In this way the
youths place themselves in tune with the hypermasculine
world of the gang.

But the dozens functions as more than an exorcism. It also
develops one of the devices by which the nascent man will
have to defend himself—the verbal contest.[8] It is not an acci-

8. For a discussion of such problems in a vein similar to these arguments,
see Hortense Powdermaker, "The Channeling of Negro Aggression by the
Cultural Process," *American Journal of Sociology,* XLVIII (1943), pp.
750–58. For another thesis, see Rohrer and Edmondson, *The Eighth Generation,* pp. 158 ff. The use of this type of insult contest may be a facet of
all oral cultures. Johan Huizinga in *Homo Ludens, A Study of the Play
Element in Culture,* p. 65, in discussing the widespread nature on this type
of insult contest, says: "The nobleman demonstrates his virtue by feats of

dent that this play conflict should first arise at the period of emerging sexual awareness. Through the dozens the youth has his first prolonged and self-dramatizing opportunity to declare the differences between male and female and to take sides in the struggle. The feminine world that has held and yet rejected him will now be rejected in kind and by a complete negation. (It is not unusual to completely reject something that has so nearly seduced us to its values.) This declaration of sexual awakening and independence is done with words, a traditional manly weapon of sexual power, one which the youth will have to cultivate and use often.

The verbal contests are especially important because they are indulged in by the very ones who are most conscious of their appearance of manliness. Being bested in a verbal battle in front of a group of men has immense potential repercussions because of the terror of disapproval, of being proved ineffectual and therefore effeminate in the eyes of peers. This leads to the apparent paradox that those who are most afraid of public humiliation have institutionalized a procedure of humiliation for the purpose of releasing aggressions and repressed instincts, while at the same time learning verbal skills. It is astonishing to find that the same people for whom ridicule's destructive power holds such terror institutionalize it for therapeutic purposes; they turn its primary function inside out, as it were, and ridicule properly conducted becomes a thing to be enjoyed for the health of society.[9]

This is only a seeming paradox, however, for the dozens sit-

---

strength, skill, courage, wit, wisdom, wealth, or liberality. For want of these he may yet excel in a contest of words, that is to say, he may either himself praise the virtues in which he wishes to excel his rivals, or have them praised for him by a poet or a herald. This boosting of one's own virtue as a form of contest slips over quite naturally into contumely of one's adversary, and this in its turn becomes a contest in its own right. It is remarkable how large a place these bragging and scoffing matches occupy in the most diverse civilizations."

Earlier he has equated virtue and virility, so that the sexual nature of these contests is within his plan. Elliott, *The Power of Satire*, devotes a major part of his book to showing how satire derives from just such contests. He adds the factor of the magic quality of words and the power they can have over an adversary.

9. Elliott, *The Power of Satire*, p. 78.

uation calls for an extreme license which must apply as much to the audience as to the contestants. And one would not play the dozens with just anyone, only someone with whom it was safe to play. The boys, then, are developing the tools of battle on their own home ground.

Such verbal contests remain extremely important in the lives of the Camingerly men, but their expression becomes more complex both in vocabulary and in strategy. The presence of other men continue to represent challenges to the youths' maleness, and as a result most conversations turn into word battles, albeit comic and friendly ones. In other words, the release of aggression through ritual word battles retains its group sanction and provides a release from anxiety while remaining a masculine expression. Here, for example, is a comic routine given by Kid, derived in part from a recording by the rhythm and blues singer, Bo Diddley. It uses many of the conversational devices observable in the group's discourse, but because it is a routine, it brings them to a higher pitch.

"Man, why you want to look at me like that?"
" 'Cause you ugly."
"I'm ugly? You got the nerve to call me ugly?"
"Yeah, you ugly."
"No, I ain't."
"Look, boy, you so ugly that the stork that brought you here should be locked up by the F.B.I."
"Look here, man, you was so ugly when you was a baby that your mother had to put a sheet on your face so sleep could creep up on you."
"And your girl, your wife ain't no cuter."
"Wait a minute. Don't you talk about my wife."
"Your wife is ugly. Me and your wife went out to get a drink and have a good time and she was so ugly she had to put on sneaks to sneak up on the drinks. Now you know there ain't no sense to that. She look like something I used to feed peanuts to in the zoo."
"You calling my wife ugly?"
"No, I ain't saying she's ugly. I just said she was ruined.

Now I don't know where she was, but when they was giving out looks she must have been hiding down in the cellar
somewhere. And you. When they was giving out looks you
must have been playing craps. You look like you been
slapped in the face with a sack of razor blades. You ought
to be 'shamed of yourself."

But the good talker is not just the good arguer. He is also the
storyteller, and the stories he tells represent a further ability
of his to convince and thus illustrate his masculine power. The
routine above shows some of the boastful and deprecatory
techniques with which Negro parlance abounds. It indicates
that the verbal strategy so important in Negro life involves an
attempt to parade strength through boasting and through putting the other person down.

But the above routine is not a story. Tales, jokes, anecdotes,
any fictive expression involves a strategy one step more complex. In narratives the performer uses the most subtle words
that he can within his range of experience. He is defeating
his peers through his use of words (by comparison rather than
by actual besting), but at the same time he is creating a world
wholly his own. He is master of the situation he is narrating,
director of the heroes' lives in the narration. He achieves this
kind of control not only through the force of his vocal powers
but through the creation of a narrative persona which I call,
for want of a better term, the "intrusive I."

Throughout the narratives we are conscious of a close relationship between the hero of the tale and the person doing the
narrating. In most cases, especially in the toasts, the point of
view is strictly first person, allowing the complete identification of narrator and hero. In others, this identification is put
at a slight remove by placing the narration in the third person,
but allowing the hero some attribute by which one can identify him with the narrator (a black man competing with
members of other groups, a man of words in a dupable group,
and so on).

This "intrusive I" is a convenient gambit in the narrative
game. It allows the narrator two personae at the same time, his
own as narrator or commentator and that of the hero. He can

unite the two at will if he is artful in his narration; he can also dissociate the two if he wishes. It is important in certain stories that he be able to vary his perspective, as there will be actions which he as narrator will not approve, or situations in which he would not want to be found. As opposed to the classic English and Scottish ballads, there is nothing removed, long ago, impersonal about these narratives. Even when the narrator's persona retreats from that of the hero or main character, the narrator remains, intruding as a commentator. The "I" never disappears completely, though it may recede temporarily.[10] Thus any of the battles won, physical or verbal, are won by both the hero and the narrator. Yet he is in such control of this small universe that he can be both protagonist and antagonist in this contest. He directs this battle as well as wins it. The glory is all his and the triumph is more than just a verbal one.

As Negro males grow up, their word ability grows and their strategy becomes more complex, but their weapons of struggle remain the same. The culmination of verbal growth occurs in the toast, a long narrative poem constructed with the highest wit and performed only by the best talkers. But the toast utilizes the same devices of rhyme, rhythm, word play, and repetition that we find in the earliest of verbal triumphs, the children's rhymes. The toast teller is returning to safe ground to fight his recurring battle. He is further strengthening his arsenal by placing the battle, fought in the fictive battlefield, wholly under his control.

The man of words is an important member of the Camingerly male group. His ability with words is as highly valued as physical strength. There are two possible outlets for his ability: as a secular bard or singer, an entertainer who performs on the street corner with the gang or at parties, dances, and other heterosexual occasions; and as a preacher. It may seem strange that preaching demands the same type of word control and has the same emotional basis in sexually oriented contest as singing, but such is the case. Not only do both require the

10. Odum and Johnson, *The Negro and His Songs,* pp. 279 ff., use the term "the Dominant Self" in a similar sense but in reference to Negro songs.

ability to persuade and to construct effective imaginative playgrounds (for example, in the use of Bible stories); both also involve the overt contest of words. One of the most important phenomena in regard to the Negro preacher is the preaching contest where two, three, or more preachers appear on the same platform to see who can create the greatest emotional appeal and who can convert the most sinners.

What is not surprising is that the two groups of good talkers violently hate each other. The preacher of course regards the street corner bard as a corrupt sinner. The other goes even further. He gets back by telling stories about the hypocrisy of the preacher, of his effeminacy, homosexuality, and inefficacy with words.

The difference between the two talkers is that the preacher directs his words to women as well as to men. He is able to use the sexual capacity of words for overt sexual purpose, and in the world of the streets he is consequently renowned for his sexual duplicity. The bard usually does not have the same opportunity. Most of his word creations are for the entertainment of other men. These men only make alliances with the opposite sex when their biological and social drives force them to. It is no wonder that fear will overcome these drives in due time; most of the women play on the fear to get as much from temporary cohabitation as possible. The homosexual, antifeminine world of the early adolescent remains the safe one for this group, and the bard remains its spokesman.

The man of words is immensely important as a representative of the dispossessed men of Camingerly. By exhibiting his wit, by creating new and vital folkloric expression, he is able to effect a temporary release from anxiety for both himself and his audience. By creating playgrounds for playing out aggressions, he achieves a kind of masculine identity for himself and his group in a basically hostile environment.

3 The Heroes

One can tell a great deal about the values of a group from its stories because they reveal what actions are approved and what are not. Conventional characters act in conventional ways. There is seldom any difficulty in discerning whether a specific action is regarded with approval or not. One of the salient characteristics of traditional fictions is their structure; since the audience must always know where it is in the progress of the action, the storyteller must provide constant organizational cues. Certain acts in any group's stories will provide such cues which also tell them whether a character is admirable and represents the group's highest values or whether he is to be laughed at or scorned. Fictive heroes may therefore be of crucial significance in understanding the value system of a group—especially when such characters act on motives which cannot, because of circumstances, be acted upon in real life.

In the oral-aural, heroic Camingerly male world, heroes are central to an understanding of the men because of the values implicit in the stories and the masculine focus of effective word use in storytelling.

The values a story proposes through its action, if transmitted and appreciated by the group, will represent those of the group. But values are hardly static; they are mutable, and they mutate as the situations and conflicts of the group change. The conflict of the hero must in some way echo the conflict of the narrator and his audience in order for the story to be listened to, applauded, and remembered. The fictive expression of the narrative is more complex strategically than other play expressions (because of its submerged, sublimated, vicarious nature), but it still reflects the same kinds of problems as the lore involving the simpler strategies. Just as our simpler play offers an opportunity to symbolically act out a conflict in contest terms, the fictive experience allows us to identify with those who are also doing a similar acting out. As a psychic experience the fictive expression offers examples of approved desired action (the active expression of which is in most cases denied us because of various inhibitory factors). But it can go much further because it can offer an end to the conflict, a resolution. In dialectic terms, a synthesis can emerge: in psychic terms, a transformation or reintegration. Thus one must look not only to the hero's position in the conflict, but also to the results (victory, reconciliation, marriage, retribution) in an analysis of values in narratives.

With what sort of heroes do the Camingerly men identify when expressing themselves? The heroes of this group fit into two major categories, the trickster (or "clever hero") and the badman (or a special type of "contest hero").

The trickster figure has been the most identified hero in Negro lore throughout this country and the West Indies, perhaps because of a real prevalence of this type in Negro story, or it may be because Joel Chandler Harris collected and printed many stories about tricksters in his Uncle Remus books. His tremendous success with these works may have influenced future collections of the same type.[1] This reception may have been strongly influenced by the congruence between the white stereotype of Negroes, which saw them as tricky animals, and these stories.

At any rate, we can no longer claim that the trickster figure is the only or even the dominating hero type encountered in Negro tales. But he is still to be encountered among the Ne-

---

1. Richard M. Dorson seems to agree with this point of view: "Influenced by Harris . . . subsequent collections emphasized animal tales" in *American Folklore* (p. 176).

groes in the guise of the Signifying Monkey, the colored man John, and sometimes the preacher.[2]

The trickster or clever hero is one who triumphs or functions by means of his wits. As Orrin Klapp has noted:

> He either vanquishes or escapes from a formidable opponent by a ruse. The clever hero is usually smaller and weaker than those with whom he is matched, frequently being a diminutive animal. The victory of the clever hero is the perennial triumph of brains over brawn, *la sagesse des petits*.[3]

Perhaps the *petit* quality to which Klapp refers has implications beyond matters of size. The trickster figure functions in society not at all like a small animal; he acts like a small human being, a child. His delight in tricking is reminiscent of the pleasure children derive from tricking their peers. Indeed, in almost every sense the trickster *is* a child. He has no perceptible set of values except those dictated by the demands of his bodily needs. One could not say that he is immoral; rather he is amoral, because he exists in the stage before morality has been inculcated in his being. He is "the spirit of disorder, the enemy of boundaries." [4] "Although he is not really evil," says C. G. Jung (evil = conscious reaction to established order), "he does the most atrocious things from sheer unconsciousness and unrelatedness." [5] He is an individual just beginning the quest for ego identity; "a minatory and ridiculous figure, he stands at the very beginning of the way of individuation." [6]

The existence of this amoral, childlike hero creates important questions.[7] If the narrative functions both as an expression

2. Dorson's published collections offer the best cross section of recent Negro tales, including important stories of the type listed here.

3. "The Folk Hero," p. 20.

4. Karl Kerenyi, "The Trickster in Relation to Greek Mythology," in Radin, *The Trickster*, p. 185.

5. C. G. Jung, "On the Psychology of the Trickster Figure," in Radin, *The Trickster*, p. 203.

6. Jung, "Trickster Figure," p. 211.

7. This identity of child and trickster seems to have been recognized early, as a trickster festival mocking the church or government in the

of otherwise repressed anxieties and as a "tutor, the shaper of identities," why has the Negro chosen to represent himself and his values as childlike? Why has he chosen to appear to regress to an early stage of psychological development? There are a number of possible answers. In the guise of the small (child-like) animal, the Negro is perhaps fulfilling the role in which he has been cast by his white "masters" (the childish Uncle Tom who is convinced of his simple state and thus needs the protection of his masters). At the same time, in this role he is able to show a superiority over those larger or more important than himself through his tricks, thus partially salving his wounded ego. This reversed situation is apparent in the Marster-John cycles where the black man is tricking the white man, or in the Brer Rabbit stories where the small animal is getting the better of larger animals. This might be the function of the trickster on the sociological level: a veiled reaction against overdomination while preserving the role in which he has been cast.

The psychological satisfaction of the trickster story is similar to the sociological one. As Melville Herskovits says of this figure: "Psychologically the role of the trickster seems to be that of projecting the insufficiencies of man in his universe onto a smaller creature, who in besting his larger adversaries, permits the satisfaction of an obvious identification to those who recount or listen to these stories." [8] The trickster, then, may represent to the Negro, through identification, the small, often assailed hero in control of his world through guile (the only defense available to the Negro under the slave and post-slave systems).

But it is not the trickster's smallness or his guile that really provides the Negro with his greatest source of anxiety release. It is his amorality. Reaction against authority, in his deprived situation, is forbidden. But this revolt is vitally important to the psychic well-being of the individual and the group. The only

---

Middle Ages was called among other things *festum puerorum*. (Jung, "Trickster Figure," p. 198.)

8. "Trickster," in *The Standard Dictionary of Folklore, Mythology and Legend*, p. 1123.

rebellion available then is through the actions of a figure who has undergone an apparent regression to the childlike (or animal) state where he is not responsible for his actions because he has not yet learned the difference between right and wrong. His acts are unconscious; therefore they preclude his ability to make choices. "He is both subhuman and superhuman, a bestial and divine being, whose chief and most alarming characteristic is his unconsciousness." [9] The controlling factor of his being is apparently the rampant id, that element of our psyche outside the confines of the prison of society. He lives, then, in the permissive world accorded to children. The trickster provides a full escape for Negroes who have been offered no opportunity to feel a control over their own lives, no method for developing their identities through aggressive action in a situation productive of hostility. As such, the trickster may reflect the real childlike state of a severely stunted ego, or a veiled revolt against authority in the only terms available. At the same time the performer and audience are enabled to express some of their hostile impulses in this acceptable form.

But the badman, not the trickster, is the most popular hero among the Camingerly Negroes. The badman represents a conception quite different from the trickster. He is in many ways a contest hero: "the [contest] hero is placed in the position of publicly defeating all rivals. The winner is acclaimed hero or champion. The rivalry may be in skill, fortitude, virtue, or in main strength but such proof of the hero by contest with other humans is almost universal." [10]

The badmen of this group, Stackolee, The Great MacDaddy, Jesse and Frank James, are like the classic conception of the contest hero in that they are powerful, overcome all rivals, and are secretly acclaimed as heroes because of their strength and will. Here the resemblance ceases, for the badman does not seem to work for the benefit of society.

Where the trickster is a perpetual child, the badman is a perpetual adolescent. His is a world of overt rebellion. He commits acts against taboos and mores in full knowledge of what he is doing. In fact he glories in this knowledge of revolt. He

9. Jung, "Trickster Figure," p. 203.
10. Klapp, "Folk Hero," p. 19.

is consciously and sincerely immoral. As a social entity he is rebelling against white men's laws. As a male he is revolting against woman's potential domination. As a poor man he is reacting against his perpetual poverty. He copes in a contentious world.

But his expression is not uncontrolled like the trickster's; rather it is directed not in positive terms, as with the usual contest hero, but against anything that attempts to constrain him. His characteristic manner of expression is through his physical prowess. He is the "hard man," able to accept the challenges of the world because of his strength. Anything that threatens his domain threatens his ego and must be removed. Where guile and banter are the weapons of the trickster, arrogance and disdain serve the badman. He does not aim to be a god but rather to be the eternal man in revolt, the devil. He is the epitome of virility, of manliness on display.

The rebellion against authority exemplified in the badman is much more overt than in the trickster. He shows the open defiance exhibited in real life among Negroes in the activities of gangs and the establishment of gang leaders, and, with some of them, later in their lives as criminals. The values of this group in revolt are implied in the conduct of its badman heroes. Life as well as lore admits a more open expression of revolt than in the past, and this is echoed in the qualities of these heroes.

Let us apply some of the above generalizations to specific narratives. First, look at a tale of a trickster, "The Signifying Monkey and the Lion." The opening makes it clear what sort of creature the monkey is:

> Deep down in the jungle, so they say,
> There's a signifying motherfucker down the way.
> There hadn't been no disturbing in the jungle for quite a
> bit,
> For up jumped the monkey in the tree one day and
> laughed, "I guess I'll start some shit."

The name "signifying" shows the monkey to be a trickster, signifying being the language of trickery, that set of words or gestures achieving Hamlet's "direction through indirection" and used often, especially among the young, to humiliate an adversary.

The monkey, using this device of the child, invokes his powers in an attempt to stir up trouble. The dialogue that ensues in not untypical of the process of signifying. The monkey is a master of the technique. Without any known provocation, he involves the lion in a fight with the elephant:

> Now the lion come through the jungle one peaceful day,
> When the signifying monkey stopped him and this is what
>   he started to say:
> He said, "Mr. Lion," he said, "a bad-assed motherfucker
>   [elephant] down your way,"
> He said, "Yeah, the way he talks about your folks is a cer-
>   tain shame.
> I even heard him curse when he mentioned your grand-
>   mother's name."
> The lion's tail shot back like a forty-four
> When he went down that jungle in all uproar.

The fight that ensues between the lion and the elephant is almost epic. The lion gets badly beaten, as could be expected. The monkey, signifying, proceeds to rub salt in the lion's wounds from the safety of his tree:

> When they was fussing and fighting, lion come back
>   through the jungle more dead than alive,
> When the monkey started more of that signifying jive.
> He said, "Damn, Mr. Lion, you went through here yester-
>   day, the jungle rung.
> Now you come back today, damn near hung."
> He said, "Now you come by here when me and my wife
>   trying to get a little bit,
> Tell me that 'I rule' shit. I just tried it out. You ain't shit."
> He said, "Shut up, motherfucker, you better not roar,
> 'Cause I'll come down there and kick your ass some more."

But the monkey's signifying leads him to get excited and he falls and is captured by the lion. He must use all his guile to get out of this situation, first calling on the sympathy of the lion and then on his pride:

The monkey looked up with a tear in his eyes.
He said, "Please, Mr. Lion, I apologize."
He said, "You lemme get my head out the sand,
Ass out the grass, I'll fight you like a natural man."
The lion jumped back and squared for a fight.
The motherfucking monkey jumped clear out of sight.

In many versions, the story ends here. In some others, however, the monkey once again, while signifying from his tree-retreat, loses his footing and this time the lion puts an end to the monkey's ways:

Again he started getting panicked and jumping up and
down.
His feet slipped and his ass hit the ground.
Like a bolt of lightning, a stripe of white heat,
Once more the lion was on the monkey with all four feet.
Monkey looked up again with tears in his eyes.
He said, "Please, Mr. Lion, I apologize."
Lion said, "Ain't gonna be no apologizing.
I'ma put an end to his motherfucking signifying."
Now when you go through the jungle, there's a tombstone
so they say,
"Here the Signifying Monkey lay."

So in some versions the unusual situation occurs where the hero dies. This fact seems significant. The trickster, as we have noted, is the eternal child. The Negro trickster story had a real place in the antebellum and Reconstruction South where this was the sort of pose the Negro was forced to assume, the masochistic, subservient, childlike creature, the Uncle Tom who was allowed his few tricks as his idiosyncracies. But the attitudes, the values inherent in this approach to revolt have changed considerably. Because of recent developments in the lot of the Negro, especially in the Northern cities such as Philadelphia, he has been able to express his aggressions more overtly and thus escape his image as a perpetual child. With the break-up of the land-oriented matrifocal family of the slave, the men escaped from the actively accommodating or masochistic role they were driven to by the plantation-sponsored, mother-dominated home in which they were obliged to live.[11] The heroes of this earlier group reflected to a certain extent the values of the men under the slavery system. Their trickster, protagonist heroes existed in a permissive, childlike, neuter world, completely divorced from sexual conflict. To regress to such a world was the only way these men could express aggressions at all, and so these fictive expressions, which seem to have been most characteristic of that era, had aggressively infantile heroes.

The trickster finds a smaller place in the folklore of Negro city dwellers; when he does persist, his maneuvers sometimes lead him not to triumph but to death. Being childlike is as non-masculine as femininity. Lack of guts ("balls" would be more precise) in any form is lack of manliness. The trickster and his mechanisms of defense conflict with gang values, and their heroic orientation.

The trickster, when he does emerge in Camingerly narratives, is usually quite different from his form in the Old South, though some stories have persisted from that area and era. The monkey is obviously motivated by sadistic impulses. He wants to see the lion hurt. Brer Rabbit can be equally sadistic in strategy, but he must mask his aggressions if his tricks are to work. But then, the two tricksters are working with different dupes. Rabbit is contesting for his life against those not only much bigger than he but who desire to eat him. His reasons for tricking others in most of the stories are defensive in the broadest sense of the term. He must preserve himself from those who want to consume him, a projection of the same emasculation fears city dwellers exhibit in their stories. Being in a thoroughly dominated position both in the family and in

11. Wilhelm Reich agreed that behind the masochist's behavior lay a desire to provoke authority figures, but he disagreed that this was in order to bribe the superego or to execute a dreaded punishment. Rather, he maintained, this grandiose provocation represented a defense against punishment and anxiety by substituting a milder punishment and by placing the provoked authority figure in such a light as to justify the masochist's reproach. "See how badly you treat me." Behind such a provocation is a deep disappointment of the masochist's excessive demand for love based on the fear of being left alone. In Hinsie and Campbell, *Psychoanalytic Dictionary*, p. 443.

antebellum society, the trickster's only protection is a retreat to a seemingly presexual stage. He must in a sense play the clown, be the impotent man.[12]

The monkey, on the other hand, has no apparent motive for his trickery beyond a purely sadistic one, wanting to see another (and bigger) get beaten. He is the epitome of the little man talking big. His brag talk is more adolescent than childish.

Illustrative of the rejection of the older trickster expression is the change which occurs to Brother Rabbit in the imaginations of these city dwellers. The little animal becomes the hard man. Here is a comparison of two tellings of the same story. The first comes from Joel Chandler Harris and is thus a semi-artistic rehandling of a section of a Negro folktale of the Old South. The second I collected from Kid. We cannot rule out the possible influence of the Walt Disney comic strip on the transmission process here, but as Kid tells it, it is quite changed from any telling, Harris, Disney, or otherwise.

> "One time," said Uncle Remus, "Brer Fox, he tuck'n ax some er de yuther creeturs ter he house. He ax Brer B'ar, en Brer Wolf, en Brer 'Coon, but he ain't ax Brer Rabbit. All de same, Brer Rabbit got win' un it, en he 'low dat ef he don't go, he 'speck he have much fun ez de nex' man.
>
> "De creeturs w'at git de invite, dey tuck'n 'semble at Brer Fox house, en Brer Fox, he ax um in en got um cheers, en dey sot dar en laugh en talk, twel, bimeby, Brer Fox, he fotch out a bottle er dram en lay 'er out on de side-bode, en den he sorter step back en say, sezee:
>
> "'Des step up, gentermens, en he'p you'se'f,' en you better b'lieve dey he'p derse'f.
>
> "W'iles dey wuz drinkin' en drammin' en gwine on,

---

12. As Martin Grotjahn points out in *Beyond Laughter*, the comic is a father figure with the sexuality of the child. Most of the comic's symbols (baggy pants, always falling down, floppy hats, stooped-over walk, drunken state) emphasize the comic's impotence, are symbols of the "ridiculed penis." Children laugh at clowns, Grotjahn avers, because they represent father figures without the threatening aspects of their superior strength and virility, thus are on equal ground as the child in his struggle for his mother's affections. The clown operates much more complexly, it seems to me, however. The child sees in the clown a representation of himself, using (apparently) asexual tricks for aggressive purposes.

w'at you 'speck Brer Rabbit doin'? You des well make up
yo' min' dat Brer Rabbit monst'us busy, kase he 'uz sailin'
'roun' fixin' up his tricks. Long time 'fo' dat, Brer Rabbit
had been at a borbycue whar dey was a muster, en w'iles
all de folks 'uz down at de spring eatin' dinner, Brer
Rabbit he crope up en run off wid one er de drums. Dey
wuz a big drum en a little drum, en Brer Rabbit he snatch
up de littles' one en run home.

"Now, den, w'en he year 'bout de yuther creeturs gwine
ter Brer Fox house, w'at do Brer Rabbit do but git out dis
rattlin' drum en make de way down de road todes whar
dey is. He tuk dat drum," continued Uncle Remus, with
great elation of voice and manner, "en he went down de
road todes Brer Fox house, en he make 'er talk like thun-
ner mix up wid hail. Hit talk lak dis:

"'Diddybum, diddybum, diddybum-bum-bum-diddy-
bum!'

"De creeturs, dey 'uz a-drinkin', en a-drammin', en a-
gwine on at a terrible rate, en dey ain't year de racket,
but all de same, yer come Brer Rabbit:

"'Diddybum, diddybum, diddybum-bum-bum—diddybum!'

"Bimeby Brer 'Coon, w'ich he allers got one year hung
out fer de news, he up'n ax Brer Fox w'at dat, en by dat
time all de creeturs stop en lissen; but all de same, yer
come Brer Rabbit:

"'Diddybum, diddybum, diddybum-bum-bum—diddybum!'

"De creeturs dey keep on lis'nin', en Brer Rabbit keep
on gittin' nigher, twel bimeby Brer 'Coon retch und' de
cheer fer he hat, en say, sezee:

"'Well, gents, I 'speck I better be gwine. I tole my ole
'oman dat I don't be gone a minnit, en yer 't is 'way 'long
in de day.'

"Wid dat Brer 'Coon he skip out, but he ain't git much
furder dan de back gate, 'fo' yer come all de yuther creeturs like dey 'uz runnin' a foot-race, en ole Brer Fox wuz
wukkin' in de lead."

"Dar, now!" exclaimed 'Tildy, with great fervor.

"Yasser! dar dey wuz, en dar dey went," continued Uncle Remus. "Dey tuck nigh cuts, en dey scramble over one er 'n'er, en dey ain't res' twel dey git in de bushes.

"Ole Brer Rabbit, he came on down de road—diddybum, diddybum, diddybum-bum-bum—en bless gracious! w'en he git ter Brer Fox house dey ain't nobody dar. Brer Rabbit is dat owdacious, dat he hunt all 'roun' twel he fine de a'r-hole er de drum, en he put his mouf ter dat en sing out, sezee:

"'Is dey anybody home?' en den he answer hisse'f, sezee, 'Law, no, honey—folks all gone.'

"Wid dat, ole Brer Rabbit break loose en laugh, he did, fit ter kill hisse'f, en den he slam Brer Fox front gate wide open, en march up ter de house. W'en he git dar, he kick de do' open en hail Brer Fox, but nobody ain't dar, en Brer Rabbit he walk in en take a cheer, en make hisse'f at home wid puttin' his foots on de sofy en spittin' on de flo'.

"Brer Rabbit ain't sot dar long 'fo' he ketch a whiff er de dram—"

"You year dat?" exclaimed 'Tildy, with convulsive admiration.

"—'Fo' he ketch a whiff er de dram, en den he see it on de side-bode, en he step up en drap 'bout a tumbeler full some 'ers down in de neighborhoods er de goozle. Brer Rabbit mighty lak some folks I knows. He tuck one tumbeler full, en 't wa'nt long 'fo' he tuck 'n'er'n, en w'en a man do dis a-way," continued Uncle Remus, somewhat apologetically, "he bleedz ter git drammy."

The rest of the story is concerned with Brer Rabbit getting caught because of his inebriated state and then how he escapes by a ruse similar to the usual one found in the tar baby story.[13]
Here is the text from Kid:

Brother Fox had been trying to get Brother Rabbit for a long time. So he told Brother Bear one day, he said, "Brother Bear, now I know how we can trick that old rab-

---

13. Joel Chandler Harris, *Nights with Uncle Remus*, pp. 62–65.

bit into giving himself up." Brother Bear said, "How will we do it?" He said, "Now we'll invite all the animals in the forest to a party, all except Brother Rabbit. He'll be so embarrassed and hurt that he won't want to live and he'll give himself up. And we'll have rabbit stew before the week is up."

So all the invitations were around. So that Saturday evening, you know, all the animals were going down to the party. Even the skunk washed up and put the perfume on, went into the party. Brother Rabbit was sitting on the post and all. Said, "Where you all going?" "Down to Brother Buzzard's house." "Brother Buzzard?" "Yeah. Brother Fox is giving a party over there." Rabbit ran to the house and got dressed, and ran down to the house. Brother Buzzard said, "Sorry, Brother Fox and Brother Bear say they don't want you in it. I'm sorry, that's what they told me."

So the Rabbit turned away with his head turned down. He feeling sad, downhearted, tears in his eyes. Felt like he was alone in the world. But then he got mad. He said, "I know what I'll do." He went home and shined his shoes and got his shotgun and went back and kicked the door open. "Don't a motherfucker move." He walked over the table, got all he wanted to eat. Walked over to the bar and got himself all he wanted to drink. He reached over and he grabbed the lion's wife and he dance with her. Grabbed the ape's wife and did it to her. Then he shit in the middle of the floor and he walked out.

So after he left, you know, the giraffe jumped up. He said, "Who was that little long-eared, fuzzy-tailed motherfucker just walked in here with all that loud noise?" The bear looked at him and said, "Now look, no use getting loud. You was here when he was here, why didn't you ask then?" (Like guys, they like that. You always get bad after the other person is gone, but you never say nothing while they is there.)

The trickster has become in this case, the hard man.

In this apparent retreat from trickster values, agility is an attribute much more acceptably male than guile because it contributes to style. In his role as the great pool and card player, the monkey finds greater success, as in the toast of "The Monkey and the Baboon." Here, the monkey is adept at games and his agility pays off; he acquires status from his smart manner and his sharp clothes.

> Now a few stalks shook and a few leaves fell,
> And up jumped the monkey, sharp as hell.
> Had a one-button roll, two-button satch.
> You know, one of them boolhipper coats with a belt in the back.

The monkey still has power with his words, but he uses it sim‑ ply to add a brilliant finish to the veneer of his actions. For in‑ stance, he is not satisfied to win at a game of cooncan; he must cap the game by laying down his cards in the following flourish of victory:

> So hop Mr. Rabbit and skip Mr. Bear.
> It's gonna look mighty shady but there's 'leven of them there.
> [A lay of eleven cards wins the game.]

But agility is not the ultimate value to these men; more highly considered are meanness, strength, and the ability to revolt in the face of authority and possible death. Death does not matter, just style of living. If dying results from this style, that is all right. In this realm, the badman reigns. He will often say, "I'm a bad motherfucker and I don't mind dying." He is highly conscious of his role. Because of his attitudes and his meanness, he has women falling at his feet. The history of John Henry is a good illustration of this. He is the hard man, but because of his situation he does not need to act immorally, for the most part. He channels his aggressions toward the ma‑ chine which is attempting to emasculate him. His leaping into the world full grown (or nearly) is stressed in the songs about him, usually in the first few stanzas, and often a stanza follows promoting further the mystery of his birth ("Some say he was born in Texas") and stressing the aspect of him as be‑ ing his own man. Commentators have long played down his obvious sexual prowess, indicated by the number of girlfriends he had that remained true to him. Among the Camingerly men, he is remembered specifically for his sexual feats.

When John Henry was a baby,
You could hold him in the palm of your hand.
But when he got nineteen years old,
He could stand that pussy like a man.

John Henry told his father,
A man ain't nothing but a man.
But before he'd let a piece of pussy go by,
He'd die with his dick in his hand,
Yeh, he'd die with his dick in his hand.

Now John Henry took his girlfriend
He layed her 'pon a rock.
When he got through he looked at her,
"Umm, such good cock,
Umm, such good cock."

Now when John Henry died
They say he died from shock.
But if you want to know the truth
He died from too much cock.
Yes, the boy died from too much cock.

Now they took John Henry's body,
And they layed it in the sand.
People came from far and near
To see that good fucking man,
Yeh, to see that good fucking man.

The most characteristic and exciting of the badmen is Stackolee. Stack is a mean man, a purveyor of violence. He does not hesitate to hurt, taunt, kill if someone offers him the slightest insult or challenge. All acts are executed with the greatest show of strength and arrogance and with the smartest kind of flourish. Down on his luck when we first meet him, Stack doesn't let that affect his pride; it seems to make him even meaner and more deadly.

I walked through water and I waded through mud.
I came to a little old hole in the wall called "The Bucket of Blood."
I walked in, asked the man for something to eat.
Do you know that bastard gave me a stale glass of water and a fucked-up piece of meat.
I said, "Raise motherfucker, do you know who I am?"
He said, "Frankly, I don't give a damn."
I knowed right then that sucker was dead.
I throwed a thirty-eight shell through that motherfucker's head.

A girl comes over and offers herself in an obvious attempt to keep him there until the murdered man's brother Benny Long (or Billy Lyons) gets there. He accepts both challenges and wins them in the grandest of styles. He is as magnificent in sex as he is in battle.

"Hi there, baby, where's the bartender, if you please?"
I said, "Look behind the bar, he's with his mind at ease."
So she peeped at her watch, it was seven of eight.
She said, "Come upstairs, baby, let me set you straight."
Now, we went upstairs, the springs gave a twistle,
I throwed nine inches of dick into that bitch before she could move her gristle.
Now we come downstairs big and bold.
They was fucking on the bar, sucking on the floor.
Then you could hear a pin drop. Benny Long come in.
He walked over where his brother lay dead, and he calmly said,
"Who had a nerve to put a hole in my brother's head?"
I said, "Me, motherfucker, to put your mind at ease.
I'm that bad-ass so-and-so they call Stackolee."
He said, "I heard of you, Stack, from tales of old.
But you know you tore your ass when you fucked my hole.
But I'ma give you a chance my brother never got. I'ma give you a chance to run,
'Fore I reach in my cashmere and pull out by bad-ass gun."

Just then some old sucker over in the corner said, "Some-
body call the law."
He stretched out and put a forty-five shell through that
motherfucker's jaw.
A cute little broad came and said, "Benny, please."
He blowed that bitch down to her knees.
And out went the lights.
And Benny Long was in both of my thirty-eight sights.
Now the lights came on and all the best.
I sent that sucker to eternal rest,
With thirteen thirty-eight-bullet holes 'cross his mother-
fucking chest.

Benny is just as mean and strong as Stack, so that Stack's triumph is a fitting one. An appropriate end to a story of this sort
is Stack's violent boast:

I was raised in the backwoods, where my pa raised a bear.
And I got three sets of jawbone teeth and an extra layer
of hair.
When I was three I sat in a barrel of knives.
Then a rattlesnake bit me, crawled off and died.
So when I come in here, I'm no stranger.
'Cause when I leave, my asshole print leaves "danger."

Because Stack is the prototype hero of the Camingerly men
it seems pertinent to examine his actions and values further.
Stack's actions exhibit the importance in his life of bravery,
honor (perhaps "face" would be better here), and ability with
words. But Stack seems to be acting at all times for himself,
unlike the epic heroes whose deeds represent their group.
It is true that Stack's immediate ancestors were bullies and as
such represented the honor of a town or neighborhood, but
Stack seems to have lost this motivation. His acts are an extension of his disturbed ego.

The epic hero acts in order to protect his land, his home, his
women. Odysseus's reunion with Penelope is not fortuitous action in that drama; it is the proper and full resolution of it.
Through his protection of her and his home, his final actions
are the epitome of heroic values. Stackolee acts for nothing

but himself, and in direct rejection of women. Stack, the hard man, doesn't owe any part of his existence to home or woman. He springs into the story full grown, independent, unattached to anything or anyone. He is his own man. All the actions in the story are not only done in order to exercise his virility but in direct rejection of women or things feminine (witness the confrontation with Billy's mother and girlfriend). Billy, as far as the dramatic action is concerned, is but an extension of his mother's threat of retribution. Stack's feats, sexual and otherwise, are all motivated by women's challenges. He must prove himself, even when it means dying for it.

This brings up the two major questions about Stack's character and actions: What is the reason for his sadistic action? What is the relationship of this sadism to his self-destructive tendencies? In the broadest sense, sadism is an outlet for repressed male sexuality.

> Viewed as a perversion, sadism is a defense against castration fears. . . . What might happen to the subject passively is done actively to others—"identification with the aggressor." . . . The discharge of aggression in itself may be pleasurable, but sadism further implies pleasure in the destruction of others.[14]

Not even active proof of virility, such as in the first shooting or in the bedroom scene, is enough to assuage this man's severly dislocated ego. He indulges sexually because the girl offering herself does so as a challenge, aggravating his problems rather than soothing them.

Stack's activities are not only sadistic but they are consciously self-destructive. When he says, "Got a tombstone disposition and a graveyard mind, I'm a mean motherfucker and I don't mind dying," he is voicing the interrelationship of the two. Meanness and dying are part of the same style of life. He not only doesn't mind dying, he wants to, and in most versions, he does.

In our discussion of the rejection of women and family, we have noticed that in many ways the men do not emerge un-

14. Hinsie and Campbell, *Psychoanalytic Dictionary*, p. 653.

scathed. They are fixed in a permanent love-hate situation, one that causes a vacillation between violent attraction to and equally violent rejection of women. This duality can be fully expressed in the sadistic act because both the attraction and the repulsion remain under the control of the actor. But the sadistic action itself must leave its mark, because ultimately it is antisocial and ends with a complete rejection. This must be atoned for, and Stack attempts to do this by dying, or at least coming so close that he attains part of the release of death. What he himself cannot do because it would be overt masochism, he has others do for him by placing himself in a position where he may be hurt or killed. This way he has his cake and is able to eat it as well. The guilt accrued for his actions (activated by the attraction part of his ambivalent feelings, and expressed through the agency of society or the superego) is assuaged by the punishment accompanying his actions, and he is able to be punished in a style that fits the dominant image of himself.

But the punishment of living dangerously under the threat of death functions on another level. The love-hate situation Stack, as representative hero, finds himself in creates almost unbearable anxieties. His main expression of this tension is, of course, in his overtly aggressive actions. But death would provide a much fuller release. And the audience identifying with him might find in his death the kind of regenerative or transforming experience that would lead them out of their emotional impasse. Stack would then be functioning as a scapegoat. But even in those versions where Stack dies (none were collected in Camingerly, but many have been in other communities), he goes to hell and begins his evil, hypervirile ways all over. This totally heroic male is both unregenerated and untransformed by experience, and as such may reflect the persisting condition of the young men who tell stories about him and who must continue to live in this totally male world.

But as we know from the "Signifying Monkey" toasts, Stack is not the only hero type; there are alternative models of aggressive behavior among the Camingerly men.

In one story, the toast of the Negro stoker Shine aboard the *Titanic* at the time of its sinking, we can observe motivations somewhat different from those of the badman. Briefly, the story is that Shine is the one who informs the ship's captain about the holes in the hull after the ship crashes with the iceberg. The captain keeps sending him down to pump, and he keeps re-emerging, giving the captain further information on the size of the hole. Finally Shine jumps in the water and begins swimming. He is then offered three temptations from those still on board—money from the captain and sex from the captain's wife and his daughter. All of these he turns down because of the practical demands of his predicament. He is then challenged by the shark and the whale but is able to outperform them. He swims safely to shore.

In Shine we have a hero who has guile and a trickster's command of the language, but he is no trickster. We have a hero who has amazing physical powers, but he is not mean like a badman. He is able to perform acts which qualify him as a much more complete hero than any of the others we have encountered. First of all, he performs feats, is a legendary hero. Shine's amazing action of swimming away from the sinking, even outswimming the creatures whose natural habitat he has entered, qualifies him firmly as a performer of feats. His declining of the temptations of money and sex add other attributes to his status as hero; he is a passer of trials, of tests. Further, Shine undergoes a real transformation, is reborn. His act of jumping overboard is a conscious rejection of white commands, followed by a rejection of status symbols. He undergoes a symbolic slaying of himself to be reborn in the ocean (not a surprising place to be reborn).

Shine exhibits in his actions a sense of task which is conspicuously absent in the actions of any of the other heroes. Stackolee, presented with a similar situation, would certainly have accepted the offer of sex and stolen the money. But Shine seems to perceive a direction to his actions. His abilities not only indicate an amazing physical and verbal talent but also show a capacity to turn his back on just those status symbols for which the other heroes have been fighting. After all, Stack and the monkey are reacting against the insecurity caused by financial and psychological poverty. But those very insecurities are represented, and apparently mastered, in the things Shine rejects in his replies to the captain, his wife, and his daughter. He has an opportunity to exhibit his superior abilities in a much grander manner.

Shine makes it very clear that he is turning his back on white people. He answers the offer of the captain's wife with:

> You know my color and you guessed my race.
> You better jump in the water and give these sharks a chase.

It is also clear throughout that this triumph is achieved in the name of his race. He is pointed out as a Negro on a ship that was renowned for not allowing members of that race aboard as passengers. He was thus isolated, away from his people, being tested. Do we not then have in this toast a message of some sociological and psychological significance? Here is a Negro story that overtly pictures the enemy as white. The white man has been one of the authority figures against whom he has been rebelling. But here he achieves that greater act of rebellion, the turning of his back. This is then something of a declaration of independence.

The tone of the story is pronouncedly defiant; the note on which it ends is a derisive joke:

> When news got to Washington that the great *Titanic* had sunk
> Shine was standing on the corner already one-half drunk.

The pleasure involved in this story is the irony that Shine made it to shore and the white people, the oppressive yet less strong, didn't.

Though "Shine" is unusual in the toast tradition, there are a number of jokes that treat the same conflict theme. Here, too, there seems to have been a trickster tradition contemporary with the Brer Rabbit type stories that parallels them also in theme and technique. In these stories, which are still in the repertoire of black raconteurs both old and young, the comic conflict arises between Old Marster and one of his slaves, often named John. Since the slave is in a subordinate position, his tactics must often be covert, and his victories seem very small (see in this regard "The Coon in the Box," p. 000). Not highly valued by the Camingerly performers, these stories have been almost completely supplanted in the men's repertoires by stories about more overt confrontations between black and white. The men claim to know a number of the Marster-John stories but they tell few. In their place are the stories about "Negro, White Man, and Jew" in which the three-man formula is used to emphasize the superior capacity in wit or strength of the Negro, or the even more overt stories about the Harlemite in the South. Characteristic of the first type is Charley's story about "Chinaman, Jew, Negro":

> There was this Chinaman, a Jew, and a Negro. They was caught fucking the farmer's wife. So the farmer said, "Well, uh, Chink, how would you like to die?" So the Chinese said, "Er, uh, well, my father, he was a swordsman, so I'd like you to chop my dick off." So he said, "O.K." So he asked the Jew, he said, "What was your father?" So he said, "My father owned a steel mill, so you have to weld my dick off." So he got to the Negro. He said, "What about you?" He said, "My father was a lollypop maker, so you have to suck my dick off." [15]

An example of the Harlemite story, also from Charley, I call, "He Gets What He Orders":

> Remind me of the time, this here guy was down South. He was from New York. He was the kind of guy, he didn't care about nothing from nobody. There were these two guys in front of him, you know, at this Mississippi store. Guy had stopped at the filling station. He said, "I want some cigarettes." "If you what?" "If you please, Mr. Charlie."
>
> The guy in front of him said, "Could I have some hot dogs please, sir?" He said, "If you what?" "If you please, Mr. Charlie." He said, "All right."

15. This is one of the most common (for the most part, unprinted) jokes in the ingroup, outgroup mold. Legman notes that a version of this story, with the Jew given the triumph line, is printed in the original *Anecdota Americana* (1927), Vol. I, p. 314, and is quoted and discussed by G. Legman in "Rationale of the Dirty Joke," in *Neurotica*, 9 (1951), and "The Castration Complex," p. 56. In this form the story ends leaving the logical conclusion, with the Jew saying: "Me? I'm a nobody. I peddle lollypops."

Next guy walked up, he said, "Could I have a pound of hot sausage, please, sir." He said, "If you what?" "If you please, Mr. Charlie." He said, "All right."

So this here city slicker, you know, he didn't pay them no mind. He walked up to the counter, you know. He said, "Look here, throw me a pack of them Pall Malls right there, will you?" "If you what?" "If you got 'em, mother-fucker, now what."

This gravitation toward the hard-man solution is one of the most salient characteristics of the Camingerly narratives. They have chosen to espouse the approach of the social type Harold Firestone has appropriately designated "the gorilla," [16] this being one of the pimp's names for the hard man, the tough guy and his life style. This is not the only available model for the young men, however. In certain groups, the flexibility and style of the pimp is more highly valued, than the gorilla approach, especially the pimp's ability to cope with whatever experience comes along, however adverse. This approach is beautifully exemplified by "The Signifying Monkey," but as noted, though his doings are greatly enjoyed, he is killed off in many of the versions told by these performers. Rather than illustrating a complete rejection of trickster values within the ghetto world, these stories illustrate that there is a choice of heroes and life styles available and that the good talkers in Camingerly have opted for the hard-man style. Insofar as the pimp's approach is the modern representation of the guile of Brer Rabbit, one cannot say that this style of coping has been rejected; but one can note that this one group of narrators has seemingly rejected it for the more hard-line approach.

Both of these styles of coping are expressed in comic form, perhaps because the joke is the most characteristic form of narrative in the United States at this time. But it also seems appropriate, considering the male environment in which the stories are told and the men's ambivalent attitudes toward their antagonists (especially white men and women).

16. Cf. Howard Firestone, "Cats, Kicks, and Color" in Howard Becker, ed., *The Outsiders*. (For a more discursive treatment of the pimp-gorilla contrast, see my *Positively Black*.)

The laugh allows one to accept and reject at the same time. It permits identification and at the same time reservation, thus utilizing the fullest capacity of the fictive strategy. Even "Stackolee" is full of laughs, and Stack's actions are seen to be both significant and funny. These are protest heroes that people these stories, and comedy is a fine expression for protest. As Wylie Sypher points out, "The Comic rites are necessarily impious, for comedy is sacrilege as well as release." [17]

However, Sypher here is talking primarily of such pieces as satyr plays and other pieces with a saturnalian impulse. All of what we call comic is certainly not impious, directed against the excesses of society and its restrictions. Much of the derision of the comic may be, in fact, directed against the self or against the image of the power figure who is rendered inept. Comic pieces can easily vacillate between these modes of aggression, these objects of derision. This is especially evident in these toasts and stories which have been described. Motivation and direction of humor varies from the exhibitionistic actions of the monkey to the impious yet self-destructive acts of Stack. In this group aggressive behavior cannot be uniformly institutionalized into protest through lampoon. The ambivalent situation of the men causes a constant shift to occur in the direction of attack. Aggression is unified only through the persistence of the comic purpose and humorous tone.

In view of this ambivalence, however, it may seem strange that in the narratives described here there is such a predominance of rejection (both through symbolic action and through laughter). A nearly complete reversal from the antebellum trickster approach seems to have been affected in the stories of this group. But this is not true of all Camingerly stories. The narratives, it is true, are rejective, but the songs, the lyric expressions, are still highly suppliant. The "see how much you have hurt me baby" feeling which has been pointed out so often in Negro song (especially the blues) still predominates in the popular songs most appreciated by the men—those

17. Wylie Sypher, "The Meanings of Comedy," in *Comedy.* Essays by George Meredith and Henri Bergson, p. 223.

sung by the city bluesmen, B. B. King and Ray Charles, Jimmy Reed and Lloyd Price. But then the narratives are usually told only in the company of men and seem to state, "Look at me, I am a superman." The songs are directed toward the women, and most of them seem to say, "I'll come to you, baby, and on your own terms, too." Both are necessary fictions, given their audiences.[18]

18. For a contrary view, and one that has much to recommend it, see Charles Keil, *Urban Blues*. That I agree with Keil at certain key points I have made clear in my analysis of the development of soul singing in *Positively Black*.

Section **2: the texts**

4 Style and Performance

the first section of this work examined the social milieu of a group of young Negro storytellers along with certain elements of the narratives in order to place these pieces and their performers in as full a light as possible and to explore the process by which their traditional literature interacts with other aspects of their lives. Specifically, the object was to show how the family life of the group created a situation of emotional ambivalence that had great effect on the traditional modes of expression, especially in the oral literature. There, some aspects of the texts were outlined or underlined, not so much to render the stories themselves comprehensible but rather to show more fully the relationship between text and teller.

This section is devoted to a presentation of the stories themselves, and all discussion therefore centers upon them. All the narratives collected in Camingerly, other than those given in the first part, are printed here. Through discursive headnotes to individual pieces an attempt will be made to trace their history and to reveal meanings that might otherwise be lost. Words or expressions of esoteric meaning can be found in the Glossary. As G. Legman has been so helpful in matters of annotation, I have presented his comments, where relevant, in his own words. The reader must therefore bear in mind that Legman's remarks are given in something of an alien context, as they were originally conveyed in personal letters. They will simply be prefaced by his name and a dash.

The stories are divided into two categories, the toast and the joke. This division is dictated by stylistic and generic considerations. For purposes of clarification, as well as to attempt to tie in matters from the first section, the stylistic patterns and conventions are described in the introductions to each genre.

The problem of style in literature, oral or written, has been especially clouded by romantic and impressionistic attempts at definition. Ultimately style is *not* definable as the form of expression a writer will fall into when he finds his "true voice." It is also not something revealed in its fullest sense through some adjectival or metaphorical approach. Style is rather the recurrence of linguistic entities, which provide an objectively describable pattern in terms of sounds, words, rhythms, syntactical constructions, and even perhaps units of meanings. The introductions of the genres attempt to point to the stylistic elements that recur most often and to indicate those that always occur, thus defining the genre.

Any consideration of style, however, creates theoretical problems. Because style has been seen as the dressing of the artist, the literary analyst has been driven to stylistic perceptions in the work of the individual artist. To unite a writer's method with his themes and central vision—his "world"—one must, I suppose, do just such an analysis. However, to do so is to ignore or at least take for granted the existence of a certain number of patterns a specific language and culture exhibits. These patterns are as truly stylistic as any individual configurations of them are. For the folklorist at least, these cultural linguistic patterns are more important than those refinements made by the individual artist, because these embody the forms accepted by the past and utilized in the present; they are the structures of tradition. It is by means of these patterns that the simplest levels of communication are preserved and the forms of the past transmitted to the present.

This point needs clarification. Certain linguists make a distinction between casual and noncasual utterances, between "common usage and uses of language for more restricted purposes and often enough, perhaps characteristically more elevated purposes." [1] The distinction echoes the linguists' pre-occupation with common usage (at least as the point of departure for their descriptive grammars). Language has structure and it is best describable in utterances that are part of general discourse. But linguists have long realized that there are certain preset exceptions of usage in every language, where what appear to be the rules for conversational languages are abrogated. These are noncasual utterances, and in them one can find the established and accepted deviations in the language structure.

The usual method for defining the noncasual aspects of a language are through syntactic constructions and certain elements of diction that are permissible under the special circumstances in which such utterances are invoked. Much more reliable, however, would be to see noncasual language as that exhibiting expressive style, for these diction and syntactical changes are just two areas of change used to create the kind of recurrent patterns that distinguish noncasual utterance. There are elements common to casual and noncasual utterances, but when they are encountered in the latter they serve to define it, while when they crop up in the former they do so to no purpose or plan. It is the elements of balance and other features of conventional order that call attention to a work of art as art, and these are the devices of style. These elements, too, denominate noncasual utterance. Rhyme, for instance, may occur in normal discourse, but if it does so with any regularity it will come as a surprise to the speakers and will involve either a humorous response or a further conscious attempt to use the device, which of course would change the expression to noncasual.

The utterances folklorists call folklore are noncasual. They are prepatterned pieces which, because of their traditional and ceremonial nature, are able to utilize the language of more restricted or elevated purpose. This linguistic distinction becomes an important one for folklorists, because one of the best indications of cultural imperatives is through the linguistic

1. For a discussion of these problems and further bibliography, see C. F. Voegelin, "Casual and Noncasual Utterances within a Unified Structure," in Thomas Sebeok, ed., *Style in Language*, pp. 57–68.

patterns of style, and style is most clearly perceivable in non-casual utterance. There are so many language elements that can be repeated and patterned that an enumeration of such stylistic elements can go a long way in pointing out the patterns of expressive activity of a group—their attractions or *tropisms*.

Within the total realm of noncasual utterance a wide variance of freedom or fixity of formal patterning can occur. Both a folktale and a ballad are noncasual, therefore utilizing accepted formal patterns, but one can see clearly that the folktale is freer in expression (that is, closer to casual language) than the ballad. The ballad, being wed to a tune and all the formal restraints that go with it, is more severely limited in the way it may express and develop its story. Thus both are delimited by the stylistic elements involved, but the ballad, being more fixed, will have potentially more recurrent patterns and thus is liable to be described stylistically in a much more complex manner. In the present study, just such a contrast is observable between the highly fixed and formal toast and the freer joke.

There is a further dimension to the problem of style: the problem of the importance of the style of the individual performer-creator. If a language has a range of stylistic possibilities, then the individual can, by choosing certain stylistic elements and eschewing others, find something of his own voice. Yet only the artist in a sophisticated and eclectic society really has this wide range of choice; the folk performer is working within a tradition that severely delimits the number of different stylistic configurations permissible by the group. This point was well examined in an exchange between Richard M. Dorson and Roman Jakobson. The former pointed out in reference to folk performers:

> In the past we have supposed that most people in a group, in a subculture, told about the same tales in the same way and that the style was uniform for all members of the group. But when we look into it a little more closely and begin to consider individual performers, we see that there is a good deal of difference, variation and individual style.

So it seems to me that we can make such a distinction *once the group repertoire has been established.*

To which the latter replied:

> In any popular tradition there are several stereotyped styles of performance and corresponding selections of epic or lyric genres, and from these "stock types" (*emplois*) the individual chooses the one particularly suited to him. Likewise the observers of language are often prone to exaggerate the imprint of personality. . . . The strong tendency of the individual to adopt his language to the milieu, and in any dialogue to approach his interlocutor, considerably reduces the notion of the so-called "idiolect." [2]

There were certain elements of style exhibited by all the men and boys whom I heard perform in Camingerly. All seemed to be carried away by the impetus of words into near euphoria. Word sounds seemed to exist for themselves apart from sense, and all noncasual discourse seemed to gravitate toward rhyme or clever turn of phrase. Performing was performing, and there was no attempt by the teller to confuse the reader by introducing pieces that seemed to involve casual speech. Voice pitch and other elements of vocal production were, for each performer, different in a very important way from his usual manner of speaking, whether through utilization of a wider range of pitch levels and loudness, great emphasis on story line or its embroidery, or simply sheer rapidity of narration. Sentence units for the most part are very short. When they are lengthened, they are done by conjunctions, not by any method of subordination. The emphasis is on action, description being used only to heighten the effect. Because of a peculiarity in Negro speech which utilizes in certain cases the same verb forms for both past and present, a feeling of ongoing action pervades these stories.[3] This emphasis on action

---

2. Dorson and Jakobson, in Sebeok, *Style in Language*, pp. 52–53. The emphases are mine.

3. It was often impossible to transcribe texts faithfully in this regard, as these verbs were often heard by me one way one time and another way another time. I fear that I often heard them in a way that would more nearly agree in tense with what came before.

and "nowness" has a great effect on the diction. Active verbs dominate. Modifiers are generally intensifiers. There are frequent injected sounds and exclamations also used to intensify and further the action.

Individual performers, however, did show some peculiarities in style as well as subject. Many of the informants have been discussed earlier in passing.[4] Bobby Lewis was responsible for the narration of few of the stories himself but was immensely valuable in helping me gather the material. At the time of this study he was seventeen and eighteen years old. He had, when he was about fourteen, taken a trip to Florida with Charley, working his way down and back. Though small and young, he regarded himself as very much a man, especially a lady's man. Like all of these men, Bobby had been a member of the Twelfth Street Gang and had fought for it often, but he seems to have abandoned fighting a few years before I arrived. Bobby explained that this was because too many of the boys had departed for the service or for parts unknown.

As a storyteller, Bobby was not recognized by his peers as outstanding. His main trouble seemed to be that he tried too hard and yet could not remember stories, especially the toasts, very well. Thus his sense of the story's direction was often impaired and this was reflected in his faltering method of delivery. When he did perform, which was not often (and I imagine he performed more often to me than to his peers), he was definitely attempting to emulate Kid's style and method.

John H. "Kid" Mike was by far the most prolific and effective of my informants, probably because of from his acceptance by the group as an outstanding talker, which led him to see himself as a professional entertainer. As a result he was nearly always performing, his roles varying from the bumptious clown to the scathing satirist to the boastful badman. He knew some of the routines of the Negro nightclub performer Redd Foxx, as he had heard them on records; the same is true of his performance of the Bo Diddley piece on p. 00.

Kid was born and raised in Philadelphia and has always lived somewhere near Camingerly. At the time of this study he

---

4. I do not use full names here in certain cases as this was their request.

was twenty-seven and twenty-eight. He was on the short side, muscular and stocky, who when he didn't see himself as a professional entertainer pictured himself as a professional softball player. He had been married a few years before, but was at present living with his mother. His wife had taken him to court many times for nonsupport and on a few recent occasions had him thrown into jail. He claimed that she was living with another man and harassing him for spite. At one time during our stay in Camingerly he disappeared for a while, returning to say that he had been in a hospital with tuberculosis.

Kid's rendition was very theatrical. He used as many dramatic devices as possible, changing voices for different characters or varying situations, utilizing the full range of his voice's pitch and intensity, and he would speed up and slow down at will. He was a masterful rhymester and quipster, but he was also capable of almost endlessly embroidering a story if he wanted to. He was the only one in the neighborhood I ever heard who felt he constantly needed to fill in character motivation in his jokes.

An interesting pattern in his personal repertoire was his predilection for stories in which the young man has relations with an older woman ("Granny" usually) and for those in which the female is the active of the pair and the male more passive. This style would suggest the possibility of a wish to resign his male role except in relation to maternal figures, and it seems especially significant in the light of his marital history and his return to his mother's household.

Charley is an open contrast to Kid in attitudes, style, and delivery. On the short side, light-skinned, Charley was a brilliant musician and had performed in a quartet, The Turbans, that had made a few records. He could take any group of boys and give them different singing parts out of his head, and the result was a fine arrangement. His voice was very flexible and he was able to sing anything from bass to falsetto melody. When he was not singing, however, Charley was very shy and commonly expressed himself through a short breathy giggle. Yet he had a wide and varied repertoire of stories. Whereas Kid used every theatrical trick to put across his story, Charley relied almost completely on effects of lesser intensity. His voice was soft and he drawled. Though he had just as great a control on his material, he would often punctuate his narration with a nervous "eruh."

Charley had traveled south with Bobby, though he was four or five years older. He was the most mobile of the regulars of the neighborhood, moving to many different places during our two-year residence, most of them some distance from Camingerly. He usually lived with sisters in one or another neighborhood in Philadelphia. Yet he had been raised around Camingerly and returned regularly to visit friends. He was not much of a hand with the girls, with all of his talents. He seemed definitely afraid of them on the few occasions I saw him in mixed company.

His taste in jokes tended toward the most childish, with a strong emphasis on the clownish doings of drunks and the sexual activities of prepubescent children. He told numerous stories involving drunken or baby talk. This suggests the possibility of a dream dimension in fictive terms focusing on a regression to the presexual stage or a resignation to the nonsexuality of inebriation.

Arthur was the third outstanding taleteller I encountered. Whereas Charley's delivery was deliberately slow, Arthur's was absolute staccato madness, a veritable machine-gun delivery. He spoke so fast that it was tremendously difficult to understand his words. Of the three, we knew Arthur the least well. He was around for only a short time during our stay. He was short and very much the dandy, and he had learned to do "processing," hair straightening. He went on a crusade to Virginia to teach the boys there how their hair should be worn, and he only returned during the last couple of months we lived in Camingerly. He was not always available for recording sessions and the only things collected from him were toasts.

The rest of the texts included here came from a number of other sources. Javester, a friend of Bobby's, brought me a manuscript from a man at work which included a number of items I have included here, *punctatim et literarum*. "Boots" and Victor were younger members of the community, singers in one of the quartets that met at our house. Harry was an elderly man who regularly sat across from our residence in a portable chair. He gave me a couple of items from a manuscript he carried in his wallet. Petey I have discussed earlier, in the first chapter. He was a young fellow who got married during our sojourn. He brought Freddie around for a couple of recording sessions. Freddie was a school chum of his who knew many stories but did not tell them very well, as will be noticed in the texts attributed to him.

5 The Toast

the toast may be the most neglected form of traditional narrative; it has been almost totally ignored by folklore scholarship. Indeed, beyond my own preliminary report and an article by Debra Galoob,[1] one of my students, the only publication I have located that prints any texts of the verses that follow is *The Book of Negro Folklore* by Langston Hughes and Arna Bontemps.[2] Richard M. Dorson, in his article "Negro Tales," mentions that one of the tales printed was "also given . . . in the form of a rhymed story or 'toast' . . ." and he prints some tale texts close to toasts.[3] This situation probably exists because the toast by its very nature (and quite often its subject) calls for the use of obscene words.

The toast is a narrative poem that is recited, often in a theatrical manner, and represents the greatest flowering of Negro verbal talent. Toasts are often long, lasting anywhere from two to ten minutes. They conform to a general but by no means binding framing pattern. This consists of some sort of picturesque or exciting introduction, action alternating with dialogue (because the action is usually a struggle between two people or animals), and a twist ending of some sort, either a quip, an ironic comment, or a brag. There is generally a unity, in the

1. "The Toast," in Beck, ed., *Folklore in Action*, pp. 1 ff; Debra Galoob, "Back in '32," pp. 24–33.
2. Hughes and Bontemps, *The Book of Negro Folklore*.
3. Dorson, "Negro Tales," p. 87.

consecutiveness of action; there is no "leaping and lingering" as in sung traditional narratives. Toasts are not sung, and it is perhaps the lack of reliance on the structure of a tune that allows their freedom of form.

But toasts do have a structure. Like so many other forms of oral narrative they are organized by conventions, ones that Albert Lord would consider "epic." [4] These conventions allow for a feeling of much freedom within a fairly restricted form.

At first glance it seems that there is no conception of length or duration of the individual line. A fairly typical couplet, such as the following, has a line of five stresses followed by a line of three:

> Shine went up on deck, said "Captain, I was downstairs
>   eating my peas
> Till the water come up to my knees."

On further analysis, however, the dominant line pattern is seen to be one of four stresses:

> Dówn in the júngle near a dríed-up créek

> The signifying mónkey hadn't slépt for a wéek.

This line provides a flexible pattern; lines involving greater or fewer stresses are countenanced. The importance of the stress system is not that it provides an unvarying mold but that it establishes an expectation pattern. This kind of verse is called *isochronic*.

The pattern is a useful one, as a four-stress line will divide and balance easily, and the balanced line is the core of the wit of these pieces. Very often lines are divided in the middle with a stop (comma, semicolon, period) or a conjunction.

> Now a few stalks shook, and a few leaves fell,
> Up popped the monkey one day, 'bout sharp as hell.

Balance and caesura are used for a number of effects. Often there are balanced actions, paralleled by a balance in subject-

---

4. Lord, *The Singer of Tales*. Much of the analysis in the next few pages is indebted to this perceptive work.

verb-object positions. "The monkey grabbed a stick, and the baboon snatched the chalk." Or simple syntactic (paratactic or oppositional) balance occurs: "Hand full of chives, pocket full of herbs."

However, the major structural unit is not the line but the couplet, and the principle of balance extends to it. Rhyme, uniting the two lines of the couplet, creates an initial balance. Further balance can be developed within these bounds by using the first line of a couplet to introduce a character (or an action) and the second to describe him (or it). I use here lines from "Jesse James" to illustrate.

> There was the Dalton Brothers, four of a kind.
> They shot a motherfucker for a raggedy dime.

And here the principle of balance is carried further, for the next couplet parallels the first in subject, modifiers, and syntax:

> There was John Dillinger in the corner, counting his gold.
> He shot *his* motherfucker when he was ten years old.

The couplet that follows the above two shows how balance can be preserved yet varied, for here the name comes after the modifying line, and the first line breaks, with its violent irregularity, the metrical pattern which otherwise might get boring:

> There was a bad motherfucker in the corner we all should
>   know.
> His name was Geronimo.

The balanced, four-stress line easily falls into dogtrot rhythm, but the freedom by which the lines are expanded and contracted and the almost endless variety of patterns and durations of nonstressed syllables eliminate the possibility of aural fatigue. Further, because the caesura in a four-stress line falls most often in the center, the toast teller will seldom provide many consecutive lines with a strong caesura. The most common device he uses is to take a balanced line with a strong caesura and play it off against a line with little or no break in it, at the same time preserving balance between the two lines in sound and syntax:

He said, "I'ma hold my jacks, spread my queens.
I'ma do switching in this old fucked-up deck the world's
never seen.
I'ma hold my deuces, lay down my treys.
Get down on your motherfucking ass in a thousand ways."

As noted, the couplet provides the basic structural unit of the toast in most cases. Even where there is no strong line or couplet balance, the thought, action, or description is encompassed within the confines of the couplet. Thus, most lines or couplets begin with the subject of the sentence followed immediately by the active verb, with the modifiers generally following to complete the unit. Personal pronouns are the most frequent first words of the lines in any toast.

These verses are improvisational in character.[5] They are the sort of narrative not learned by rote or even by plot line. The primary purpose of the toast teller, it is true, is to tell the story as quickly, fluidly, and dramatically as possible. But he doesn't exactly remember the toast, having "learned it by heart." Rather he has learned the conventions, the formulas, and the themes (or commonplaces) and by means of these has reconstructed or retold the narrative.

The improvisational nature of the toast makes any one text simply a chance rendering of a story highly transitional by nature—a rendering that will probably never be reproduced exactly, even by the same informant. Variation is the essence of the toast's character. This variation from one occasion to another is especially great if the social situation of the telling is changed (for instance, talking on the street corner as opposed to sitting around a room speaking into a tape recorder).[6] This point was brought home to me once when Kid recorded "Shine" early in a session, before he had really hit his stride.

5. These toasts may be popular among Negroes because of their predilection, otherwise evinced in calypso, for improvised pieces of a contest nature. A cross-cultural approach would probably be very revealing, but obviously is not within the confines of this study.

6. Albert Lord validly objects to the use of the term "variation" in references to extemporized narratives of this sort, as the word implies the existence of a fixed form which can be varied from. I use it because the alternatives don't seem any more helpful, and because the concept of variation is still useful, even without the acceptance of the fixed text.

His telling, as always, was effective but not as highly dramatized or elaborate as a version he recorded for me another time. (The variation in his use of conventional elements from one telling to the other was a good indication of his control over the conventions.)

Here follow two versions of "Shine" performed by Kid on two separate occasions:

> It was back then a long time when the great *Titanic* was sinking away.
> Shine, a little man, was off on the port side.
> He come over and he said, "Captain, Captain, the water's over the first fireroom door."
> He said, "Shine, Shine," he said, "have no doubt,
> For we got forty-nine pumps to pump that old water out."
> Shine went down and came up again.
> He said, "Captain, that damn water's still coming in."
> Captain said, "Shine, Shine, have no doubt.
> I told you we got ninety-nine pumps to pump the water out."
> Shine said, "There was a time, your word might be true,
> But this is one goddamn time your word just won't do."
> Shine jumped overboard, throwed two kicks and one stroke,
> Was off like a motorboat.
> Captain came up on deck. He said, "Shine, Shine, save poor me.
> I'll give you more money than a man want to see."
> Shine said, "There's money on land, money on sea,
> But I keep on stroking, that money on land be best for me."
> Captain's daughter came up on the deck
> With her drawers in her hand, brassiere around her neck.
> She said, "Shine, Shine, save poor me.
> I'll give you more pregnant pussy than any black man want to see."
> Shine said, "You know my color, and you guessed my race.
> You better come in here and give these sharks a chase."
> Shine kept a-swimming. Come past a shark's den.
> Shark looked at Shine and invited him on in.

Shine said, "I heard about you. You the king of the ocean,
the king of the sea,
But you got to be a stroking motherfucker to outstroke me."
When the word got to Washing' times the great *Titanic* was
sunk,
Shine was on Broadway, one-third drunk.

(*Second Night's Version*)

One day when the great *Titanic* was sinking away,
Captain was in his quarters one lonely night,
This old man came up the port side.
He said, "Captain, Captain, the water's over the first fire-
room door."
He said, "Shine, Shine, have no doubt.
We got forty-nine pumps to pump the water out."
Shine went down and he came up again.
He said, "Captain, look! That damn water's still coming
in."
Captain said, "Shine, Shine, have no doubt,
Now we have ninety-nine pumps to pump the water out."
He said, "Captain, there was a time when your word might
be true,
But this is one damn time your word won't do."
So Shine he jumped overboard. He took two kicks, one
stroke,
He was off like a PT boat.
Captain came up on the deck. He said, "Shine, Shine, save
poor me.
I'll give you more money than any black man want to see."
Shine said, "You know my color and you guessed my race.
Come in here and give these sharks a chase."
Captain's daughter came up on deck,
Drawers in her hand, brassiere around her neck.
She said, "Shine, Shine, save poor me.
Give you more pregnant pussy than a black man want to
see."
Shine said, "I know you're pregnant, 'bout to have a kid,

But if that boat sink two more inches, you'll swim this
    coast just like Shine did."
The Captain's wife came up on deck. She said, "Shine,
    Shine, save poor me.
I'll let you eat pussy like a rat eats cheese."
Shine said, "I like pussy, I ain't no rat.
I like cock, but not like that."
Shine kept a-swimming.
Shine came past the whale's den.
The whale invited old Shine in.
Shine said, "I know you're king of the ocean, king of the
    sea,
But you gotta be a water-splashing motherfucker to out-
    swim me."
So Shine kept on stroking.
Now Shine met up with the shark.
Shark said, "Shine, Shine, can't you see.
When you jump in these waters you belongs to me."
Shine said, "I know you outswim the barracuda, outsmart
    every fish in the sea,
But you gotta be a stroking motherfucker to outswim me."
Shine kept a-swimming.
When the word got to Washington that the great *Titanic*
    had sunk,
Shine was on Broadway, one-third drunk.

In both these recitations Kid was directing the toast just
to me and the microphone. I heard him and others tell this
same toast in a poolhall environment and it was at least twice
as long (or so it seemed at the time).

Performance can be judged in terms of the ability to extend
or contract the line, both for variety's sake and for the purpose
of adding a conventional flourish or to make a description
more direct and more dramatic. As mentioned, the four-stress
line predominates, but it is not the absolute rule. Within that
line the performance can add all sorts of intensives and other
modifiers which are unstressed and therefore do not affect the
stress pattern.

His ability to recount and embellish is further aided by the conventional structure of the line and couplet. The balance often achieved within these units conforms to certain types that provide the framework for the formulas exhibited in these verses. A line or couplet that is balanced conjunctionally, paratactically, or appositionally is easier to remember than one without such self-conscious construction; it also establishes that construction as a pattern for future expressions and situations. These cosntructions are the formulas of the toasts.

The themes are another way in which the narrator will recount his story successfully. These are larger units, in which similar situations in different toasts are treated in a similar manner. When such situations are repeated in one toast, incremental repetition occurs. "Squad Twenty-two," for instance, begins:

> I ran over to Lombard Street to get my gat,
> I ran back to South Street to get my hat.

and later says:

> Now I run back to South Street to put down my gat
> And back over to Lombard Street to put down my hat.

More often, such similarities exist in different toasts. A common situation is some strong man trying to shut somebody up. When this occurs in a barroom, as in "Stackolee," it ends in violence:

> Just then some old sucker over in the corner said, "Somebody call the law."
> He stretched out and put a forty-five shell through that motherfucking jaw.
> A cute little whore came over and said, "Benny, please."
> He blowed that bitch down to her knees.

In a courtroom scene, the structure is similar, the results different:

> Just then my sister-in-law jumped up, started to cry
> I throwed her a dirty old rag to wipe her eye.
> My mother-in-law jumped up, started to shout.
> "Sit down, bitch, you don't even know what the trial's about."

The courtroom is a locale returned to again and again in the toasts. The judge's sentencing is invariably announced with a retort from the convicted.

> "Fifty-five ain't no time.
> I got a brother in Sing Sing doing ninety-nine." [7]

As a theme is an improvised form, the same situation is recounted with variations:

> "Judge, ninety-nine years ain't no goddamn time.
> My father's in Alcatraz doing two-ninety-nine."

Occasionally entire scenes are thematic, being found in similar forms in two or more toasts; the hero's descent to hell and his defeat of the devil, the fight with the bartender, the courtroom and jail scenes are some that occur repeatedly.

A further device by which the toast is remembered by informants is by the use of cliché. The pattern of the four-stress rhymed line, often divided in two, elicits many descriptive images that are used repeatedly for both rhyme and stress purposes. A gun is never a gun; it is a forty-four or forty-five or thirty-eight depending upon which rhyme is needed. A man is never shot; gunplay is rather described as putting a "rocket through his motherfucking head."

Often the clichés called for are proverbial. Such phrases abound as *like a rat eats cheese, king of the sea, off like a PT boat, faster than a streak of lightning, more dead than alive, like a ten-ton truck,* and the self-consciously Negro proverbs *spend money just like I was white* and *stay in your class.*

Yet, as is readily observable, not all images used are clichés. The language used in these poems is, as in many public utterances, highly self-conscious and artful. The well-turned phrase is constantly sought, and he who calls forth the best of phrases is the best of the toast tellers. Often the balanced line is created simply for poetic effect, such as the line from "Stackolee" and one version of "Jesse James":

7. This comes from a commonplace blues verse. See Oliver, *Blues Fell This Morning,* p. 176. The whole courtroom scene may be a commonplace from early Negro song; see for instance Mary Wheeler, *Steamboatin' Days,* p. 111.

I walked through water and I waded through mud.

Often the sense of a line is obscured in order to enhance its sound.

The bed gave a twist, the springs gave a twistle.
I throwed nine inches of joint to the whore before she
    could move a gristle.

In the toast of "The *Titanic*," fact is sacrificed for a more euphonious opening. This tragedy, which actually occurred on April 14 and 15 begins:

The eighth of May was a hell of a day.
When the *Titanic* was sinking away.

or:

It was a hell of a day in the merry month of May
When the great *Titanic* was sailing away.

This is by no means great poetry, but the interrelationships of the "a" sounds and the "m" sounds in the second are consciously and artistically conceived. Sometimes these artful effects are used to emphasize a comic point, as in the couplet from Charley's "*Titanic*":

Shine said, "You may be king of the ocean, king of the sea,
But you got to be a swimming motherfucker to outswim
    me."

Consistent with this attitude toward sound and sense in words is the emotional content of the poems as a whole. The poems are created to excite the emotions, by their sound, by their diction, by their breath-taking, and by their subject matter. The emotions they primarily call forth are amusement and amazement. The subject treated is freedom of the body through superhuman feats and of the spirit through acts that are free of restrictive social mores (or in direct violation of them), especially in respect to crime and violence. The heroes of most of these stories are hard men, criminals, men capable of prodigious sexual feats, bad men, and very clever men (or animals) who have the amorality of the trickster. The diction of the toasts does everything to heighten the effect of these characters. The values of iconoclasm are strongly echoed in the abundance of forceful and obscene words. Such words show the performer to be the kind of strong man that the hero of the tale is. Furthermore, they are lively words that blend well with the abundance of active verbs and expressions found here; *swinging, running, stomp, kill, knock, jumped* are the verbs that predominate in these highly active pieces. In the same way, the proverbs and clichés are commonly utilized for the purposes of either furthering the action or the iconoclasm, or both. *Like a bat out of hell, pick on someone your own size, clean out of sight, fight like a natural man, like a bolt of lightning, a stripe of white heat, like a ten-ton truck* all behave in this violent way. Here is the concreteness common to much folk-speech, used for desired effect.

Because of the confines of the form, the images and diction of these pieces seem even more vivid, more precise, more imaginative than those found even in the tales and anecdotes. More is borrowed from the economy of the Negro ballad than from the narrative method of the tale. There is much in common in technique between the standard Negro ballad stanza (found in "Delia Holmes," "Frankie and Johnnie," and many others.):

> Send for the yellow-tired buggy, send for the yellow-seated hack.
> Gonna carry her to the graveyard. Ain't never coming back.

and such a couplet as this (from "The Great MacDaddy"):

> I was standing on the corner, wasn't even shooting crap.
> When a policeman came by, picked me up on a lame rap.

especially in regard to economy and artistic embellishment.

There is much about the toast as an entertainment form that is strongly paralleled in the professional medium of the blackface minstrel stage. It is impossible to say with our present knowledge of early Negro lore whether such narrative recitations existed among the Negro before the beginning of the minstrel shows and were borrowed by white performers for the minstrel stage, or whether they were an invention of the whites, later borrowed by the Negro and recast. At any rate, we know that in the later history of the blackface show, recitations, often comic ones, became a part of the show. As Carl Wittke, the historian of the minstrel stage, says, a

> favorite device of the endmen was to entertain their audiences with the recital of a poem. . . . Frequently the interlocutor would recite a popular favorite correctly, in order to give the endmen the opportunity to improve on his rendition by . . . new versions.[8]

Such verse not only found its way into the interplay between the interlocutor and the endman; the monologist during the olio part of the program was known to break into verse.[9] With what we otherwise know of the effect of minstrel show materials on Negro lore, it seems possible that such recitations may have provided an impetus for the toast tradition.

A further possible influence of the blackface show may be seen in the common characteristics of some of the dialogue. In such toasts as "Stackolee" and "The *Titanic*" there is much dialogue between two characters. Often this approaches the form of the "straight man" and "gagman" jokes, or in more appropriate terms, "Mr. Interlocutor" and "Mr. Endman" jokes. This is most evident in "The *Titanic*" where the captain, his wife and daughter, the shark, and sometimes the whale, serve "feeder" or "set-up" lines for Shine.

> Shark said, "Shine, Shine, can't you see,
> When you jump in these waters you belongs to me."
> Shine said, "I know you outswim the barracuda, outsmart
>   every fish in the sea,
> But you gotta be a stroking motherfucker to outswim
>   me."

This same element can be seen, with a lesser comic effect, in "Stackolee," which in general is more concerned with action than dialogue. After Stack has shot the waiter:

8. Wittke, *Tambo and Bones*, p. 164.
9. Wittke, *Tambo*, p. 171.

Little lady came in and said, "Where's the waiter, please?"
I said, "He laying behind the counter with his mind at
ease."

It is not being argued that the minstrel show is the point of origin of the toast but rather that it exhibits, in some of its facets,
similar tendencies and may have affected the early history of
the toast. On the other hand, somehow the present form derived in some way from the custom of the dedicatory speeches
or verse toasts pledged with a drink, some of which were quite
long and flamboyant.[10] We know that this custom was taken
over by the Negro at least as early as the beginning of this
century.

10. Legman relates these toasts to the toast tradition in general, even
though they have lost their salutory function. He says: "In the first place
they are clearly related to the quatrain saws of the late 16th and early 17th
century almanac type, beginning 'When a man grows old,' and so on—as
these folk-witty apothegmatic statements are just what 'goes' when giving a
toast at drinking. Also, *toasts* in just this sense continued in all convivial
company until the end of World War I in the U.S., when they were killed
by prohibition and the surreptitious drinking thereafter. Even the British,
who did not have prohibition, will hardly venture more, nowadays, than a
tight-lipped 'Cheers,' and I understand that the Upper-and-Lower 'U'
snobbery school has definite strictures on any more flamboyant toasts being
given.
  "However, throughout the 17th and 18th centuries, and well into the
19th—until the period of the British moral reform of the 1830's, which was
intended to stave off the threatened working-class revolution (aborted into
the labor-union movement then and since)—heavy drinking was *de rigueur*
among all classes, and most song and jest books included pages and pages
of these ornate 'toasts.' As late as the 1870's, in the usual anglicized reprints
of Burns' *Merry Muses of Caledonia*, a page of such toasts will be found.
Scotland was, in fact, a particular center of these toasts, especially among
the secret societies, of drinking, singing, and sexual conviviality, such as the
stupefying 'Beggar's Benison' society, of Anstruther, Scotland, in the early
18th century, whose *Records* were printed at the dissolution of the society
in the 1890's, precisely with a few pages of these long and ornate toasts. In
America the college fraternities kept the tradition alive, and still do,
especially in the Southern colleges, such as Virginia, with such fancy items
as 'High-riding horses and porcupine saddles fo' ouah enemies!' At the
present time in Scotland there is still a secret, or semisecret society, the
'Horseman's Word,' of which the Scottish folklorist, Hamish Henderson,
has actually tape-recorded a session; and it is a point of honor with the
members to 'propose' long and ornate erotic toasts, which go on for a
paragraph of brag of mythical sexual autobiography."

> Toasts are given at drinking parties; but all through the
> South they are given at all kinds of gatherings, even at
> school "jus' fo' pastime." [11]

The sense of the word here indicates that the custom of toast-
ing begun at the drinking parties had already expanded. Perhaps it grew further to include any verse recitation and from
there became particularized into the form as we know it. There
did, and does exist among Negroes the custom of creating occasional poems and other long verse forms. Fauset quotes one
from Nova Scotia[12] Negroes and Dorson from Michigan
Negroes.[13] Perhaps the name "toast" became associated with
these longer rhymes.

On the other hand, the name may have been derived from
the numerous books of after-dinner speeches, jokes, and toasts,
which include such recitations as "The Shooting of Dan Mc-
Grew" or "The Face on the Barroom Floor." Whenever I
asked any older members of the neighborhood if they knew any
toasts, they would say they used to know those toasts about
"Stackolee" or "The Face on the Barroom Floor," and I did find
one who remembered most of "The Drunkard." Many of them
claimed to have books of toasts in their homes (which at
first I took to mean their own individual collections, but on in-
vestigation proved to be either jokebooks or books of these
recitations).

The relationship of these rather theatrical narrative poems to
the toast can be seen in another way. It is certain that "Paul
Revere's Ride" is a parody of the famous Longfellow poem;
in the same way some of the fornication contest toasts are parodies of the type of verse as "The Shooting of Dan McGrew"
or "The Face on the Barroom Floor." Such origins are a good
deal clearer in texts collected from white informants. A good
example is found in *Count Vicarion's Book of Bawdy Ballads*

11. Portia Smiley, "Folklore from Virginia, etc.," *Journal of American
Folklore*, XXXII (1919), p. 375.

12. Fauset, *Folklore from Nova Scotia*, p. 100.

13. Dorson, *Negro Folktales in Michigan*, p. 13.

(Paris, 1956) XIV, "Eskimo Nell." [14] Closer analysis might show a similar relationship between all the toasts and the works of popular verse.

The toast is today, as its ancestors were, an entertainment. It is a social entity, not to be performed alone in the fields or while washing dishes but on the street corners with the gang on long summer evenings, in the poolhall after everyone has run out of money, and occasionally at parties. Though for the most part toasts are male entertainment, the female members of the neighborhood like to hear them performed, and it is only the matriarchs and the sternly religious who look down upon them. There is a tendency not to offend the female sensitivity by performing them before women, but the women often try to goad the men into giving them a show. It is a favorite pastime of some young girls to sneak to a place where, unobserved, they can hear the boys performing these pieces.

Because the object of the toast teller is primarily to entertain, he will narrate with such emphases that it will be just a little funnier (by the addition of incongruous or picturesque expressions) or a little more superhuman or explosive. And there is no doubt that the audience is being entertained when one hears a toast performed well. All sorts of vocal appreciation is expressed at the high points of the narrative.

A real question is whether the audience believes that such events actually happened. Most will reply, if asked, that the stories are fictions, but perhaps because they don't want to be suspected of not being in tune with the beliefs of the investigator. However, some whom I asked thought that probably there were men named Stackolee and Billy Lyons who lived and did the things described in the toasts. All who were asked regarded the toasts about animals as humorous ways of describing people, but none would go so far as to say that the jungle really represented city life.

The element of belief is intricately bound up with the vicarious enjoyment the members of the audience obviously exhibit while hearing these stories. The desire to be sexually

14. Legman says of such recitations and parodies, "there are plenty of 19th century white recitations. . . . There are also certainly plenty of white recitations of a highly erotic kind, and not all of these are parodies."

superpotent or above the restrictions of (an imposed) society is obviously manifested in the reactions of both the performer and the audience.

The question of belief or vicarious participation is important because of its effect on structure. The ballad form has not been congenial to the Negro, it would seem. Few are the ballads of Negro origin, and those that exist lack much of the direction of those from the European tradition. There are such Negro ballads as "Betty and Dupree" and "Delia Holmes," but even here where exciting stories are being documented, the lyrical element encroaches, a phenomenon I have earlier referred to as the "intrusive I." We hear about the doings of these men and women, but insistently we find the singer entering the song to make an emotional point:

> Some say he was born in Texas
> Some say he was born in Maine.
> But I don't give a damn where that poor boy was born.
> He was a steel-driving man.

It is the impersonality of the European ballad form, seemingly, that is anathema to Afro-American performers. The toasts are devices to call attention to performance abilities, and most of the stylistic criteria will reflect the personal perspective: the performer must be able through his improvisational abilities, his artful control over the active vocabulary, and his repertoire of commonplaces and themes to hold the audience.

It would be a mistake to imagine that just because a performer launched into a toast, his audience would allow him to finish it. To be sure, he is given a certain amount of license, but if he has too many pauses or proves to be "lame" in any other way, he'll be edged out of the center of the scene. This contest orientation, discussed earlier in regard to playing the dozens, is further observable in the context of these longer performances. Not only does one performer challenge another and one toast or joke suggest another, but if a performer knows a toast that has just been performed and feels he can tell it with a new twist and greater verve, he will not hesitate to perform that toast again immediately. For instance, Kid might give his rendition of "The Signifying Monkey and the Lion":

Deep down in the jungle so they say
There's a signifying motherfucker down the way.
There hadn't been no disturbin' in the jungle for quite a bit,
For up jumped the monkey in the tree one day and laughed,
"I guess I'll start some shit."
Now the lion come through the jungle one peaceful day,
When the signifying monkey stopped him and this what he started to say.
He said, "Mr. Lion," he said, "a bad-assed motherfucker down your way."
He said, "Yeah! The way he talks about your folks is a certain shame.
I even heard him curse when he mentioned your grandmother's name."
The lion's tail shot back like a forty-four
When he went down the jungle in all uproar.
He was pushing over mountains, knocking down trees.
In the middle of a pass he met an ape.
He said, "I ought to beat your ass just to get in shape."
He met the elephant in the shade of a tree.
"Come on, long-eared motherfucker, it's gonna be you and me."
Now the elephant looked up out the corner of his eye,
Said, "Go on, birdshit, fight somebody your size."
Then the lion jumped back and made a hell of a pass.
The elephant side-stepped and kicked him dead on his ass.
Now he knocked in his teeth, fucked up his eye,
Kicked in his ribs, tied up his face,
Tied his tail in knots, stretched his tail out of place.
Now they fought all that night, half the next day.
I'll be damned if I can see how the lion got away.
When they was fussing and fighting, lion came back through the jungle more dead than alive,

When the monkey started some more of that signifying jive.

He said, "Damn, Mr. Lion, you went through here yester-
day, the jungle rung.

Now you come back today, damn near hung."

He said, "Now you come by here when me and my wife
trying to get a little bit,

T' tell me that 'I rule' shit."

He said, "Shut up, motherfucker, you better not roar

'Cause I'll come down there and kick your ass some more."

The monkey started getting panicked and jumped up and
down,

When his feet slipped and his ass hit the ground.

Like a bolt of lightning, a stripe of white heat,

The lion was on the monkey with all four feet.

The monkey looked up with a tear in his eyes,

He said, "Please, Mr. Lion, I apologize."

He said, "You lemme get my head out the sand

Ass out the grass, I'll fight you like a natural man."

The lion jumped back and squared for a fight.

The motherfucking monkey jumped clear out of sight.

He said, "Yeah, you had me down, you had me last,

But you left me free, now you can still kiss my ass."

Again he started getting panicked and jumping up and
down.

His feet slipped and his ass hit the ground.

Like a bolt of lightning, stripe of white heat,

Once more the lion was on the monkey with all four feet.

Monkey looked up again with tears in his eyes.

He said, "Please, Mr. Lion, I apologize."

Lion said, "Ain't gonna be no apologizing.

I'ma put an end to his motherfucking signifying."

Now when you go through the jungle, there's a tombstone
so they say,

"Here the Signifying Monkey lay,

Who got kicked in the nose, fucked-up in the eyes,

Stomped in the ribs, kicked in the face,

Drove backwards to his asshole, knocked his neck out of
place."

That's what I say.

To this Charley would not hesitate replying with his rendition of essentially the same story, but with an added scene and a different ending:

Deep down in the jungle where the coconut grows
Lives a pimp little monkey, you could tell by the clothes
   he wore.
He had a camel-hair benny with a belt in the back,
Had a pair of nice shoes and a pair of blue slacks.
Now his clothes were cute little things,
Was wearing a Longine watch and a diamond ring.
He says he think he'd take a stroll
Down by the water hole.
And guess who he met? Down there was Mr. Lion.
The monkey started that signifying.
He said, "Mr. Lion, Mr. Lion, I got something to tell you
   today."
He said, "This way this motherfucker been talking 'bout
   you I know you'll sashay."
(He told the lion)
He said, "Mr. Lion, the way he talking 'bout your mother,
   down your cousins,
I know damn well you don't play the dozens.
He talking your uncle and your aunt's a damn shame.
Called your father and your mother a whole lot of names.
I would'a fought the motherfucker but looked at him with
   a tear in my eye.
He's a big motherfucker, he's twice my size."
The lion looked down with a tear in his eye,
Said, "Where's this big motherfucker that's twice my size?"
That little monkey said, "I'll show you the way."
He went down and the elephant was standing by a tree,
And the lion said, "Hey, motherfucker, I hear you been
   looking for me."
Elephant looked at the lion and said,
"Go on chickenshit, pick on somebody your size."
The lion made a roar.
The elephant side-stepped and kicked his ass on the floor.

The lion looked up with a tear in his eyes.

Says, "I'm gonna beat you, motherfucker, though you're twice my size."

He looked back and squared off to fight.

The elephant kicked his ass clean out of sight.

Came back for ride or roar.

Elephant stomped his ass clean on the floor.

The elephant looked about, said, "What the fuck is this?"

The lion said, "You know you's a bad motherfucker, put up your fists."

They fought three days, and they fought three nights.

I don't see how in hell the lion got out of that fight.

Coming back through the jungle more dead than alive,

Here goes the monkey in the tree with that same signifying.

He said, "Look at you, you goddamn chump.

Went down in the jungle fucking with that man

And got your ass blanshed and drug in the sand.

You call yourself a real down king,

But I found you ain't a goddamned thing.

Get from underneath this goddamned tree

'Cause I feel as though I've got to pee."

The lion looked up, said,

"That's all right, Mr. Monkey, if that's the way you want to play

The sun's gonna shine in your ugly ass some day."

Monkey looked down, said, "Long as the trees grow tall, the grass grows green,

You's the dumbest motherfucker the jungle's ever seen."

Said, "You motherfucker, I heard you down there pleading for your life.

At the very same time I had my dick in your wife.

You motherfucker, when that man knocked you over the hill,

I was gonna throw a party 'cause I thought your ass got killed."

The lion strode through the jungle to pick himself up.

The monkey called him back, said,

"Hey, you motherfucker, and oh, by the way,

Don't you come 'round here with that hoorah shit,

Every time me and my wife get ready to get a little bit."
Monkey started jumping up and down.
The left foot slipped and his ass hit the ground.
Like a bolt of lightning, like a streak of heat,
The lion was on him with all four feet.
Monkey look up with a tear in his eye,
Said, "Mr. Lion, I'se just kidding, but I apologize."
He said, "No, you're a signifying motherfucker and you always will.
You gonna fuck around some day and get somebody killed."
The monkey jumped back, and said, "Get your feet off my chest and my head out the sand
And I'll get up and beat you like a natural-born man."
Now the lion squared back, he was ready to fight,
But the poor little monkey jumped clean out of sight.
He said, "I told you, long as the trees growed tall, grass growed green,
You's the dumbest motherfucker the jungle ever seen.
Dumb motherfucker, I done tricked you again."
So the lion said, "All right, Mr. Monkey, if that's the way you want to play.
The sun's gonna shine in your ass some day."
Now what do you think? Down on Rampart Street
Who did Mr. Lion chance to meet—
The signifying monkey.
He stomped to the right and he stomped to the left.
Stomped the poor monkey clean to death.
Now I know some people think there is where the story ends.
But I'm gonna show you when it just begins.
You know how news travels in the jungle far and fast,
When it reached the monkey's baboon cousins at last.
He looked in the mirror with a tear in his eyes,
He says, "I'll get this motherfucker, he's just about my size."
He told his main whore he had to go
Down to the coconut grove to the water hole.
He packed up his whiskey and his bottle of gin,
He had a long ways to go, but a short time to make it in.
Coming through the jungle, swinging on the limbs,

Come the baddest motherfucker the jungle ever seen.
So by the time he got down to the coconut grove,
All the animals having a party 'round the water hole.
So Brother Lion was there, him and his wife,
When the baboon came up. In his hand he was carrying his knife.
He said, "Hey there, bad motherfucker, you did my cousin in.
Now I come down here to fight, to do you in."
So the lion said, "Look here, Mr. Baboon, I don't want to fight,
I want you to get your ass out of my sight."
He said, "Tomorrow I want you to come down here early in the morning.
And be ready to fight."
So the lion went on home, preparing for the next day.
He knowed he had to fight, he had to fight in a hell of a way.
So now coming back to the fight, turn back down to the coconut grove,
Who was standing there looking so outright and fine,
But old Brother Monkey and Billy Lion.
While over there with real bad sight,
They naturally had to pick on Brother Bear to referee the fight.
So he introduced them.
He said, "In this corner we got Brother Lion,
He been bit by a tiger, scratched by a lion,
Tied in a barrel of lye, shot in the ass with a forty-five.
He's a bad motherfucker, but he don't want to die.
And in this corner we got Brother Baboon.
So far he's done licked every ass from earth to the moon.
He's better known as Big Jim,
He's the baddest motherfucker that ever swing from a limb."
So when Brother Bear jumped back off the grass,
Signal for the two motherfuckers to tear their ass.
Now they begin to fight and they begin to scuffle.
Soon the lion's jaw begin to ruffle.

After a while I saw a mighty right to the lion's chin,
And everybody thought the lion had come out to an end.
But now when the bell rang for the first round,
The lion went back to his corner.
In his corner they were using Hadacol,
While in the baboon's corner they were saying a prayer
   to the Lord.
Everybody thought that Big Jim was through.
But when they came back out, that's when it turned to.
Brother Lion hit Brother Baboon to the face, one to the
   ribs,
Kicked him in the mouth, bust all his jibs.
Hit him in the ribs, hit him in the head.
That time the lion fell out for dead.
Brother Lion's wife jumped up in a mighty roar,
Said, "You just knocked my husband down to the floor."
She said, "I'ma have you put in jail.
And there ain't nobody here gonna go you bail."
So the monkey is standing on the corner with the same old
   signifying,
Said, "Don't worry, I got a friend and his name is Billy
   Lion.
He's the richest man 'round here in town. He'll get you
   out."
But where it ends, the baboon's still in jail,
And the monkey not trying to get a dime to go his cousin's
   bail.

With this contest situation, toast-telling sessions may go on
at great length, and sometimes the deeds of Shine or Stackolee
are celebrated for up to an hour. Because of the importance of
variations in performance even on the same occasion, and because each text exhibits a different handling of conventional
themes and situations and characters, it is useful to give variant
texts for some of the toasts.

"The Titanic"

Most versions of "The *Titanic*" fit into the same general pattern: a prologue about the terrible day on which the ship sank; the introduction of Shine, the mythical Negro stoker on board the ship; a description of his argument with the captain about whether the ship was sinking; his jumping into the water and his amazing swimming ability described;[15] the captain's offer of money to save him which he refuses; the offer of the captain's wife and/or daughter of sexual relations with him if he will save them, which he likewise refuses; a conversation with the shark and/or whale where he claims to be able to outswim them (which he apparently does); and a final ironic twist in which it is mentioned that Shine swam so fast that by the time news of the sea tragedy arrived, Shine, was already inebriated in some specific location.

As far as I have been able to ascertain, only one complete text of this toast has previously been printed: in the *Book of Negro Folklore* in a text collected by Langston Hughes on Eighth Avenue in Harlem in 1945.[16] In one text of this collection, a millionaire (in Hughes' version he is specified as Jay Gould) is added to the *dramatis personae*. It is he who offers monetary reward, and it is his daughter who offers herself sexually and is rejected. The text as printed shows strong evidence of being bowdlerized. The common lines

15. Legman: The speedy-swimmer joke is not original with this text. It exists in France, concerning a man who falls off a boat and is waiting for it when it docks, printed in a number of 1920's French joke collections. There is also a similar French joke called "The Mast of Marseille," which was long ago printed in the *Intermediaire des Chercheurs* (the French *Notes & Queries*), about the man who falls off the boat, thinks of his girlfriend, uses his handkerchief as a sail on his resulting erection, and his thumb up his rectum for a rudder, and sails home to Marseille. I don't know if he also arrives ahead of the boat, but it wouldn't be out of keeping with the Munchausen tone.

16. Hughes and Bontemps, *The Book of Negro Folklore*, p. 366. I have a number of other unprinted texts, one sent to me by Kenneth S. Goldstein from the recitation of E. H., a white truck driver from Texas, one from Roosevelt Wattley of Austin, Texas, and one collected by Debra Galoob in Longview, Texas.

That's when the Captain's daughter came on deck;
Hands on her pussy, and drawers 'round her neck.

become

Jay Gould's millionary daughter came running up on deck
With her suitcase in her hand and her dress 'round her
neck.

The Hughes version lacks the dialogue between the shark and
Shine and ends in a beautiful piece of modern irony:

When all them white folks went to heaven,
Shine was in Sugar Ray's Bar drinking Seagram's Seven.

It is impossible to date accurately the origin of this piece.
The date of the sinking seems to indicate that it must be
around forty-five years old. And, indeed, the story could be
older, with a change in the name of the ship to make it more
timely.

In *Gumbo Ya-Ya* the authors report from the *singing* of one
Carolina Slim a song about the *Titanic* which the singer claims
to have written.[17] The stanzas quoted are:

I always did hear that the fi' of May was a wonderful day,
You believe me, everybody had somethin' to say,
Telephones and telegraphs to all parts of town,
That the great *Titanic* was a'goin' down.
The captain and the mate was standin' on deck havin' a
few words.
'Fore they know it, the *Titanic* had done hit a big iceberg.
Had a colored guy on there called Shine, who came from
below,
And hollered, "Water is coming through the fireroom do'."
Shine jumped off that ship and begun to swim,
Thousands of white folks watchin' him.
Shine say, "Fish in the ocean, and fish in the sea,
This is one time you white folks ain't gonna fool me."

17. Saxon, Dreyer, and Tallant, *Gumbo Ya-Ya, A Collection of Louisiana Folktales*, pp. 374–75.

This is certainly a not-too-remote relation of our toast. The authors possibly felt, as Hughes and Bontemps seem to have, that it would be improper to print anything so raw, as they indicate that there were further verses. As the book is made up of material collected by the WPA, we can at least date the story in the same basic outlines as far back as the 1930's.

There is further secondary material to indicate that the story could be found in somewhat similar form even earlier. This dating can be deduced from a number of fragments from other sources. Carl Sandburg in *The American Songbag* prints a Negro song about the *Titanic* which he claims was sung by American Negro soldiers during World War I.[18] One stanza says:

> Up come Bill from de bottom flo'
> Said de water wuz runnin' in de boiler do'.
> Go back, Bill, an' shut yo' mouth
> Got forty-eight pumps to keep the water out!

In a minstrel song that was popular throughout the South in the 1920's we find another momentary glimpse of the toast. In this song, usually called "The Traveling Coon," the hero is something of a trickster.[19] His exploits seem to be derived from popular tall tales.[20]

Found among the most common verses are the following:

> The coon got on the *Titanic*
> An' started up the ocean blue,

18. Sandburg, *The American Songbag*, p. 254.

19. This song can be found in many collections and on many records with practically identical texts. See: Howard W. Odum, *Rainbow Round My Shoulder*, p. 235 (does not have verses quoted); Odum, *Wings on My Feet*, p. 286; Newman I. White, *American Negro Folk Songs*, p. 350; White, ed., *The Frank C. Brown Collection of North Carolina Folklore*, Vol. III, *The Folksongs*, p. 515.

I have also heard it on the following records: Victor 2095-7-B, as sung by Luke Jordan; Columbia 142028, as sung by Doc Walsh; OKEH 40237-A, as sung by Henry Witter; Riverside RLP 657, "Traveling Man," as sung by Billy Faier. Text on the latter from Walsh.

20. The most notable one included in all texts is the one about going to the spring to get water, a hole springing in the bucket, and how the traveling coon ran to the house, got another bucket, and caught the water before it hit the ground.

But when he saw the iceberg,
Right overboard he flew.

The white folks standin' on the deck
Said, "Coon, you are a fool."
But 'bout three minutes after that
He was shootin' craps in Liverpool.[21]

The problem presented by this material is whether these fragments are echoes of the toast in an old version or the toast is made up of fragments derived from these sources, a question unanswerable with the knowledge we are now able to gather.

We do know that there were a great many songs and ballads in broadsheet form concerning the sinking. The Lomaxes say of the event that it was "the most widely celebrated tragedy of that era, the event which seems to have caught the imagination of the Negro. . . . From the variety of ballads on this subject that have been discovered, we can only suppose that there must have been numerous songs composed and broadcast." [22] It was reported that one week after the event a blind preacher was seen on a train selling a ballad he had composed on the disaster.[23] There are three broadsheets of songs about the sinking in the Frank C. Brown collection.[24] Besides these numerous creations, there are also parodies of previously existing songs that talk about the tragedy.

Where wus you when the big *Titanic*
Went down?
Where wus you when the big *Titanic*
Went down?
Standing on the deck singing
"Alabama Boun'."[25]

21. White, *American Negro Folksongs*, p. 350.
22. John and Alan Lomax, *Negro Folk Songs as Sung by Leadbelly*, p. 181.
23. A. E. Perkins, as quoted in White, ed., *Brown Collection*, Vol. II, *The Ballads*, p. 662.
24. White, ed., *Brown Collection*, pp. 662–68. "A" text is a parody of "The Golden Vanity."
25. White, *Negro Folksongs*, p. 348.

Most of these songs concerning the *Titanic* are moralistic. They say in effect, "See what God can do, even to the rich." Such common verses as

> When that ship left England it was making for the shore,
> The rich had declared that they would ride with the poor.
> So they put the poor below,
> They were the first to go.[26]

do not necessarily contain any social message; rather, they are carrying the message of a God-fearing people.

Yet the *Titanic* disaster did evince social commentary, especially in Negro compositions. This may have been because the story was circulated that Jack Johnson, the Negro Heavyweight Champion of the World, was not allowed on the ship and thus his life was saved, an irony that appealed to the Negro sense of humor. Leadbelly in his song about the disaster says:

> Jack Johnson wanted to get on boa'd:
> Captain Smith hollered, "I ain't haulin' no coal."
> Cryin', "Fare thee, *Titanic*, fare thee well."

and later:

> Jack Johnson heard the mighty shock,
> Might'a' seen the black rascal doin' th' Eagle Rock.
> Cryin', "Fare thee, *Titanic*, fare thee well."

> Jack Johnson heard the mighty shock,
> Might'a' seen the black rascal doin' th' Eagle Rock.
> Cryin', "Fare thee, *Titanic*, fare thee well."

> Black man oughta shout for joy,
> Never lost a girl or either a boy.
> Cryin', "Fare thee, *Titanic*, fare thee well." [27]

This irony may indeed account for the popularity the story of the tragedy has had among the Negro.[28]

---

26. White, *Negro Folksongs*, p. 347.
27. John and Alan Lomax, *Negro Folk Songs*, p. 182.
28. There seems to have been a number of white songs on the tragedy, but their currency in tradition is small indeed. See *Brown Collection*, pp.

Yet this irony is only the germ of the one exercised in our toast. A great deal of the humor in the piece depends on the same triumphant irony that the Negro escapes while the whites all drown (with the crowning touch that Shine was already home and nearly drunk by the time news had arrived there). Yet this irony is made so much more effective by the fact that before the ship has gone down Shine has been offered money and sex and refuses them.

In the figure of Shine the young Negro has a character who exhibits in abundance many of the characteristics he highly values. Shine is more than a mere trickster with anxious repartee. He is to be regarded, because of both his actions and his name (generic for any male Negro), as a representative hero of his group. This toast may not be the only piece about him, but it may be the most lively and memorable of them. Though I have not encountered any other full toasts about Shine, pieces of others have come my way. Kid sometimes appends his *"Titanic"* toast with the following:

> Shine had two cents in his pocket.
> He went to a place called "Dew-drop Inn."
> He asked the broads to give him cock for a lousy fin.
> She took Shine upstairs and she gave him a fuck, and all
>   this pats.
> He came out with the syphs, the crabs, lobstertoes, and a
>   hell of a case of the claps.
> He went to the doctor. Said, "Doctor, Doctor, can't you
>   'stand.
> Please remember I'm a fucked-up man."
> Doctor got his bag, rips in his tools.
> He says, "Sit here on my three-legged stool."
> He started hammering and cutting, breaking and sawing.
> Shine said, "Doc, is that the best you can do?"
> He said, "Quiet, motherfucker, 'cause your nuts go too."

663–66; Henry, *Songs Sung in the Southern Appalachians,* p. 88; Henry, *Folksongs from the Southern Highlands,* pp. 426–27; Gardner and Chickering, *Ballads and Songs of Southern Michigan,* p. 295. Many of the above are related to the song very popular at campuses and camps, and which may be of Negro origin itself, as many early recordings testify; see *Folkways,* FP 221, #22, as sung by W. V. Smith.

In a version I collected in Texas, the descent into hell, usually in "Stackolee" (with its relation to "The Farmer's Curst Wife"), is connected to Shine:

> At half-past four Shine came in the B & O,
> And rolled up to the whorehouse door.
> And said, "Come here all you whores, and don't you pout
> 'Cause I'm a peter-pushing papa, and a water trout.
> I measures thirty-six inches across the chest,
> And I don't borrow nothing but sickness and death.
> I've got a tombstone disposition and a graveyard mind;
> I'm one motherfucker that don't mind dying."
> When Shine was dead from drinking his gin,
> The devil said, "You're a long time coming but you are
>   welcome in."
> He sent the devil for a glass of water.
> When the devil came back, he was fucking the devil's
>   daughter.
> The devil stooped over to pick up a glass,
> He rammed his dick in the devil's ass.
> Two little imps standing against the wall
> Said, "Get that black motherfucker out of here before he
>   fucks us all."

Such additions make Shine into more of the badman than he previously appeared.

In addition to the versions given above from Bobby and Kid, the following were recorded:

> It was a hell of day in the merry month of May
> When the great *Titanic* was sailing away.
> The captain and his daughter was there too,
> And old black Shine, he didn't need no crew.
> Shine was downstairs eating his peas
> When the motherfucking water come up to his knees.
> He said, "Captain, Captain, I was downstairs eating my
>   peas
> When the water come up to my knees."
> He said, "Shine, Shine, set your black ass down.

I got ninety-nine pumps to pump the water down."
Shine went downstairs looking through space.
That's when the water came up to his waist.
He said, "Captain, Captain, I was downstairs looking
    through space,
That's when the water came up to my waist."
He said, "Shine, Shine, set your black ass down.
I got ninety-nine pumps to pump the water down."
Shine went downstairs, he ate a piece of bread.
That's when the water came above his head.
He said, "Captain, Captain, I was downstairs eating my
    bread
And the motherfucking water came above my head."
He said, "Shine, Shine, set your black ass down.
I got ninety-nine pumps to pump the water down."
Shine took off his shirt, took a dive. He took one stroke
And the water pushed him like it pushed a motorboat.
The Captain said, "Shine, Shine, save poor me.
I'll give you more money than any black man see."
Shine said, "Money is good on land or sea.
Take off your shirt and swim like me."
That's when the Captain's daughter came on deck;
Hands on her pussy, and drawers 'round her neck.
Says, "Shine, Shine, save poor me.
Give you more pussy than any black man see."
Shine said, "Pussy ain't nothing but meat on the bone,
You may fuck it or suck it or leave it alone.
I like cheese but I ain't no rat.
I like pussy, but not like that."
And Shine swum on.
He said, "I hope you meet up with the whale."
Old Shine he swim mighty fine.
Shine met up with the whale.
The whale said, "Shine, Shine, you swim mighty fine,
But if you miss one stroke, your black ass is mine."
Shine said, "You may be king of the ocean, king of the sea,
But you got to be a swimming motherfucker to outswim
    me."
And Shine swim on.

Now when the news got to the port, the great *Titanic* had
   sunk,
You won't believe this, but old Shine was on the corner,
   damn near drunk.

[Arthur]

The eighth of May was one hell of a day
When the *Titanic* was sinking away.
Babies was crying and mothers was dying.
Boy, what a hell of a day,
The *Titanic* was sinking away.
Well, on aboard that ship they had a man named Shine.
He ran up to the Captain, said, "Captain, Captain, don't
   you know,
There's a leak in your boiler-room floor?"
Captain looked at Shine, said, "Shine, Shine, have no fear.
Got three pumps to keep the water out of here."
Shine went down and closed the boiler-room door,
And he didn't fear no more,
Till the water come up to his waist.
He said, "Captain, Captain, don't you know,
You got nine holes in your boiler-room floor."
Captain said, "Shine, Shine, have no fear,
We got nine pumps to keep the water out of here."
He went down below. The water came up to his neck.
He said, "Captain, Captain, don't you know,
You got ninety-nine holes in the boiler-room floor?"
Captain said, "Shine, Shine, have no fear,
We got ninety-nine pumps to keep the water out of here."
He said, "Captain, Captain, I know your word is true."
He said, "But if you want the water out of here, you got
   to get down there and pump it till your ass is blue."
Shine jumped overboard and begin to swim.
Now the millionaire on board, with his daughter was pack-
   ing his trunk.
He land in the motherfucking porthole, damn near drunk.
She went up on deck with her drawers below her knees.
She said, "Shine, Shine, save poor me.
I'll give much pussy as pussy can be."

Shine says, "Pussy on land, there's pussy on the sea,
But the pussy on land's the pussy for me."
So Shine started to swim, he begin to stroke.
He begin to wiggle like a motorboat.
And the Captain run up, said, "Shine, Shine, save poor me.
I'll give you much money as money can be."
Shine said, "Captain, that might be,
But you got to jump in this motherfucking water and swim
    like me."
He swam, he swam, he begin to stroke.
He was beginning to move like a motorboat.
Till he swum up to a shark.
He said, "Mr. Shark, of all the fishes in the sea,
I'll be damned if you can outswim me.
Your eyes may shine, your teeth may grip
[*couldn't remember any more*]"

                                     [Charley]

STACKOLEE

The history of the notorious badman Stackolee (or Stagolee)
is indeed a curious one. From the stories and songs concerning
him, one can see that he was a bully, a self-appointed guardian,
the cock-of-the-walk of a neighborhood or a small town.

Stagolee was a bully man, an' ev'ybody knowed.
When seed Stagolee comin' to give Stagolee de road.
Oh, dat man, bad man, Stagolee done come.[29]

Such a personage used to be common in Southern towns'
Negro communities and still flourishes in parts of the South.
He has his roots in primitive tribalism (leadership by prowess
or apparent control of people and/or nature), and his modern
urban counterpart is the gang leader. The bully is not respon-
sive or responsible to white laws or society; he is a law unto
himself, and his only obligation is to uphold, by his physical
powers, the honor of the neighborhood or town. When he is not

29. *Journal of American Folklore,* XXIV (1911), p. 288.

fighting, he may be terrorizing his own neighbors; but even though he may be mean by nature, he apparently remains extremely attractive to women. (The portrait of "Crown" in "Porgy and Bess" seems to be an accurate picture of this type.)

In his guise as guardian, the bully is liable to attack from those that would depose him, either from the same neighborhood or from another. He is a bad man both by nature and in the sense that his acts almost always violate the white man's laws. But he is not really to be judged by such morality, at least by his own people, as the apparent (approved) amorality of toasts and songs about Stack testifies.

Odum and Johnson describe Stack in terms of the bully. They say:

> The notorious character is sung as a hero of the tribe. His deeds are marvelous, his personality is interesting. He is admired by young and old in song and story and undoubtedly has an important influence upon the group.[30]

Stack's most celebrated exploit, the fight between Stack and Billy Lyons, was a fight between two bullies. "Bully" and "Billy" are so similarly pronounced that they could be easily interchanged; Billy's last name may originally have been "lion" (it is not untypical for a leader of this sort to take on the name of an animal), and thus Billy Lyons may originally have been "Bully Lion." [31] "Lyon" is just as typical a spelling as "Lyons," and Richard Dorson spells it as the animal.[32] One of the earliest versions of the song simply calls him "big bully":

30. Odum and Johnson, *The Negro and His Songs*, p. 196.
31. It is interesting to note that in Onah Spencer's piece, "Stackolee," which is a semiliterary rehandling of traditional material (originally published in *Direction*, IV [Summer, 1941], pp. 14–17, and later printed by Botkin in *A Treasury of American Folklore*, pp. 122–30, and Hughes and Bontemps, *The Book of Negro Folklore*, pp. 361–63), there is a stanza:

> "Jailer, jailer," says Stack, "I can't sleep.
> For round my bedside poor Billy Lyons still creeps.
> "He comes in shape of a lion with a blue steel in his hand,
> For he knows I'll stand and fight if he comes in shape of man."

32. Dorson, *Negro Folktales in Michigan*, pp. 160–62. Also notice the introduction of Billy Lion into the animal toast.

I got up one mornin' jus' 'bout four o'clock;
Stagolee and big bully done have one finish' fight.
What 'bout? All 'bout dat rawhide Stetson hat.

Stagolee shot bully; bully fell down on de flo',
Bully cry out: "Dat fohty-fo' it hurts me so."
Stagolee done kill dat bully now.[33]

Most versions of the song involve Stack's killing Billy because the latter won Stack's Stetson hat. The earliest versions, however, are not so explicit. The two texts published by Odum in 1911 never specify any of the victims: in one it is simply:

Stagolee started out, he give his wife his han';
"Goodbye, darlin', I'm goin' to kill a man."

Stagolee killed a man an' laid him on de flo',
What's dat he kill him wid? Dat same ole fohty-fo'.[34]

Most versions begin with some sort of introduction about Stack's badman characteristics:

Stagolee, he was a bad man, an' ev'body know,
He toted a stack-barreled blow gun an' a blue steel forty-
        four.[35]

Stackerlee, he was a bad man,
He wanted the whole round world to know
He toted a thirty-two twenty
And a smokeless forty-four.[36]

I remember when I was a little boy,
Sittin' on my mother's knee,
She often told me the story
About that bad man, Stackerlee.[37]

33. Odum and Johnson, *The Negro and His Songs*, pp. 196–98. First printed JAF, XXIV (1911), p. 288. Also reprinted Leach, *The Ballad Book*, pp. 755–56, and Scarborough, *On the Trail of Negro Folk Songs*, pp. 92–93.

34. Odum and Johnson, *The Negro and His Songs*, p. 197.

35. John and Alan Lomax, *American Ballads*, p. 96.

36. "Negro Prison Songs," collected and annotated by Alan Lomax, Tradition Records, TLP 1020, Side B, Band 7.

37. "Blues in the Mississippi Night," collected and edited by Alan Lomax, United Artists, UAL 4027 (end of Side A).

There usually follows a description of the gambling in which Billy wins the hat. Often it begins with a "discovery" stanza:

> It was late last night
> I thought I heard my bulldog bark.
> Stagolee and Billy Lyons,
> Squabblin' in the dark.[38]

and proceeds to the apparent victory of Billy. Stack gets his gun and comes back to shoot Billy, and Billy often pleads for Stack not to kill him.

> Stagolee found Billy,
> "Oh, please don't take my life.
> I got three children
> And a very sick little wife." [39]

The shooting itself is often described graphically:

> Stagolee shot Billy,
> Oh, he shot that boy so fas'
> That the bullet came through him
> And broke my window glass.[40]

In some versions there follows a trial scene, and in some other versions Stack is killed and goes to hell, where he beats the devil at his own game, either to be expelled or to rule in hell.

There are a number of texts of the ballad in print. Odum's versions, printed in 1911, have served as the texts for many other books and collections.[41] The Lomaxes include two collated texts in *American Ballads and Folk Songs*.[42] Wheeler has a number of versions, one of which has Stack as the hero of "Bully of the Town."[43] Alan Lomax, in his most recent volume, has a text of a chain-gang work song version.[44] Onah

38. Lomax, "Blues in the Mississippi Night."
39. "Angola Prisoners' Blues," collected by Dr. Harry Oster and Richard B. Allen, Folk-Lyric Record, LFS A-3, Side A, Band 2.
40. Oster, "Angola Prisoners' Blues."
41. *New York Times Magazine* (June 5, 1927). Albert Friedman published a collated version of these texts in *The Viking Book of Ballads,* pp. 381–82.
42. John and Alan Lomax, *American Ballads,* pp. 93–99.
43. Wheeler, *Steamboatin' Days,* pp. 100–102.
44. Lomax, *Folk Songs of North America,* p. 306.

Spencer has a long text in his saga of "Stackalee," which has been reprinted by Botkin and by Hughes and Bontemps but which presents special problems concerning its semiliterary rehandling. It is really only through the many recordings that one can fully realize the popularity of the ballad.[45]

Stack was not only a bully; he seems to have been of the roughest type, the levee bully. His place of origin is not precisely known, but he is always associated with some town on the Mississippi. Most commentators place him from Memphis. Alan Lomax says unequivocally, "Legend has it that Stacker Lee . . . was the most dangerous Negro tough of Memphis in his time, and that he shot and killed Billy Lyons, because Billy stole, or, in some accounts, spat in Stack's milkwhite Stetson hat." [46] A letter accompanying a text of the song as sung earlier than 1910 said:

> The origin of this ballad, I have been told, was the shooting of Billy Lyons in a barroom on the Memphis levee, by Stack Lee. The song is sung by Negroes on the levee while they are loading and unloading the river freighters, the words being composed by the singers. The characters were prominently known in Memphis, I was told, the unfortunate Stagalee belonging to the family of the Lee line of steamers, which are known on the Mississippi from Cairo to the Gulf.[47]

45. Charles Finger, *Frontier Ballads*, p. 91. Further printed references are: Spaeth, *Weep Some More, My Lady;* Gordon, *Folk Songs of America,* (printed from *New York Times Magazine*); Burt, *American Murder Ballads.*

Recordings of the song include: Alan Lomax, *Negro Prison Songs from the Mississippi State Penitentiary*, Tradition Records, TLP 1020 (collected 1947); Frank Hutchinson, original issue, OKEH 45106 (w80-359A), recorded in early 1927 (this is on *American Folk Music*, Vol. I, *Ballads,* Folkways, FP 251); John Hurt, OKEH 8654; Johnny Dodds and his Chicago Boys ("Stack O'Lee Blues") DE-1676; Woody Guthrie, ASCH-347 (also Folkways 781); Alan Lomax, *Listen to Our Story*, BR-1024; Paul Clayton, *Bloody Ballads*, Riverside RLP 12-615; Cisco Houston, Folkways 42; Furry Lewis, Brunswick 59001; Ed McCurdy, Elektra 108; Ma Rainey, Riverside 12-108; Logan English, Riverside 12-643; Jesse Fuller, Good Time Jazz L-12031; Archibald (perhaps a pseudonym for Speckled Red) Imperial X5358.

46. Lomax, notes to *Negro Prison Songs.*

47. John and Alan Lomax, *American Ballads*, pp. 93–94.

There were many such conjectures as to his birth and occupation. "His real name was Stack Lee and he was the son of the Lee family of Memphis who owned a large line of steamers that ran up and down the Mississippi. . . . He was a nigger what fired the engines of one of the Lee Steamers. . . . They was a steamer runnin' up an' down de Mississippi, named de Stacker Lee, and he was one o' de roustabouts on dat steamer. So dey called him Stackerlee." [48] Certainly there was such a steamer with his name; Edna Ferber even included it in *Showboat*. Wheeler has a song about the boat in *Steamboatin' Days*.[49]

The ballad and the toast stem from the same dramatic situation, the killing of Billy by Stack, but they do not share much else. In some versions of the ballad the shooting takes place in a barroom, and the locale of the toast is the particular bar-cafe, "The Bucket of Blood." Gone is the controversy over the Stetson; the fight between bullies is sufficient rationale (based on the fact that Stack has shot Billy's brother). The ironic verse

> Stagolee tol' Mrs. Billy, "Ef you don't b'lieve yo man is dead,
> Come to de barroom, see de hole I shot in his head." [50]

is also found in the toast, but the words are put into the mouth of the bartender's mother:

> She said, "You don't mean to tell me my son is dead."
> I said, "If you don't believe it, look at those motherfucking rockets in his goddamn head."

Only in one text is any courtroom scene included, and then it is for a different purpose than that found in the ballad.

The three texts of the toasts included here are similar in many respects. They all begin with a description of the times; a catalog of Stack's earthly belongings; the walk down the street; the entering of the "Bucket of Blood"; the serving of the

48. John and Alan Lomax, *American Ballads*, p. 93.
49. See *Midwest Folklore*, 10:77. Also see Wheeler, *Steamboatin' Days*, pp. 102–103.
50. John and Alan Lomax, *American Ballads*, p. 97.

unfortunate meal and the consequent killing of the bartender; the arrival of the dead man's mother and her warning about the coming of her other son, Billy Lyons (or Benny Long); the deploying of the girl to keep Stack there by "taking him upstairs"; the arrival of Billy; the fight; and Billy's demise. Each adds little interesting scenes. The endings of many texts are conventional boasts which may well have traveled from the river with the stories of Stack.

Nothing like the toast has ever appeared in print. D. K. Wilgus has sent four texts from the Western Kentucky Folklore Archives which are very similar to the Camingerly texts. Three of his texts have the same general plan of Charley's text here. The fourth has the outlines of the first two here with the boast at the end, and also has the type of signature to be found in Arthur's version of "The Monkey and the Baboon." There are two texts in the Texas Archives, one collected by myself from a student who had it from a Negro marine in San Diego in 1959. The other was collected by Debra Galoob and is printed in bowdlerized form in her article (19   ).

There are, however, two places in which toastlike versions of the Stackolee Story appear in print. The first of these is an article by Richard Dorson, "Negro Tales." He includes two texts which show clearly that the ballad and the toast are related. His first text includes verses from the ballad, including the one about the bulldog barking and arguing in the dark, and goes on to a number of lines of boasts including the one commonly found in the toast about rattlesnakes crawling off and dying.[51] His second text is sometimes in verse form, sometimes in prose, and also includes verses from the ballad.[52] The prose passages show, by their occasional rhymes, some contact with a toast; this is also shown in the references to clocks and time, found often in the toast, but not, so far as I have found, in the song. Hughes and Bontemps include a similar text that seems to be in toast form, but which tells the story

51. These boasts are some widely known ones. *JAF*, 40:293, has the similar: I was born in a backyard/Suckled by a bear/I got nine sets of jaw teeth/An' three coaches of hair. See the rattlesnake boast in Thorp, *Songs of the Cowboys*, p. 17, in a song called "Buckskin Joe."

52. Dorson, *Western Folklore*, pp. 160–62.

in the ballad and ends with Stack running hell after vanquish-
ing the devil and having intercourse with his wife.[53] Kid gives
a similar narrative about Stack and Billy in joke form (and then
as a toast):

> Now you know, everybody heard the joke about Stacko-
> lee. Well, they didn't tell you that Stackolee died and Billy
> died and they went to hell. Devil said to Billy, "I seen you
> every day and I know you was coming. I knowed you
> was on your way." So he told Billy he could have all the
> fun he wants, just to keep away from his wife.
>
> So Billy was goofing around one day and got hold of the
> devil's wife, started working. Got through, he got hold of
> the devil's daughter, started to working. Got through,'
> grabbed hold of the devil's niece, he started working. He
> was running around Hell trying to catch the devil's wife.
> She said, "Devil, get him down." When three little jumpy
> little bastards jumped out of the wall and said, "Get that
> motherfucker before he fucks us all."

> Back in '32 when times was hard
> I had a sawed-off shotgun and a crooked deck of cards,
> Pin-striped suit, fucked-up hat,
> T-model Ford, didn't even have a payment on that.
> Had a cute little broad, she throwed me out in the cold.
> I asked her why, she said, "Our love is growing old."
> So I packed all my little rags, took a walk down Rampail
>   Street.
> That's where all the bad motherfuckers went down to
>   meet.
> I walked through water and I waded through mud,
> Come a little hole-in-the-wall, they call the "Bucket of
>   Blood."
> I walked in and asked the bartender, "Dig, chief, can I get
>   something to eat?"
> He threwed me a stale glass of water and flung me a
>   fucked-up piece of meat.
> I said, "Raise, motherfucker, do you know who I am?"

---

53. Hughes and Bontemps, *The Book of Negro Folklore*, pp. 361–63.

He said, "Frankly, motherfucker, I just don't give a damn."
I knowed right then that chickenshit was dead.
I throwed a thirty-eight shell through his motherfucking
    head.
So a broad walked over, she said, "Pardon me, please.
Can you tell me where the bartender is, please?"
I said, "Sure, whore, behind the bar with his mind at ease."
She looked back and screamed, "No! My son can't be
    dead."
I said, "You don't think so? Look at the hole in that mother-
    fucker's head."
She said, "Who did this terrible crime, may I ask you
    please?"
I said, "Me, bitch, and my name is Stackolee."
She said, "Oh, I heard of you, Stack, from the tales of old.
Be here when my son Benny Long get back."
I said, "Bitch, I'll be here till the world go to pass.
You tell your son, Benny Long, that I said, 'Kiss my ass.' "
Just then a cute little broad came over, a terrible smile.
She looked me up and down and said, "You look like you
    ain't had none, Daddy, in quite a while."
I said, "Now raise, bitch, don't hand me that shit.
I'm used to pussy quite a bit."
She looked at her watch, it was quarter to eight.
She said, "Come on upstairs, I'ma set you straight."
The bed gave a twist, the springs gave a twistle.
I throwed nine inches of joint to the whore before she
    could move a gristle.
We came back downstairs. They was fucking on the bar,
    sucking on the floor.
Just then you could hear a pin drop, for that bad-ass
    Benny Long walked in the door.
Now he walked over to the bar where his brother lay dead,
And quietly said,
"Who had nerve to put a hole in *my* brother's head?"
I jumped up and screamed, "Me, motherfucker, put your
    mind at ease.
I'm known as a bad motherfucker called Stackolee."
He said, "Oh, I heard of you, Stack, from tales of old.

But you know you done tore your ass when you fucked
my hole.
I'ma give you the chance my brother never had. I'ma give
you the chance to run,
Before I throw open my bad-ass cashmere and pull my
bad-ass gun."
Just then some little short motherfucker way over in the
corner jumped up and hollered, "Somebody call the
law."
Benny Long throwed a forty-five shell through the mother-
fucker's jaw.
His broad walked over, she said, "Benny, please."
He beat that whore down to her motherfucking knees.
Just then everything got black, 'cause out went the lights.
I had that old bad-ass Benny Long in my thirty-eight sights.
When the lights came back on and all the best,
I had sent that old bad motherfucker to internal rest.
Thirteen thirty-eight-bullet holes 'cross his motherfucking
chest.
His boys jumped up and said, "Ain't this a shame.
Here's a man got our boss Benny Long there on the floor
dead.
This jive-ass motherfucker's reputation we haven't ever
heard."
They dove in their coats and went down for this shit.
I said, "Cool it, motherfuckers, let me tell you a bit.
I was born in the backwoods, for my pet my father raised
a bear.
I got two sets of jawbone teeth, and an extra layer of hair.
When I was three I sat in a barrel of knives.
A rattlesnake bit me and crawled off and died.
'Cause after I get up and leave, my asshole print leaves
'danger.' "

[Kid]

Back in '32 when times was hard
Had a sawed-off shotgun with a crooked deck of cards.
Had a pin-striped suit, old fucked-up hat,
And a T-model Ford, not a payment on that.

I had a cute little whore, throwed me out in the cold.
When I asked her why, she said, "Our love is growing old."
I took a little walk down Rampart Street,
Where all them bad-assed motherfuckers meet.
I walked through water and I waded through mud.
I came to a little old hole-in-the-wall called the "Bucket of Blood."
I walked in, asked the man for something to eat.
Do you know that bastard gave me a stale glass of water and a fucked-up piece of meat.
I said, "Raise, motherfucker, do you know who I am?"
He said, "Frankly, I don't give a damn."
I know right then that sucker was dead.
I throwed a thirty-eight shell through that motherfucker's head.
Now a cute little whore came up and said, "Where's the bartender, please?"
I said, "Look behind the bar, baby, he's with his mind at ease."
She grabbed her head.
She said, "No, my son can't be dead."
I said, "No? Look at the hole in that motherfucker's head."
She said, "Who did this crime, may I ask you, please?"
I said, "Me, bitch, and they call me Stackolee."
She said, "I heard of you, Stack,
But you better not be here when my son Benny Long gets back."
I said, "Bitch, I'll be here when the world go to pass.
And you can tell Benny Long he can kiss my ass."
Still another cute little whore came up, said, "Where's the bartender?
Hi there, baby, where's the bartender, if you please?"
I said, "Look behind the bar, he's with his mind at ease."
So she peeped at her watch, it was seven of eight.
She said, "Come upstairs, baby, let me set you straight."
Now we went upstairs, the springs give a twistle.
I throwed nine inches of dick into that bitch before she could move her gristle.
Now we came downstairs big and bold.

They was fucking on the bar, sucking on the floor.

Then you could hear a pin drop. Benny Long came in.

He walked over where his brother lay dead, and he calmly said,

"Who had the nerve to put a hole in my brother's head?"

When I jumped up, I said, "Me, motherfucker, so put your mind at ease.

I'm that bad-ass so-and-so they call Stackolee."

He said, "I heard of you, Stack, from the tales of old,

But you know you tore your ass when you fucked my hole.

But I'ma give you the chance my brother never got. I'ma give you a chance to run,

'Fore I reach in my cashmere and pull out my bad-ass gun."

Just then some old sucker over in the corner said, "Somebody call the law."

He stretched out and put a forty-five shell through that motherfucker's jaw.

A cute little whore came over and said, "Benny, please."

He blowed that bitch down to her knees.

And out went the lights,

And Benny Long was in both of my thirty-eight sights.

Now the lights came on and all the best.

I sent that sucker to eternal rest,

With thirteen thirty-eight-bullet holes 'cross his motherfucking chest.

This boy said, "Who is this sucker whose name we haven't heard

Got our boss laying there dead?

We ought to kill this motherfucker to fuck him up."

I said, "Cool it, motherfucker, let me tell you a bit.

I was raised in the backwoods, where my pa raised a bear.

And I got three sets of jawbone teeth and an extra layer of hair.

When I was three I sat in a barrel of knives.

Then a rattlesnake bit me, crawled off and died.

So when I come in here, I'm no stranger,

'Cause when I leave, my asshole print leaves 'danger.' "

[Arthur]

In 1938 when things was hard
I had a crooked pair of dice and a stacked deck of cards.
I waded through water and I waded through mud
Until I came to a place called the "Bucket of Blood."
Now I went in to get myself a little something to eat
And the waiter brought me back a muddy glass of water
    and a tough-ass piece of meat.
I said, "Say, motherfucker, do you know who this might
    be?
This is that bad motherfucker named Stackolee."
The waiter looked at me and said,
"I heard 'bout you from 'cross the way,
But I feed you hungry motherfuckers each and every day."
Now I pull out my gun and layed three rockets in his
    motherfucking head.
He fell out behind the counter dead.
Little lady came in and said, "Where's the waiter, please?"
I said, "He's laying behind the counter with his mind at
    ease."
She said, "You don't mean to tell me my son is dead."
I said, "If you don't believe it, look at those motherfucking
    rockets in his goddamn head."
She fell out on the goddamn floor,
And here come walked up to me a pretty little whore.
Said, "Hello, Stackolee, I haven't seen you in a mighty
    long time."
She looked at the clock, it was about quarter to eight.
She said, "Come on upstairs and I'll set you straight."
Now I went upstairs and we begin to fuck.
I begin to push dick to this whore like a ten-ton truck.
And then everything was going 'long fine
When out walked Billy Lyon.
At first I thought it was the motherfucking law,
The way the hinges jumped off the goddamned door.
I looked around, said, "What the fuck this might be?"
He said, "You know, you bad motherfucker, I know your
    name is Stackolee."
I said, "And by the way, what's your name, look so fine?"
He said, "Shut up, motherfucker, this is Billy Lyon."

Now some dirty bitch turned out the light,
But I had Billy Lyon in my goddamned sight.
One little bitch hollered, "Stackolee, please."
I shot that bitch clean to her knees.
The other one hollered, "Call the law."
I shot that bitch in the goddamned jaw.
Now three of them old Mississippi police came in all loud
     and raunchy.
"Let's kick this motherfucker's ass and go on home."
Well I guess it was 'round nine o'clock, or somewhere
     'round ten
I was standing before some jive-ass judge and ten other
     men.
One motherfucker said, "What may the charges be?"
One said, "Murder," one said, "Rape," one said, "Murder
     in the third degree."
Then the old judge said, "Well, how might he die?"
One said, "Hang him," one said, "Give him gas."
Little lady jumped up in the courtroom and said, "Run
     'lectricity through the rotten motherfucker's ass."
I grabbed that bitch by the seat of her drawers
And threw her out the courtroom door.
Judge said, "Stackolee, I see you're a man without any fear,
So I'ma give you ninety-nine years."
I looked at him, said, "Judge, ninety-nine ain't no god-
     damn time.
My father's in Sing Sing doing two-ninety-nine.

                                              [Charley]

THE SIGNIFYING MONKEY

These toasts about the adventures of the Signifying Monkey
may be the last lively gasp of the Negro tradition of animal
stories in American provenience. As in the famed series about
Brer Rabbit or even Anansi, the animals act like animals often
only to show the similarities of themselves to humans. As in
these older tales, these toasts present a milieu that is half natural habitat, half world of man, and characters that sometimes

act like the animals whose names they bear and sometimes like human beings. The shift between these oppositions is done without any sense of existing conflict at all.

> Deep down in the jungles, way back in the sticks,
> The animals had formed a game called pool. The baboon
>   was a slick.
> Now a few stalks shook and a few leaves fell.
> Up popped the monkey one day, 'bout sharp as hell.

The animals seem as much at home in the jungle or on the street; the monkey is equally adept at climbing trees and shooting pool. Though he is portrayed as a tree climber, he is the sharpest of dressers by human standards.

> He had a one-button roll, two-button satch.
> You know, one them boolhipper coats with a belt in the
>   back.

or

> He had a camel-hair benny with a belt in the back,
> He'd a pair of nice shoes and a pair of blue slacks.
> Now his clothes were cute little things,
> Was wearing a Longine watch and a diamond ring.

The baboon is easily his match, though:

> The baboon stood with a crazy rim,
> Charcoal gray vine, and a stingy brim,
> Hand full of dimes, pocket full of herbs,
> Eldorado Cadillac parked at the curb.

Much like his predecessors Brer Rabbit and Anansi, the monkey is a trickster figure; his mode of life, his existence depends upon his agility, mental and physical. Though not solely the possession of the Negro, the trickster figure has figured very greatly in black folklore. The fact that the monkey fits into this type is patent. He is not only a clever hero, smaller and weaker and a diminutive animal but his adventure with the lion qualifies him as a rogue.

It is interesting to note that this hero is a monkey. In the minds of a certain segment of the white population of the world, the Negro has been associated with the monkey. Perhaps because of his African jungle heritage and the casual resemblance between some Negroid and some simian physical characteristics, the words "monkey" and "ape" have been used as derogatory words in relation to the Negro, and have achieved a meaning and notoriety not very different from "nigger." In much the same way that nigger has come to mean, among Negroes, any bad kind of Negro, so monkey has come to mean any Negro that will unduly play around, especially for the amusement of whites. As one Negro youth is reported to have said, "If you can act big enough monkey, you can get anything you want [from whites]." [54]

Probably because of this concept, Negro children often feel mystically related to monkeys, and call each other apes or monkeys in jest (just as they humorously chide each other on being black). As we had a pet monkey ourselves, we were able to see much of this "identification." Beyond the common taunt found among children and adults of any group of "Look, there goes your brother" when the monkey passed, many of the Negro children developed a real kinship feeling with the monkey, erupting with such statements about the monkey as, "Is he Negro?" or "He is colored, and I am a monkey." The same children would often look through a book of monkey pictures we had and comment on each, assigning someone's names to the pictures, such as "There's you," "There's her," "There's Lydia," "There's me." The identification was certainly a racial one, for certain monkeys were excluded from the name-attaching ceremony because they were "white monkeys"—that is, they did not have such pronounced Negroid features.

Of the two toasts concerned with the doings of the monkey, the only texts in print are of "The Signifying Monkey and the Lion." Once again our printed text comes from Hughes and Bontemps.[55] That text, obviously rewritten to a slight degree, still preserves most of the feeling of the original. It has an interesting moralistic ending:

54. Simpson and Yinger, *Racial and Cultural Minorities,* p. 470.
55. Hughes and Bontemps, *Negro Folklore,* p. 363.

"Monkey," said the Lion,
Beat to his unbooted knees,
"You and your signifying children
Better stay up in them trees."
Which is why today
Monkey does his signifying
A-*way-up* out of the way.

Richard Dorson prints a tale, "The Elephant, the Lion, and the Monkey," that tells the same story, with the change that the Monkey tells the Elephant the Lion is playing the dozens on him.[56] The toast must have a fairly wide distribution, for D. K. Wilgus has sent two Kentucky texts very similar to the ones printed here, and a shorter text from New Jersey. Kenneth S. Goldstein has sent a fragmentary text as recited by Ernest Hobbs. Ed Kahn also sent a partial text. I have three Texas versions, two from Austin and one from Longview which was printed in bowdlerized form in Debra Galoob's article, "Back in '32 When the Times Was Hard" (19   ).

On an early race record, "Can't You Read," sent to me by Mack McCormick as sung by Big Maceo (Maceo Merriweather, Bluebird 8772, Victor 3209, recorded June 24, 1941), the following verse occurs:

Now the monkey and the elephant, they went out for a little drive.
Elephant hit the monkey right square in his eye.
The monkey looked up with a tear in his eye.
"Now lookahere, big boy, you oughta get someone your size.
One of these days I'm gonna climb me a tree.
Remember big boy, you got to march right under me.
When you march under me you better march careful and fast.
I hear the wind abreakin' cause a . . ."

This record was probably a new issue of records made in January, 1930, by Lonnie Johnson and Spencer Williams (OKEH 8762) and Barbecue Bob (Columbia 14523-D) called "Monkey

56. Dorson, *Western Folklore*, 13:87–88.

and the Baboon," and these seem to indicate the existence of this toast for at least three decades.

Two recent pop records are close to the texts here, one of which has an interesting etiological ending with the lion chasing the monkey into the tree, establishing his permanent residence there (Motif A 2433.3.19).[57] Bruce Jackson sent me a highly bowdlerized prose text of "The Signifying Monkey and the Lion," printed in *The Lancer*, the Indiana State Prison inmate magazine (Vol. III, No. 3 [March 1946], p. 37).

There is a derivative verse, current in white tradition in the Eastern United States, which stems only in part from these toasts. The beginning is a direct borrowing:

Up jumped Willie from a coconut grove,
He was a mean cocksucker by the color of his clothes.
He had a twelve-inch peg and a two-button stitch;
Man, he was a cool-looking son of a bitch.

but the subsequent action places the piece firmly in the fornication contest tradition. The ending is often the stock toast ending:

Now when Willie died, he went to hell
And he fucked the devil's wife, and he fucked her well,
And on his grave this is seen,
"Willie, the human fucking machine."

The texts of "The Signifying Monkey and the Lion" printed here are uniform except in some small particulars of the fights and in respect to the variable ending. In the latter part of one text, all pretense of the jungle is given up. In the last few lines, the Lion becomes "Billy Lion," the protagonist of the "Stackolee" story, and this fight may indeed have come from another bully story and have been an autonomous toast just added to this story for interest.

The story is strongly reminiscent of two international tale types. One (Type 6) is a tale in which an animal captor is persuaded to talk and thus the captive is released. The monkey

---

57. Oscar Brown, Jr., on *Sin and Soul*, CL 1577 (LP), Columbia 3-41977 (single); Smoky Joe with the Clyde Leoppard Band, Flip #228.

uses a very similar strategy for his escape (see Motif K 56.1.1). The other (Type 59) involves a strategy similar to the one the monkey uses in the early part of the toast. In this tale, "Jackal carries false challenges, etc., between the lion and the bull so that they kill each other" (see K 213.2).

The texts of "The Monkey and the Baboon" also are similar to the ones found in Camingerly for the most part. Except for the fragmentary text printed by Debra Galoob, I have never seen a text in print. The Big Maceo record cited above also has a stanza which goes:

> Way back in nineteen hundred and ten
> The monkey and the baboon they came walking in.
> The monkey told the baboon "Let's shoot a game of pool."
> The monkey could shoot but the baboon wasn't no fool.
> Next thing came along was a little mule.
> He said, "You know I'm so mad I even caint wear no shoes."
> Next thing came down was Mr. Cat.
> We're gonna have to put the stuff going on here like that.
> Next thing came, there was a little mouse.
> Let's all get drunk, break up the doggone house.
> Can't you read.
> Can't you read.
> If you keep on reading, I'm bound to put you out.

The toast can be understood only by a knowledge of the strategy of the games of pool and cooncan. In pool, of course, the object is to sink as many balls in their numerical order as possible without missing. To have a run like the one described in this toast is truly phenomenal, as is only seen among pool sharks.

Cooncan is a favorite rummy game among the Negroes in this area (and throughout the South). It is very complicated, and as it is amply described in Hoyle, I will omit such description here. The dialogue that surrounds the cooncan game is the sort that one can hear during any game among Negroes, full of attempts to get "one-up" or to "out-psych" the opposing players.

THE MONKEY AND THE BABOON

Deep down in the jungles, way back in the sticks,
The animals had formed a game called pool. The baboon
    was a slick.
Now a few stalks shook, and a few leaves fell.
Up popped the monkey one day, 'bout sharp as hell.
He had a one-button roll, two-button satch.
You know, one them boolhipper coats with a belt in the
    back.
The baboon stood with a crazy rim,
Charcoal gray vine, and a stingy brim,
Hand full of dimes, pocket full of herbs,
Eldorado Cadillac parked at the curb.
He said, "Mr. Monkey, if it ain't my friend.
We gonna play some Georgia Skin."
"Raise! That ain't my game.
Me and you can play some cooncan."
"Why should we argue and fight, acting like a fool,
We'll just step in the hall and shoot a game of pool."
So the baboon reached over to break the rack.
The monkey kicked him square in the ass and he snatched
    him back.
He said, "Unh, unh, not here."
So they was fussing and fighting over who was going to
    make the break.
The giraffe was the houseman. You know naturally he had
    a stake.
So he said, "Well flip for it."
So he flipped a coin about three feet in the air.
The baboon was itching to try to make a pin.
It was a two-headed coin, the monkey had to win.
The monkey grabbed a stick, and the baboon snatched
    the chalk,
And around the table them two motherfuckers started to
    walk.
The monkey broke the rack. Got the one, two, three, four,
    and five.

Brought tears in the baboon's eyes.
Now the six, seven, and eight
Was a natural take.
The nine and ten
Flew right in.
The 'leven ball crossed corner, the twelve just as well.
The thirteen in the side pocket, combination, like a bat
    out of hell.
Baboon jumped up, said, "It's a goddamn shame,
I can't beat this ugly motherfucker in no kind of game.
We gonna play some cooncan."
The monkey told the baboon, "You know Brother Buzzard
    who live across the creek?"
He said, "I cooncanned him for a solid week."
He said, "But you ain't gonna act right,
'Cause it took all me and my blade could do to keep out
    of a fight.
But you go find yourself a stump to fit your rump,
I'ma cooncan you tonight till your asshole jump."
He said, "I'ma hold my jacks, spread my queens,
I'ma do switching in this old fucked-up deck the world's
    never seen.
I'ma hold my deuces, lay down my treys,
Get down on your motherfucking ass in a thousand ways."
He said, "Now skip Mr. Rabbit, hop Mr. Bear,
Looks shitty, but there's 'leven of them there."

                                                    [Kid]

Deep down in the jungle, way back in the sticks
The animals had a poolroom and the baboon was a slick.
But they didn't know, deep down in the jungle in the
    coconut grove
Lived a little pimp monkey, you could tell by the clothes
    he wore.
He had a camel-hair benny with the belt in the back,
Had a pair of nice shoes, and a pair of blue slacks.
He said he think he'd take a little stroll.
In just a few minutes he passed the poolroom door.
Now the baboon was setting on the stool

Waiting for the next damn fool.
Celery seen, celery done,
Who wanted to try Brother Devil one?
He said, "Come here, Mr. Monkey, you come here late.
But you're just in time for one more break."
The monkey said, "Houseman, I want you to hold my gun.
I don't want to kill the motherfucker, I just want to shoot
   him one."
He said, "And by the way, while you're at that, I want
   you to chalk my cue.
If I break this motherfucker, there's gonna be a tip for
   you."
He broke the balls and ran the one, two, and three.
He said, "Hold this cue stick while I go and pee."
He pissed on the table, he shit on the floor.
Came back and run the three and four.
Now he shot the balls, and he shot 'em all, and turned
   around and shot the five.
Brought hot, scalding water from the baboon's eyes.
He banked the six and seven cross-side.
He took the motherfucking eight for a goddamn ride.
He shot the nine, he shot the ten.
He only had five more balls to shoot on in.
He shot the 'leven, he shot the twelve.
By that time, the baboon said, "To hell! Go to hell!"
He said, "Wait a minute, rack the ball."
He said, "Do you know how to coon?"
"Get you a rump to fit your stump
And I'll coon you till your asshole jump."
The monkey said, "Well, you ain't saying a thing."
So they started out. Brother Baboon said, "Monkey, when
   I fall out on you I'm gonna spread four queens
And this a king."
Well, the game's going 'long all right, he made a mistake.
And that's when this monkey made a hell of a break.
Now there was a spider on the wall, with a fly beside his
   head.
He saw that break and he dropped dead.
He said, "Jump Brother Rabbit and leap Brother Bear,

It may look like shit, but there's 'leven cards there."
He said, "Somebody go get this motherfucker's wife,
'Cause I'm just about to win his goddamned life.
I done won all his silver, done won all his gold.
If we play long enough, win his goddamned soul."

[Charley]

Deep down in the jungle, way back in the sticks,
That's where the baboon was a slick.
Now a few stalks shook, and a few leaves fell,
And up jumped the monkey, sharp as hell.
Had a one-button roll, two-button satch.
You know, one of them boolhipper coats, you know, with
      a buckle in the back.
There was Mr. Baboon, he was sharp as a pin.
Charcoal gray vine with a stingy brim.
He had a pocket full of money, handfull of herbs,
Eldorado Cadillac parked at the curb.
He said, "Mr. Monkey, if it ain't my friend.
Come on, Dad, let's play some Georgia Skin."
He said, "Raise, motherfucker, that ain't my game.
Come on, let's play some cooncan."
He said, "No, don't be no fool.
Let's go in the hall and play a game of pool."
They was fussing and fighting 'bout who was going to
      make the break.
They asked the houseman, naturally he had a stake.
The monkey grabbed the stick, and the baboon grabbed
      the chalk.
Around the table them two motherfuckers started to walk.
Now the monkey reached back
He broke the rack.
He sank the one, two, three, four, and five.
He brought tears to the baboon's eyes.
The six, seven, and eight
Was a natural take.
The nine and ten
Flew right in.

He played the 'leven in the corner and the twelve just as
    well,
Put the thirteen ball in the side, like a bat out of hell.
Knocked his stick on the floor,
Said, "Count 'em, house, you'll find well over sixty-four."
The baboon said, "Goddamn, I can't beat this man in no
    kind of game.
Come on, let's play some cooncan."
He said, "You know Brother Rabbit across the creek?
Well, I cooncanned him for a solid week.
But you ain't gonna act right,
'Cause it took all me and my blade to do to keep out of a
    fight.
Come on. I'ma find a stump to fit your rump
And I'ma cooncan you till your asshole jump."
He said, "I'ma spread my deuces and dish my treys,
I'ma get down on you in all kinds of ways.
I'ma spread my jacks and dish my queens,
I'ma put a switch in the deck the world never seen.
So hop Mr. Rabbit and skip Mr. Bear.
It's gonna look mighty shady, but there's 'leven of them
    there.
If anybody asks you who pulled that toast,
Just tell them old bullshitting Snell, from coast to coast.
I live on Shotgun Avenue, Tommygun Drive,
Pistol Apartment, and Room 45."

                                       [Arthur]

To be said at end of "The Monkey and the Baboon" sometimes:

Now I was walking through the jungle the other day, come
    along a coconut tree.
That old dirty motherfucking baboon tried to shit on me.
So I looked up and said, "Raise, do you know what you're
    doing?"
He said, "Dig, kid, did you see me lose my money the other
    day?"
I said, "Yeah." He said, "Don't come fucking me in that
    kind of way."

He said, "Furthermore, due to that you're a slick, and I'm
supposed to be smart,
You knowed I was going to shit, 'cause you heard me when
I fart."

[Kid]

THE SIGNIFYING MONKEY AND THE LION

Down in the jungle near a dried-up creek,
The signifying monkey hadn't slept for a week
Remembering the ass-kicking he had got in the past
He had to find somebody to kick the lion's ass.
Said the signifying monkey to the lion that very same day,
"There's a bad motherfucker heading your way.
The way he talks about you it can't be right,
And I know when you two meet there going to be a fight.
He said he fucked your cousin, your brother, and your
niece,
And he had the nerve enough to ask your grandmom for
a piece."
The lion said, "Mr. Monkey, if what you say isn't true
about me,
Bitch, I'll run your ass up the highest tree."
The monkey said, "Now look, if you don't believe what I
say,
Go ask the elephant. He's resting down the way."
The lion let out with a mighty rage,
Like a young cocksucker blowing his gauge.
He ran through the jungle with a mighty breeze,
Kicking gorillas in the ass and knocking giraffes to their
knees.
Then he saw the elephant resting under his tree.
He said, "Get up, motherfucker, you and me."
The elephant looked up from the corner of his eye
And said, "Scram, chickenshit, fuck with someone your
size."
The lion squatted and made a pass.
The elephant ducked and knocked him flat on his ass.

Then he jumped in his stomach and stepped in his face
And tore his asshole clean out of place.
He mashed in his face like a forty-four,
Plucked out his eyes and dared him to roar.
The lion crawled through the jungle more dead than alive,
And swore to stop the monkey from signifying.
Now that's when the monkey really started his shit.
"Jive-king of the jungle, ain't you a bitch,
All swelled up like you got the seven-year itch.
You was up there all jobbing and jiving and swinging your
    arms
While the elephant was hitting you like a young King
    Kong.
Going around talking about you can't be beat.
Well I want you to know that me and my wife had a ring-
    side seat.
And another thing. Every time me and my old lady try to
    get a little bit,
You come 'round here with that roaring shit.
Git away from my tree before I pee."
The lion looked up and said, "Mr. Monkey, if you piss on
    me
While under your tree I pass,
I'll climb that tree and kick your motherfucking ass."
The monkey said, "Mister Lion, if I piss on you while you
    pass,
You'll climb this tree and *kiss* my ass."
The monkey started jumping up and down.
His foot missed the limb and his ass hit the ground.
Faster than a streak of lightning and a bolt of heat,
The lion was on the monkey with all four feet.
Then the monkey's wife started her shit,
"See that, monkey, that's what you git
Going around signifying and shit."
The monkey said, "Now look! You shut up, because there's
    one thing I'll never be able to see.
That's how I leaped and missed a whole damn tree.
Bitch, I believe you pushed me."
The monkey looked up with tears in his eyes

And said, "I'm sorry, Mister Lion, I apologize."
The lion said, "There ain't no use for you to be crying,
Because I'm going to stop you from signifying.
Now before I put you away to rest,
I want to hear your dying request."
The monkey said, "Get your motherfucking feet out my
    eyes and my nuts out of this sand,
And I'll wrestle your ass all over this land."
Then when the lion got ready to fight
The monkey jumped up and went clean out of sight.
But in the distance you could hear the monkey say,
"As long as these weeds and green grass grow,
I'm going to be around to signify some more.
And another thing, Mr. Lion, you ain't no hell by the way
    you creep,
'Cause I know where three elephants sleep."

                                                    [Arthur]

The monkey said to the lion one bright summer day,
"There's a big motherfucker across the way,
You and him will never be right
Because I know when you get there, there'll be a hell of
    a fight.
Now here is something I really has to say.
He talks about your mother in a bitching way.
He called her a no-good bitch and he meant it for a fight.
You ask my opinion, I'll say, 'Man, it wasn't right.'"
Off drove the lion in a terrible rage,
Creating a breeze which shook the trees
And knocked the giraffe to his knees.
He confronted the elephant up under the tree,
And said, "Motherfucker, it's you or me."
He drove at the elephant and made his pass.
The elephant knocked him flat on his ass.
He kicked and stomped him all in his face.
He busted two ribs and pulled his tail out of place.
They cursed and fought damn near all day.
I still don't see how that lion got away.
He dragged himself back, more dead than alive,

When the monkey started his signifying.
"Well, I be damned, kid, you don't look so well.
Looks to me like you've been catching hell.
When you left here the whole forest rung.
Now you come back damn near hung.
That elephant sure kicked the shit out of your ass,
But that bad, bad cocksucker sure put you in your class.
You've got more scratches on your ass than a dog with the
    seven-year itch.
You say you're King of the Jungle, now ain't that a bitch.
Every night when I'm trying to steal a bit
Here you come with your ratcoon shit.
Now motherfucker, if you make another roar
I'll jump down and kick your ass some more."
The monkey laughed and jumped up and down.
He missed a limb and his big ass hit the ground.
Like a bolt of lightning or a flash of heat,
The lion hit the monkey with all four feet.
The monkey screamed and rubbed his eyes,
And said, "Please, Mr. Lion, I apologize."
"Shut up, motherfucker, and stop your crying,
'Cause I'm gonna kick your ass for signifying."
The monkey's last words as he was dying,
"I tore my ass by signifying."
Now the monkey is dead and in his grave.
No more meddling will he crave.
On his tombstone these words are wrote,
"He's dead as he lived, by his signifying shit,
Now take my warning and stay in your class,
Or you'll get knocked right square on your ass."

[Harry]

SQUAD TWENTY-TWO

Judging by the streets mentioned in this toast, this is a local production. South and Lombard are the two major east-west
streets in the neighborhood.

The attitude toward the police expressed here is the prevalent one among the Negroes of this area. A long history of very bad incidents has produced much antagonism between the police and the neighborhood people.

> I ran over to Lombard Street to get my gat.
> I ran back to South Street, put on my hat.
> While I was walking along who did I run into but a little
>   old boy who was holding a ten-spot in his hand.
> So I grabbed that motherfucker and away I flew,
> And guess who I run into?
> Those bad motherfuckers from Squad Twenty-two.
> Now in the back was my man.
> He didn't even raise his hat or tip his hand.
> So they put me in the wagon and they took me on down
>   to the county jail.
> I didn't have a punk, fag, or sissy to go my bail.
> So a guy in the cell told me the thing to do,
> Was to get in tight with the captain of Squad Twenty-
>   two.
> I talked my shit and I talked it well.
> He let me out of jail, so I flew home like a bat out of hell.
> Now I run back to South Street to put down my gat,
> And back over to Lombard Street to put down my hat.
> Now I takes the short cut home and jumps into bed,
> And this is what the rotten bitch I live with said,
> Said, "Charley dear, wonderful one,
> While you was gone I dreamt you got shot in the ass by a
>   big gun.
> And by the way, the man that was carrying the gun was
>   from Squad Twenty-two."
> Now my blood began to boil, my ass began to itch.
> I jumped up and shot that rotten bitch.
> Now I know you fellows think that's the wrong thing to do,
> But I don't want to hear another motherfucking word
>   about Squad Twenty-two.

>   [Charley]

A HARD-LUCK STORY

Bruce Jackson sent me a text of this story from his Indiana prison collection, and it is closely related to other stories reciting the hardships of being without money The story relies for its effect on the final line (the most constant feature of these versions). The tone of the story is similar to the song "Nobody Knows You When You're Down and Out," and Robert Shaw, an Austin, Texas, ragtime piano player, says a version of the toast between stanzas in his rendition of the song.

Here are some Camingerly versions of this story.

Look out, bitch, and don't say a word,
'Cause I'm beating your ass about some shit I heard.
Long time now you been pulling this shit.
I'ma give you an ass-whipping you never will forget.
I send you to the store ask for butter, you bring back lard.
I'll lay beside you, my dick won't get hard.
You got nerve to ask me for a dime.
You're kinda pigeon-toed, knock-kneed, and blind.
Receiving the call off of each and every line,
That your grandmammy's pussy done run your grand-
       pappy's line.
You got a nerve to ask me for a dime.
You got to walk the water, like Christ walked the sea,
Hold both thunder and lightning and bring it back to me.
Then I'll introduce you to a friend of mine.
He might lend you a nickel, he won't lend you a dime.
By that you know, you ain't no more bitch of mine.
                                                    [Arthur]

I was once a man with plenty of wealth,
Going 'round showing my friends plenty good time.
And so one day when I realized I didn't have a thing,
I decided to walk down the street and ask a friend of
       mine,
To loan me a dime.

He said, "You're a friend, a friend it's true,
But to get one of these thin dimes, here's what you're
 gonna have to do."
He said, "You have to walk the waters, like Jesus walked
 the sea.
Got to hold both thunder and lightning and bring it back
 to me."
He said, "Put the Empire State Building down in a sack.
Jump up a camel's ass and snatch the hump out of that
 motherfucker's back."
He said, "When you receive a letter from your grand-
 father, saying your grandmother's pussy's running
 blind
Your mother's sick and your father's dying,
Then I'll introduce you to a friend of mine
Who might loan you a nickel, but not a dime."

                                                [Kid]

When I was rich, I was right.
I used to spend my money just like I was white.
One day I got broke.
Not a friend did I have.
But you know what all good hustlers do.
They always keep a quarter too.
So I was walking down Rampail Street,
When two chock whores I chanced to meet,
They said, "Hello, Charley, I haven't seen you in a mighty
 long time.
Stand me maybe a dime?"
I said, "Before I give you a dime, this is what you got to do.
You got to go up on the Empire State Building and jump
 clean down on your head.
Then say, 'Charley boy, I ain't dead.'
You got to swim a ocean, 'round and around.
From the Pacific, you got to swim the deep sea channel
 and tell me you ain't drowned.
You got to eat ten links of catshit, and you better not frown.
You got to go way up high,
And find the rock that David killed Goliath,

If you do all this in a half-hour time,
Might loan you a nickel but not a goddamn dime."

[Charley]

The next three toasts are further badman stories, but of a
different sort from "Stackolee." These are the stories not of
bullies fighting each other, but of modern criminals outwitting the police or dying at their hands. Even when they do
die, they do it with a kind of glory, boasting as they go. In
many ways these toasts are extended boasts.

Here, just as in so many other aspects of the neighborhood,
are the strong effects of the popular entertainment media.
Dillinger, Slick Willie Sutton, the Dalton Brothers, the James
Brothers, Geronimo are the heroes of these pieces. And the
Jesse James portrayed here is not the modern Robin Hood of
the ballad; he is just as mean as any of the others.

Many of the lines will be familiar. Jesse winds up at the
same bar at which Stackolee killed Billy, and he seems to be
uttering the same dialogue. Both the "MacDaddy" and the
"Big Man" toasts contain the stock courtroom scene. The final
lines of "MacDaddy" are also associated with the "Stackolee"
tradition.

"The Big Man" may be a strictly local toast, as evidenced by
the reference to Fifth and South. Kid claimed to have written
this one, but he claimed to have written "The *Titanic*" also, as
well as others. The final curse is certainly not local; it is part of
a longer one that is widely known.

THE BIG MAN

I met a cute little girl, she took my heart,
So I decided my life I wanted to share a part.
Now the fellows told me, "Now look here, Kid,"
She wasn't no good for me.
I didn't care what the boys had to say,
I went down to the judge to read the matrimony one day.
So I come off from work and I was tired.
I come in the house and I see my best friend laying my
    bed inside.

So I shot him in the head and she ran out down the street.
I cut her in the throat, chopped off her feet.
So 'round about two o'clock that morning, I was standing
  on Fifth and South,
My man walked up saying, "Kid, is you the one that busted
  your lady in the mouth?"
I said, "That's me." He said, "Come on, I got a warrant for
  your arrest."
He just read a few lines, then he stopped and he wouldn't
  say a word.
Now tomorrow morning, after the judge read it, you heard.
So the judge looked down at me, my wife started to crying,
Mother-in-law jumped up, she began to shout,
My lawyer said, "Sit down, bitch, you don't know what the
  trial's about."
The judge told me, he said, "Kid, I'ma give you some time.
Here go fifty-five years to get that whooping off your
  mind."
I said, "Fifty-five years ain't no time,
I got a brother in Sing Sing doing ninety-nine.
If you think that's a kick, here's a better.
I got an uncle in Alcatraz waiting for the chair."
So he took me up and he gave me cell number 32.
So right up 'bout four, five years had passed,
When I got a letter from that old nasty bitch.
She said, "Kid, I came to your trial,
Now I didn't come there to place a bet.
Just came to see how much time your ass was going to get."
She said, "Things out here sure is hard.
I'm out here on the street, trying to make a bite,
Fucking, eating chicken every night."
So it got on my nerves, made me mad,
So I got my pencil and paper, my scratch pad.
I wrote her back a letter, and here's what I said.
"For your dirtiness towards me that can't be accounted for.
May the crabs grow 'round your body and start to eat.
May the lice grow up around your back, eat down to your
  feet.
May you get corroded and blood run from your nose.

Then before your life's a wreck, may you fall backwards to
   your asshole.

                              Your motherfucking man."

                                              [Kid]

THE GREAT MACDADDY

I was standing on the corner, wasn't even shooting crap,
When a policeman came by, picked me up on a lame rap.
He took me to the jailhouse, 'bout quarter past eight.
That morning, 'bout ten past nine,
Turnkey came down the line.
Later on, 'bout ten past ten,
I was facing the judge and twelve other men.
He looked down on me, he said,
You're the last of the bad.
Now Dillinger, Slick Willie Sutton, all them fellows is gone,
Left you, the Great MacDaddy, to carry on."
He said, "Now we gonna send you up the way. Gonna
   send you up the river.
Fifteen to thirty, that's your retire."
I said, "Fifteen to thirty, that ain't no time.
I got a brother in Sing Sing doing ninety-nine."
Just then my sister-in-law jumped up, she started to cry.
I throwed her a dirty old rag to wipe her eye.
My mother-in-law jumped, she started to shout.
"Sit down, bitch, you don't even know what the trial's
   about."
'Pon her arm she had my six-button benny.
Said, "Here you are, MacDaddy, here's your coat."
I put my hand in my pocket and much to my surprise,
I put my hand on two forty-fives.
I throwed them on the judge and made my way to the door.
As I was leaving, I tipped my hat to the pictures once more.
Now outside the courtroom was Charcoal Brown.
He was one of the baddest motherfuckers on this side of
   town.
The juries left out, and the broads gave a scream,

I was cooling 'bout hundred-fifteen miles an hour in my
     own limousine.
Rode here, rode there, to a little town called Sin.
That's when the police moved in.
We was fighting like hell till everything went black.
One of those sneaky cops come up and shot me in the back.
I've got a tombstone disposition, graveyard mind.
I know I'm a bad motherfucker, that's why I don't mind
     dying.

[Kid]

JESSE JAMES

When the West was at its best
And every time a locomotive hit a rump-stump bump
And was unable to go any further
Jess and his brother Frank would take over.
"Frank, you guard the rear
While I stomp the shit out the engineer."
Man jumped up, said, "You can have my money, but spare
     my life."
He said, "I don't want neither, I want to fuck your wife."
He said, "Do this, well I'd rather be dead."
That's when Jesse sent four rockets through his head.
Fucked the wife, fucked her well,
Fucked her till her pussy swelled,
Got Frank to wipe the chickenshit from around his dick.
But don't get me wrong.
The James Brothers weren't the only badmen on the train.
There was the Dalton Brothers, four of a kind.
They shot a motherfucker for a raggedy dime.
There was John Dillinger in the corner, counting his gold.
He shot *his* motherfucker when he was ten years old.
There was a bad motherfucker in the corner we all should
     know.
His name was Geronimo.
A man jumped up and said, "Call the law."
Jesse sent two rockets through that motherfucker's jaw.
He looked over at the conductor.

He said, "Conductor, don't you breathe or shit."
Conductor went to move, dead he lay.
Jesse dived out the window, swam through water, swam
　　through mud.
He was looking for the place they call the "Bucket of
　　Blood."
He went in the bar expecting to eat.
The bartender gave him a muddy glass of water and a
　　fucked-up piece of meat.
He pulled out a gun, he shot the bartender from front to
　　back.
Lady came in, said, "Where's Pete?"
Said, "Pete's behind the bar, fast asleep."
She said, "Pete ain't dead, Pete ain't dead."
He said, "Just count the six bullets in that raggedy mother-
　　fucker's head."
She said, "My son Pete's dead, I can't go on."
Jesse put his foot on her ass and aimed her for the door.
He punched and shot a cat.
Shot a dog from front to back.
He was in this bad old Texas town, where the dudes go
　　down.
"You just pack your rags and leave this town."
[*Couldn't remember rest*]

[Freddie]

The next three pieces are of the familiar fornication contest
pattern. That this is common lore in the Anglo-American tradition is amply shown by a glance at the most recent and
available collection of such lore, *Count Vicarion's Book of
Bawdy Ballads.*[58]

SCHOOLTEACHER LULU AND CRABEYE PETE

Schoolteacher Lulu come to town,
Ninety-nine men couldn't fuck her down.

---

58. Edited by the British modernist poet, Christopher Logue.

In that town lived Crabeye Pete.
Crab to his head and dick to his feet.
All the pimps and the conventionists holding a convention
    in town,
Betting that Crabeye Pete would fuck Lulu down.
They was hold a convention at Carnegie Hall,
Come one, come all.
Now they was standing around 'bout noon,
Here comes Pete from the greasy spoon.
Now they got on the ground, they begin to fuck,
And my man was pushing dick to her like a ten-ton truck.
Lulu threw the bulldog curve.
Pete held on but he lost his nerve.
Then she threw the bulldog twist.
Pete held on but he broke a motherfucking wrist.
They fucked and they fucked and they fucked and they
    fucked.
Pete was still trying to put that dick to her like a ten-ton
    truck.
But when it was all over poor Pete was dead.
So we took Pete up on the mountain and buried him deep
    in the sand.
And on his grave we described, "Here Lies the World's
    Greatest Fucking Man."

[Charley]

Gunfight at O.K. Corral

Now here's a story, a story of old,
When the men were men, and the women were bold.
It was back in a town that was peaceful and quiet
When one lonely night a man came walking down the
    street.
He had about a yard and a half of joint hanging down by
    his feet.
He walked to the hotel, and he asked the fellow sitting
    quiet,
"Pardon me, mister, is this where the broad named Big
    Whore lays her head?"

He said, "Well, tell her I'll see her tomorrow morning at
    O.K. Corral, we'll start our bread."
That morning about nine past nine, Butterbean Susie let
    out a fart,
To let them know the fucking was to start.
Just then, 'bout ten past ten,
Everybody knowed the fucking was about to begin.
Just then the earth gave a quiver, the ground gave a crut,
Everybody in town knew Big Dick had busted his nut.
Big Whore Sue screamed and grabbed her head,
Big Dick wiped the blood off his dick, said,
"Get the bitch, 'cause this whore is dead."
He got up, put his thing down his pants, gently at ease,
Got up and wiped the dirt off his knees.
As he was strolling out of town, he tipped his hat,
He said, "I fucked many and I fucked 'em well,
But everyone I fucked have caught hell."

                                  [Kid]

JUST LOOKING FOR A JOB

Now I was walking down the road one day 'cause things
    was hard.
I was just looking for a motherfucking job.
I knocked on this here door,
And what do you think, here come a pretty little whore.
She had on a nice little evening gown.
She said, "What you doing, hanging around?"
I said, "Well, Miss, I don't mean no harm."
I said, "I'm just coming 'round looking for a job."
She said, "Oh, a job."
She said, "Perhaps you could have the deed to my house
    or the deed to my car.
The job I want you to do ain't too hard."
She said, "Come on and sit down over here."
I said, "Well, would you tell me what might this here job
    be?"
She said, "Well, you got to get down on your knees

And eat this pussy like a rat eating cheese.
You got to get way down in it and blow it like Louis blow
    his horn.
You got to peck all around, like a rooster pecking corn."
I said, "Hold it! Wait a minute, bitch, you're talking too
    fast.
The next thing you know, you'll have my foot in your ass."
I said, "I'm not a rooster, so I can't peck corn
And I ain't Louis, so go blow your own horn."

[Charley]

THE FREAKS' BALL

The next four rhymes are all versions of what is usually called
"The Freaks' Ball" (a party held by homosexuals). It seems to
have wide currency among Negroes. The fourth shows a dis-
tinct relationship to the "Darktown Strutters' Ball" and may reflect the origins of this piece.

Lucy Lacy fucked Dick Tracy and Tessy Trueheart had a
    fit.
Now Bullshit Benny fucked B. O. Plenty and Gravel Gerty
    had a bowl of shit.
Well, the shit was so thick, it made Dracula sick
And the walls were full of slime.
While they was laughing and joking, the door flew open
And in walked Frankenstein.
He looked around to try his luck.
Grabbed the shortest broad in the crowd and started to
    fuck.
While he was twisting and twirling
His hips hit the wall, his ass hit the ceiling,
His tongue got hot, his head got stiff,
His neck started to wibbling and then that was it.
He looked around and he grabbed the smallest bitch in
    town.
He said, "I'll tell you what to do.
Now you put your left leg over my right shoulder,

And your right leg over my left shoulder and wiggle your
    ass in time.
'Cause I'm booty struck, and got to fuck,
And I got grinding on my mind."

                              [Kid]

Call up fast-fucking Fanny
To tell her gray-assed Mammy
We gonna have a ball
Down the bulldaggers' hall.
There's gonna be thirty-nine cockheads fried in snot,
Two or three pickled dicks tied in a knot.
There's gonna be long cock, short cock, cock without bone.
You can fuck a cock, suck a cock, or leave a goddamn
    cock alone.
There was Gravel Gerty and in walked Frankenstein.
He grabbed the littlest woman in the bunch.
He said, "Put your left leg on my right shoulder, and wig-
    gle your ass in time.
'Cause I'm booty struck, and got to fuck, and got grinding
    on my mind."

                          [Arthur]

Tell Bulldagging Fanny
Tell her gray-assed Granny
Tell her no-good Mammy
That we're gonna have a ball
At the bulldaggers' hall.
It was the first fuck fight
To broad daylight,
Without eating a bite.
Then we're going to have breakfast.
I'm gonna have fried snot,
Roast cock,
Three pickled dicks tied in a knot.
Come 'long lunch, I don't want no collard greens.
Just a bowl of catshit, some muddy beans.

                              [Kid]

Bullshitting Willie told cocksuckering Sammie
To come on down and bring his motherfuckering mammy,
Come on down and don't be late,
We're going to be there when the band starts playing,
Come on down and don't miss the fun,
We're going to be there when the band shits all over the
    floor,
And the leader grabs his self a fat whore.
These old girls are going to fuck and fight
Till the broad daylight.
Tomorrow night at the cheap cocksuckers' ball.

[from Javester's manuscript]

JODY THE GRINDER

Whether Jody as a character was invented by inhabitants of
the prisons or the army, he is the man who is home sleeping
with your wife. Lomax (FSNA), 595, prints the song "Sound
Off" with a Jody verse. This song is often called "Jody's Song"
or "Jody Calls." For a jail-house mention, see Library of Congress Record, AAFS L4 (A3), "Joe the Grinder." Other,
short Jody rhymes came from this group.

Now in nineteen hundred and forty-four
The World War Two was over for sure.
Now a two-timing bitch with an old man overseas,
Said, "Wake up, Jody. Wake up, please.
This shit is over, Japan is fell."
Now Jody woke up, his eyes all red.
He said, "What's that, whore, I just heard you said?"
She said, "Don't look at me like I did a crime.
You've heard me the first goddamn time."
He said, "No, that what you're talking can't be right.
'Cause the last I heard, the Japanese had just begin to
    fight."
She said, "There was a time the Japs wouldn't quit,
But Uncle Sam dropped an atomic bomb and changed all
    that shit."

She said, "Wise up, honey, just don't get mad.
I think it's time for you to pack your rags and find another
    pad."
She said, "Anyway, see who's at the door."
"Knock, knock, I'm already in.
Take a shot of my bad-ass gin."
He said, "While I was overseas fighting the enemy and
    digging that salt,
You was taking my checks and cashing them and taking
    my bitch to the Allotment Ball.
Now here's something I can't miss.
Take my motherfucking Longine off your wrist."
He said, "Hold it, motherfucker, don't start that talking
    that jive.
Let me throw you an introduction to my army forty-five.
What? Who am I? I know your name is Jody the Grinder
    and you don't give a damn.
But, bitch, tell this no-good motherfucker just who I am."
"Well, honey, if you must know.
Jody the Grinder, meet G.I. Joe."

[Kid]

THE OLD POOH-POOH

This is the old bawdy song "Ring Dang Doo" in corrupted form,
performed (badly) as a toast.

There was a girl named Jane
Who took this fellow
Down to the cellar
Fed him whiskey, wine, and gin
And give him a piece of that old pooh-pooh.

Her mother cried from within her bed,
Said, "Jane, what is this nasty thing you're doing.
You pack your rags and your bloomers, too,
And you make your living off your old pooh-pooh."

Jane went to the big city,
She tacked a sign up on the door.
"Two cents a ride, four cents a trip."
They came in twos, they came in fours.
To be correct, they came in scores.
There even was a guy named Traps
Who had the claps,
The syphs, and the blue-balls, too.
He even got a piece of that old pooh-pooh.

When she died in Carnegie Hall
They pickled her ass in alcohol.
They paraded her cock on Fifth Avenue.
And that was the end of the old pooh-pooh.

[Freddie]

I JUST LEARNED TO DANCE

Pardon me, chicks, kats, and hens,
No not now, I'll tell you when.
I am not at all trying to be real bold,
Because I just learned to rock and roll.

I also learned the latest Chinese hop,
Rattle, Shake, Crawl, and Flop.
Come on out and step over the floor,
And while the night is young let's hit the door.

I can even do the Norfolk dance.
Stand back, chicks, and see me prance.
And just to show you that I'm no hick,
Let me meet some real cute chick.

Now I will tell you the whole truth,
I come here looking for a chick named Ruth.
Move back your chairs and let everyone see
That I can shake like a limb on a tree.

I dropped in here very full of pep
In order to do the hog-pen step.

That kat you see leaning against the wall
Is not afraid the building will fall.

He sure does look like a very mean kat.
Standing there will make him really fat.
That kat sure is playing it cool.
You can see he ain't nobody's fool.

Sorry , chicks, I got to run.
Goodnight, I sure had fun.
I'll be digging you again some time,
When I'm not so full of blackberry wine.

[from a manuscript given in a female hand]

FRESH OFF THE FARM

If you know a girl named Mable,
Take her around to Jack's stable.
Tell her to stoop down slow and lay back fast
And give me that ass,
Because I am going to give it right back just like it has
    high-power gas.
You are going to stay in this hay,
So keep cool, and listen to what I have to say.
"Are you ready?" Don't be afraid, I will do you no harm,
Because you are fresh off the farm.
Just wrap your legs around my back,
And act like you are squeezing a cow's sack.
Have you ever been to Arkansaw?
Well I am going to teach you how to screw like a first-
    class whore.
I can tell what you ate
By my dick probing in your belly, and the head of my dick
    is like a seeing-eye worm used for fish bate.

[from a manuscript given in a female hand]

6 The Jokes

there is little difficulty in establishing the toasts as characteristically Afro-American because little like them has been observed in the repertoires of performers from other groups. Cultural ancestry is not so demonstrable with the jokes told by the Camingerly men because they so often are versions of international tales or jests. It therefore seems important to estabish just what is different about the stories as they are told in Camingerly and elsewhere. To do this, the concept of "oikotype" must be invoked.

If the lore of enough areas of the world were studied empirically from not only the cultural but also the structural and stylistic points of view, we could arrive at some sort of device that would allow us to look at a piece of lore and determine where it came from, from no other evidence than the internal clues provided by the piece itself. Furthermore, if we could develop our technique sufficiently we would be able to observe in a piece not only its present locus but also something of its past and perhaps even its place of origin. When one specific piece of lore of international currency has been locally isolated by means of this sort, folklorists, following C. W. von Sydow, have called it a local or *oiko*-type of that piece.

It is not really possible to isolate the oikotype of one piece without discerning those features that have made it characteristic of a specific locale or group. To say that a collected variant is an oikotype simply because it has been collected in one place a number of times and not in any other is not really enough. It is important both to isolate the oikotype and to know *why* it changed in that way at that place. To do so one must examine the folkloric conventions (or formulas, clichés, and commonplaces) and the cultural biases and imperative operative in that community or tradition. Only in this way can we isolate all of the oikotypal forms of the group, and only *then* can we begin to solve the riddle of the traditional process, oral transmission. By pursuit of this method we are able to see the relationships of the various oikotypes in each group, and through such perceptions we will be able to predict place of collection, transmission, or origin, at the same time taking a look at the effect of the cultural biases of the group on folkloric forms.

But the problems of constructing a system of oikotypification of this sort are manifold. One's sampling of lore must be full enough, both in depth and breadth, and it can be said to be truly representative of that locale or group. The corpus of the sampling must also be large enough to see *all* the traits that might affect the piece to make it truly local.

The process of oikotyping is not the same as defining. We cannot say how one corpus of folklore stemming from one group differs from the lore of all other groups, which is what the process of defintion would ask us to do. We can rather delimit those characteristics, substantive and structural, that recur and trust that if our description is full enough, no other corpus will have exactly the same configuration of elements.

The comparisons suggested in this description point to differences rather than to similarities, which are the basic elements of the comparative approach of those following the geographical-historical method. Instead of pointing to the schematic similarities of a series of pieces of lore, however, oikotyping calls for the isolation of the group's *tropisms*, those elements toward which the performers of the group are attracted. Such tropisms may be strictly formal. Dundes[1] has pointed out an important attraction of this sort in regard to

1. Alan Dundes, "The Binary Structure of 'Unsuccessful Repetition' in Lithuanian Folktales," *Western Folklore*, XXI (1962), pp. 165–73.

the structural progression or movement in Lithuanian folktales, using Propp's morphological techniques.[2] Such studies
do a great deal to establish the necessity for structural analysis on the basis of a corpus of lore of one group. But as Dundes
himself seems to realize, this type of formal analysis is only
one of many devices useful in arriving at oikotypical con-
structs. There are other structural matters equally important,
such as genre, and convention. Equally important in oikotyping are matters of texture: diction, farming patterns, poetic
models, type and frequency of repetitive devices, qualitative
and quantitative use of key words, images, and symbols.

It would be impossible because of the geographical limita-
tions of this study to establish the existence of New World or
United States Negro oikotypes, or even those for the urban
Negro. It is my hope that future studies, will enable us to delimit and describe a set of tropisms that will show what is
unique about the lore of the Negro in the New World and
how he has adapted the lore of other groups.

Most of the chapters in this book have to some extent described the tropisms of the Camingerly group, ones I feel are
at least representative of the Northern urban Negro if not of
the contemporary Negro in the United States in general.
Chapter 2 is in part a discussion of the intimate relation of the
good talker and his heroes through such devices as the "intrusive I"; this is certainly a textural tropism as described
above. The same chapter discusses another textural device
similarly important in any discussion of tropisms, the strong
reliance of these men on rhyme as a device of wit, both in
everyday speech and in their narratives. Chapter 3, about
the nature of the heroes of the group, not only points out the
tropism toward the hard-man hero and his values but indicates the lack of any satisfactory dramatic resolution in the
hero narratives. This latter insight, if broadly observed, could
be seen to be a binding structural convention. The lack of
marriage or any sort of reintegration with society is, it is true, a
convention *manqué* rather than a convention itself, but it is a
characteristic and as such must be regarded as a tropism. The

2. Propp, *The Morphology of the Folktale.*

fact that these hero stories both begin and end in midstream is itself a structural consideration and must be considered as fit material for our oikotypal discussion.

Chapter 4, as it describes one of the dominant forms in which the narratives were collected, the toast, is also descriptive of structural (direction of action) and textural (method of rhyming, framing devices, diction) tropisms. Subsequent investigations of the toast in other areas of the United States indicate that a full study of Negro tropisms and oikotypes would probably show that the toast is a characteristically Negro form. (I have never found a toast that is not demonstrably close to a Negro source. It is a form of expression that does not seem to have any firm tradition in contiguous groups. The same is true of other rhyming mechanisms of the Negro, such as the dozens, but not as pronouncedly so.)

One further oikotypical element is of great importance in discussing joke texts. The tendency toward placing stories in *cante fable* (a story with a repeated verse or song) form, which has been pointed to so often in regard to tales from other Afro-American communities, exists in these Camingerly stories. Perhaps this is a cultural retention of traits, or perhaps it is one further facet of the tropism toward rhyming.

The Uncle Remus collections and those that followed showed that the Negro had a predilection for stories in *cante fable* form. This observation is borne out in both West Indian and recent African collections. Regarding the latter, Kenneth and Mary Clarke said,

> Unfortunately, even in African materials, adequate indication of song is lacking in many of the collections made in the late nineteenth and early twentieth centuries before good portable recording equipment was available. Missionaries and others, whose knowledge of the native languages was limited at best, and whose knowledge of native music was even weaker, tended to distort or even to omit the musical portions of the tales they collected.[3]

3. Clarke, *Introducing Folklore*, p. 56.

In a fascinating early study of the ballad in Jamaica, Martha Warren Beckwith shows how the sung narratives of the British tradition fared in the West Indian climate. She found an old man, Forbes, who knew the ballad of "Little Musgrove." She describes his treatment of the song:

> Now when old Forbes first gave me the story of "Little Musgrove," he strung the verse upon a connecting thread of prose to carry along the action. Only when confronted with the phonograph did he sing the verses straight through without interruption.
>
> That his method was not adopted by chance is proved by the fact that other collectors both in Jamaica and in the Bahamas have taken down ballad stories dictated in the same form, and that I myself secured two other ballads which were recited in this fashion, . . .[4]

Though she clearly does not fully understand it, Beckwith has recognized an important pattern in West Indian Negro storytelling, a clear tropism toward the *cante fable* form.

Halpert comments upon the cause of this tropism in Miss Beckwith's article:

> . . . the popularity of the form with English-speaking Negroes is due to a joint cause: not only that, as Miss Beckwith has shown, the pattern is well known in Africa, but also that, as seems quite likely, it was a British folktale pattern and one that would be adopted even more readily than the ballad.[5]

He further points out that, "When the *cante fable* is found undistorted, . . . the interspersed verse or song usually is the dramatic core of the tale. Frequently it is the most memorable part," and indicates that, on Miss Beckwith's authority, this was the situation in Jamaica.[6] In Miss Beckwith's words:

4. Beckwith, "The English Ballad in Jamaica: A Note upon the Origin of the Ballad Form," *PMLA*, XXIX, p. 456.
5. Halpert, "The Cante Fable in Decay," in Beck, ed., *Folklore in Action*, p. 141.
6. Halpert, "Cante Fable," p. 147.

The stories contain, or usually turn upon, a song which belongs to the dialogue or is used as an ejaculation. Often its use becomes more dramatic by putting it into the lips of a fiddler or of a singing bird; but whether so presented or not, it is always there to emphasize an emotional moment and express a wish, call, or magical formula; and its repetition from time to time in the story gives the song the value of a chorus or refrain.[7]

The burden of Halpert's argument is that verses tend to remain even after stories have been lost, and that this represents "the *cante fable* in decay." He gives a number of examples from his New Jersey collection to justify this contention. In the case of the Negro tale in this country, however, this is not so much the case. The *cante fables* in the Uncle Remus collections, for instance, often have nonsense refrains (seemingly from the African) or are little songs put into Brer Rabbit's mouth as jokes or as clever commentary, quite often having little to do with the story. This is the *cante fable* in decay among the American Negro.

However, in the Camingerly stories the repeated verse or song functions in a much more structural manner, very much in the stronger *cante fable* tradition. These are jokes, short, terse, witty stories reliant upon a punch-line ending. In a great number of the Camingerly *cante fables* the song or verse supplies the material for the witty and humorous ending. This is most clearly seen in such stories as "The Curser Outcursed," "The Judge Replies," and "Open Them Doors."

The jokes can be clearly classified as *cante fables*. Many included here use repetition of phrase to build up to the punch-line ending—for instance, in "The Preacher and His Song," where the repeated line, "Oh Lord, would you drop me fifty cents?" is changed in the end to "Lord, lookahere, I don't want this shit; all I want is my fifty cents."

Many stories use this kind of wit (the punch line as a perversion of a previous line), but the phrase changed is not one that has been repeated but rather one that has come just before. The story "The Preacher and the Pickles" in-

7. Beckwith, *Jamaica Folk-Lore*, p. 458.

volves just such a device in rhyme. Not in rhyme is the ending of "Coming or Going." Occasionally just the cleverness of a rhyme is sufficient for an ending, as in "Washday in the Woods."

Just why the *cante fable* and other related witty forms are found in such profusion in this group while they are exhibited in more decay in other American Negro collections remains a question. Though to answer at this point, one can point to the important tropisms of rhyme, joke form, and word wit in general operating so prominently in the Camingerly group. In fact, the *cante fable* may not have decayed among the Negro, at least in jokes, especially bawdy ones. The use of the repeated song or verse for purposes of emotional increment, then, suggests that the song has become the *raison d'etre* for the story, the witty or foolish changes effected at the end now providing the punch lines of these jokes.

However, since the tendency toward placing stories in joke form is observable in many recent American traditions (and undoubtedly elsewhere), it seems important to examine these changes' effects on the form and meaning of the story and to see how the Camingerly stories differ from those in general American joking provenience. Let me begin by giving a text of an international tale type collected from Freddie:

This little old preacher he was coming down the road one day. So he passed this here farmhouse. So he went over, "Eruh, say, eruh, do you have any rooms to put me up overnight? I got my own food and everything. I just want a place to stay." She said, "Well, you go on down there to the shed house. Tell me it's a little haunted, but I guess you can make it over there." "Oahh. Well, could I borrow your frying pan, so I can fry my pork chops?" So she said, "Yeah."

So the preacher went on over to the shed house, so long 'bout twelve o'clock he started reading his Bible under the candlelight. So here come this ghost. He said, "Eruh," tapped the preacher on the shoulder, he said, "You seen Willy?" He said, "No, I ain't seen Willy." So the ghost looked over and went away rattling his chains and all. Came back 'bout five minutes later. He said, "You seen

Willy?" So he said, "No, I ain't seen Willy." So *he left.*
So here comes another ghost in. So he said, "Hey there,
have you seen Willy?" Reverend said, "No, I ain't seen
Willy." So he grabbed the frying pan, drink the hot grease,
ate the pork chop, grabbed some of the hot coals to wipe
his ass. The preacher looked up and said, "Well, goddamn,
you ain't Willy. Let me get the hell out of here."

This is a common folk story throughout the United States,
told in many ways, but always involving a repeated visit of a
ghost or ghostly voice or animal and its effect upon the person
trying to stay in the haunted house. Dorson says of this story:
"Believed tales of haunted houses have generated this very
popular folktale, an American oikotype of Type 326, 'The
Youth Who Wanted to Learn What Fear Is.'" [8] By his citation
of the number of American variants, Dorson indicates that the
story's oikotypicality is probably determined by its provenience
in this general form throughout the United States.

In looking into *The Types of the Folktale* of Thompson under Type 326 (p. 114 of the new edition) it becomes evident
that the protagonist and the antagonist differ considerably in
the Indo-European and the American variants. Also there is
a contrast in the pieces and their outcomes. Type 326 concerns
a boy who wants to learn what fear is and so goes through a
series of frightful experiences searching for fear. One of
these experiences is in a haunted house where a dead man's
members fall, one after another, through a chimney and ghost-
like cats continually appear, but the boy doesn't learn what
fear is until cold water is thrown on him in his sleep or until
eels are put down his back. Thus the story as collected in
the Indo-European complex is in *Märchen* form, and operates under the conventions of that form. As in such stories, we
are concerned with the experience of the young hero as an
element in the process of maturation, of confronting life. The
incidents may be fairly humorous, but the humor is secondary
to the growth experience.

8. Dorson, *Negro Folktales in Michigan,* p. 220. He notes there a number of American texts. To this add Botkin, *Anecdotes,* p. 222. Dorson has
another text in *Negro Tales from Pine Bluff,* p. 78.

The opposite is true of the American variants, where the humor of the situation is paramount. The repetitions are for the purpose of building toward the humorous withdrawal. The protagonist is taught a lesson, to be sure, but it is one of prudence. We are never concerned with his age or lack of experience. He is a comic character placed in an awkward position. There is no supernatural or logical reason why he must leave the house; only the conventions of the comic formula under which this joke functions demand it.

Just why this variation should be so typically American is impossible to say without a great deal of cultural inquiry, and even then I'm not convinced that an answer is possible because I am not sure that there is an American culture. And without a culture exercising its biases and imperatives I don't believe we can talk in terms of oikotype. However, two differences between the European and American variants can be generalized into possible tropisms that might help us to eventually identify an oikotype. These are (1) the assumption of jocularity toward supernatural occurrences, perhaps because of our rationalistic bias, and (2) modification of stories to conform to the joke pattern, where interest (in this case, humor) is derived from uncomfortable situations and play of wit, especially in punch-line endings.

This ghost story is learned and remembered because it is in joke form and jokes are an important pattern in this group; furthermore, the story assumes a jocular tone about spirits, another important attribute of the stories of Camingerly. But these are not the only reasons for the persistence of this story in this neighborhood. The story is adaptable, and has been adapted to focus on the unmanly (cowardly) preacher being exposed to ridicule, a feature observable in many of the other preacher stories collected here.

Another story collected from Freddie is very close to the one printed above, but it illustrates the effects of a further tropism, discussed in Chapter 3, the demonstration of manly deeds by hard men.

> There was once a haunted house, where nobody would go in the house because it was haunted. So one day they

put a reward up for anybody who could spend a night in the house. These three guys were willing to spend a night in the house. So they heard a voice howling out: "I didn't die right. I didn't die right."

So he got up and he started to run. Ran out. Next guy went in, heard a voice: "I didn't die right. I didn't die right."

He got up and ran out. Third man went in. He had his knife at his side. He heard a voice: "I didn't die right. I didn't die right."

He simply replied, "Fuck with me and you will die right." [9]

It is as important to understand why a group learns and remembers a story as to consider why and how they change it. Let us look at another story collected in South Philadelphia with some of its relatives to investigate this idea further. Here, to begin with, is the text as it is usually found in England and in most printings in the United States.[10]

The Man That Stole the Parson's Sheep

There was once a man who used to steal a fat sheep every Christmas. One Christmas he stole the parson's sheep, and his son, a lad about twelve years old, went about the village singing:

"My father's stolen the parson's sheep,
And a merry Christmas we shall keep,
We shall have both pudding and meat,
But the moant say nought about it."

Now it happened one day that the parson himself heard the boy singing these words, so he said, "My lad, you sing

9. Motifs H 1411, E 281 characterize this not unusual fear-test story.
10. From Addy, *Household Tales*, p. 18. This text is very close to the early American one printed by Botkin, *Anecdotes*, pp. 235–36, taken from Isaiah Thomas, Jr.'s Almanack for 1810. Johnson, *Folk Culture of Saint Helena Island*, prints a Negro version from the Sea Islands that is also very similar. It is a version of Type 1735A, *The Bribed Boy Sings the Wrong Song*.

very well; will you come to church next Sunday evening and sing it there?"

"I've no clothes to go in," said the boy. But the parson said, "If you will come to church as I ask you, I will buy you clothes to go in." So the boy went to church the next Sunday evening, dressed in the new clothes that the parson had given him.

When the service was over the parson said to the people, "Stay, my brethren, I want you to hear what this boy has to sing, it's gospel truth that he'll tell you," for he was hoping that the boy would confess before all the people that his father had stolen the sheep. But the boy got up and sang:

> "As I was in the field one day
> I saw the parson kiss a may [maid];
> He gave me a shilling not to tell
> And these new clothes do fit me well."

And here it is as collected from two informants, Charley and Freddie, from Philadelphia:

Now this here's about the reverend and the deacon. Deacon said he had a bull. So the reverend's family was in 'dation. He had a whole lot of kids, reverend didn't have no money, buy nothing to eat, so he went and stole the deacon's bull. So he invited everybody 'round. He even invited deacon over. "Come over to my house Sunday, 'cause right after church we're gonna have all kind of beef." So the reverend said, "O.K."

So he came over and he sat down, and he, you know how they do in the country, kids eat first and then the grown-ups. So the reverend sit down, and he said, "This here sure some good food. Um, um, um. You know one thing, rev?" He said, "What's that, Brother Deacon?" He said, "You know somebody stole my bull." He said, "Um, ain't that something, people just going 'round taking other people's stuff." And all the same time he's the one that stole the bull.

So the kids was outside playing, so the reverend said, "I guess I'll go and sit out there in the back for a while, see the kids play." So at that time the kids had made up this here new game. Had each other by the hand going around the circle singing,

> "Oh, Poppa stole the deacon's bull.
> All us children got a belly full."

So the deacon said, "Sing that song again. I'ma give you a nickel apiece if you sing that song again for me." So by them being kids and all, a whole nickel. You know a nickel's a whole lot of money to a kid. "Sing it again." So they start singing,

> "Oh, Poppa stole the deacon's bull.
> All us children got a belly full."

So he said, "Thank you, kids. Now I want you all to come to church next Sunday, and I'ma give you all fifty cents apiece. I want you all to sing that same song in church. 'Cause that there song carries a message." So they said, "O.K."

So they ran and told their mother that they were going to sing in church. So their mother was glad to have the children sing in church. She didn't know what they was going to sing about.

So the deacon, he was going around to everybody's house, telling them, "Reverend Jones's kids gonna be in church, and they gonna sing a song, and it's carrying a message. And I want all you all to come down hear this here. The Lord sent them children to send this message. I want you to come on down there and hear them." So he went on over to Sister Mary's house, told Sister Mary about it. Pretty soon he had gone to all the people in the community and the people had spread the word.

So finally that Sunday came. Children come to church, and they was clean. Well, by the time they got there, the church was so packed that so many people had to sit in the back of the church. So he told them, "Now when you go up there, I want you to sing loud so I can hear what you're singing, too." So they said, "Yes sir, daddy, we gonna sing loud."

So the preacher, you know how the preacher do before he bring on gospel singers. He'd go to preaching, telling you this and that, so he building up the people to hear this song. He said, "Yeah, ladies and gentlemens, you don't know. Kids can bring a message. Yes sir, kids can sure bring a message." He said, "Now just listen to this here message that Reverend Jones's kids gonna bring to you. Now sing that song, children."

They got up there:

> "Oh, poppa stole the Deacon's bull.
> All us children got a belly full."

So the reverend in the back couldn't hear them. So he said, "Sing up louder, here boy. Come on now, sing up louder so I can hear you." By that time the people down front are looking at him. So he wondered what they looking at him for. So they start singing,

> "Oh, poppa stole the deacon's bull.
> All us children got a belly full."

He said, "Look, boy, I want you to sing it louder now. You all sing that song so I can hear it." So they got to the top of their voices:

> "Oh, poppa stole the deacon's bull,
> All us children got a belly full."

So the reverend look and said, "Oh yeah? Well children—

> When you told that, you told your last,
> Now when I get home I'm gonna kick your ass."

These little boys were walking through the town singing:

> "My father stole the preacher's bull, un hunh, un hunh.
> My father stole the preacher's bull,
> And me and my brother had a belly full, un hunh."

Some lady saw them. "Son, if you sing that song in church Sunday, I'll give you a dollar." "Sure, ma'am. I'll be there."

So next Sunday, the boys got up nice, bright and early, sitting in church. The congregation was gathering around and the lady told them to start singing. Jumped up, he said:

"My father stole the preacher's bull, un hunh, un hunh.
My father stole the preacher's bull,
And me and my brother had a belly full, un hunh."

What he didn't know, his father had came to church. First time in his life that Sunday, his father was in church. Father was sitting way back in the corner of the church. So his father heard him, and stood up and he said:

"You sung your first, you sung your last,
When you get home I'ma beat your ass, un hunh."

The English and the Camingerly variants are remarkably similar, yet with some important differences. It it not too difficult to discern what tropisms were at work causing this story to be learned and remembered. We have discussed the tendency of the Negro in general, and specifically the Camingerly man, to cast his stories in *cante fable* form, and thus this *cante fable* would naturally appeal to his aesthetic. Furthermore, the clever twist of the rhyme, found in the original, is consonant with that tendency in the Camingerly *cante fable*. The repeated verse in the early version is already a structural factor in the humor of the piece, not merely textural. Just why the ending was changed is hard to ascertain, because in the earlier texts the preacher is placed in a compromised position, something which many of the other Camingerly narratives do but which is eschewed here.

Another clear, formal tropism which has affected some of the narratives collected in Camingerly is the casting of contest into Negro-white terms—in the more traditional texts, in the roles of Marster and John the slave. One portion of the international tale, "Doctor Know-All," fits (or has been fitted) into this particular pattern and thus has become the localized Negro form of the tale, here called "The Coon in the Box" and collected in similar form among Negroes throughout the United States. Here the pun on names ("Krebs" or "crab" in the German versions) is utilized to emphasize the Negro-

white contest going on ("You got this old coon at last"). Here
is the story as recited by Kid:

This here fellow was working on a farm. Colored fellow.
One night they was sitting outside, boss said, "Sam, what's
that over there behind that log?" "I can't see it, boss." He
said, "Well, there's a rumor going 'round that you are
psychic." He said, "Well, I gather that it's probably nothing but an old rabbit down there." So they went down
and they took a peek and it was a rabbit. Said, "What's
that behind the tree there?" Sam looked at the tree, "I
can't see it, I guess it ain't nothing but an old squirrel.
Maybe a black snake done got it." They look around
there and a black snake had bit the squirrel.

White man looked and said, "If Sam is psychic, I'ma
make some money off of that." So he said, "Sam, I'ma get
all the people out here and next week we gonna get something, and you gonna tell us what it is."

So the white man went and bet up all his property, saying Sam could tell them anything they want. So the one
guy, he betted him. He said, "I tell you what. I know a
thing you can't guess." So he went down got a steel box,
then he caught a buzzard. They put the buzzard under
the box.

So the white man said, "In the morning, Sam, you got
to tell us what's in that box or my land's up against it."
Sam said, "All right, boss." But Sam knew he wasn't psychic, he was just guessing. He eased out of the house 'bout
four o'clock in the morning, went and peep under the box.
Then he went back to bed. That morning he woke up
'bout ten o'clock. Sam come on out. "What's in the box
there, Sam?" Sam said, "Hmm, I don't know. Lord, let
me see now. Size of the box, I guess you got a buzzard
under there." "Sure is. Sure is psychic, ain't he?"

Guy said, "I'ma get you. Next week I'ma get you. Next
week I'ma put something under that box, see if you guess
it." "All right, captain." So that next Friday night, came
out, put a coon under the box. Sam got up 'bout four
o'clock, eased out of the house. The guy had two police-

men sitting on the box. Sam couldn't see what was under that one. Sam went back in the house, back to bed. White man came 'round, said, "Sam, if you don't win in the morning, I'm broke. Out of business. I'm ruined. And if you don't say what's under that box tomorrow," he said, "you just one hung child." Now Sam was scared.

So morning came, they woke Sam up, 'bout ten o'clock. Sam came outside, he scratched his head, he looked at the box, looked at the people. Guy whispered to his friend, "He'll never guess there's a coon under there." Sam said, "Well, Captain, you all finally got the old coon." [11]

This Marster-John pattern has persisted, changing its tendency and strategy among the Camingerly storytellers from a triumph of wits to a triumph of strength. The following story, "The Dream Contest," is a transition between the older Marster-John type and the newer, arrogant challenges. Here is the story as collected in Philadelphia, also from Kid:

White fellows, they was sitting down at the club in the South. This only colored guy in there now. They let him 'cause he had millions. Land, property, homes, factories, cars. So he told these fellows, "I bet you a thousand dollars you can't cheat him out of no money." Fellow said, "Shit, I cheat anybody I want out of some money. Give me two weeks." "All right."

Went over to the colored fellow, he said, "They tell me you're a gambling man." Said, "I'm a gambling man." He said, "Well, let's play a game called 'dream'." "How it go?" He said, "Whatever I dream, you got to make it come true." He said, "All right."

So at night, 'bout two o'clock, white man walked over, knocked on the door. He said, "Mr. John." "Yeah, what's

<hr />

11. This is a version of Type 1641, Motif N 688 (What is in dish); K 1970 (Sham miracles); K 1956 (Sham wise men). It is often found in this form among American Negroes; for representative texts see Dorson, *Negro Folktales from Michigan,* pp. 51–53; Hurston, *Mules and Men,* pp. 111–12. There are a number of texts in various articles in the *Journal of American Folklore*: 11:13; 32:370; 40:265–66; 41:542. See also Jones, *Negro Myth from the Georgia Coast,* pp. 89–90; *The Southern Workman and Hampton School Record,* 23:209.

the matter?" He said, "Last night I dreamt that you gave me your wife, your house, all your property." He said, "Well, I got to make it come true."

So the next morning, he had to move to hotel. Next night, the white man came to his apartment, he said, "John." "Yeah, what's the matter?" "You know I dreamt last night that you gave me all your money, your factory, all your stock, all your bonds, all of anything you got of any value." Colored fellow said, "I got to make it come true. This cat is getting slick. He's trying to break me. I got to think this over."

He went out to the woods, sat down on a log by the stream. He thought and thought. It came to him. He broke out for town. Boy, he was running. He ran up to Mr. Charlie's door, nearly knocked down his door. Said, "Come on downstairs, man. Look here, I was sitting in the woods and I fell asleep. And I had a nightmare. I didn't have a dream. I had a nightmare. I dreamt you gave me all my money, all my land, all my belongings, all my stocks and bonds, all my valuables, everything you dreamt I gave you, you gave back to me. Then I turned around and dreamt you gave me everything you had, clothes and money, stocks and bonds, everything. Then I fell asleep and dreamt that we don't dream no goddamn more."

The idea of a dream representing a controlled wish leading to action is a common folkloric motif (K 444). In the most common story using this motif, three men have only one loaf of bread and they agree to give it to the one who has the most wonderful dream. One eats the bread while the others are asleep and says that he has dreamt that he ate it (Type 1626). The story as we have it here is at best a distant cousin. The idea of the clever dreamer, however, unites the two and the dream bread story may have provided the idea of casting the present contest in dream form, if nothing else.

It is only by viewing the international relatives of this story that we are able to see just how the story developed to its present form. The humor of this piece relies not only on the triumph of wits of the Negro over the white man but also on the humorous situation that can arise when people start to give things away because of an established protocol. In the case of this version, the protocol is a badly worked out motivation for the contest. The importance of the protocol itself is seen in some earlier versions of the story. Here is a version from the beginning of the nineteenth century in the United States but referring back to colonial times:

> Soon after Sir William Johnson had been appointed superintendent of Indian Affairs in America, he wrote to England for some suits of clothes richly laced. When they arrived, Hendrick, king of the Mohawk nation, was present and particularly admired them. In a few succeeding days, Hendrick called on Sir William and acquainted him that he had had a dream. On Sir William's inquiring what it was, he told him that he had given him one of those fine suits he had lately received. Sir William took the hint and immediately presented him with one of the richest suits. The Indian chief, highly pleased with the generosity of Sir William, retired. Some time after this, Sir William happening to be in company with Hendrick, told him that he had also had a dream. Hendrick being very solicitous to know what it was, Sir William informed him that he had dreamed that he (Hendrick) had made him a present of a particular tract of land (the most valuable on the Mohawk River, of about five thousand acres). Hendrick presented him with the land immediately, but not without making this shrewd remark: "Now, Sir William, I will never dream with you again, you dream too hard for me." [12]

In Protestant and mercantilistically oriented countries the whole idea of the giveaway without any specific purpose is a

---

12. Harold Thompson, *Body, Boots and Britches*, p. 177, from *Funny Stories, or the American Jester* of 1804. Cf. Botkin, *Anecdotes*, pp. 58–59, from *American Anecdotes, Original and Select* of 1830. Dorson, *Negro Tales from Pine Bluff*, p. 95, has a further Negro printing similar to the present one. He discusses the Indian story in an article, "Comic Indian Anecdotes," *Southern Folklore Quarterly*, X (1946), p. 122. Baughman lists these and others in his dissertation, a motif and tale type index of English and North American tales, as K 77, "Dream Contest."

natural butt for humor, especially where the method of giving away becomes a contest device. But the humor of the
piece is not as intense, as well as not as "at home," as in countries where such largesse is much more the accepted norm of
courtesy. Here are two versions of the same story collected
recently by Américo Paredes in Mexico and given me by him,
which are much more humorous because of the Mexican attitude toward giving something away if it attracts someone's
eye. The most recent of these concerns President Kennedy on
one of his trips to Mexico:

> President Kennedy was greeted at the airport by Mexi-
> can President Lopez Mateos and as they were shaking
> hands, Jack in his most diplomatic way said, "What a
> beautiful watch you have." Lopez Mateos immediately
> gave Kennedy the watch, saying "You know, it is a custom
> in my country, when someone likes something and openly
> admires it, it is his." Later, at a state dinner in Jack's
> honor, the Mexican President leaned over to him and said,
> "You know, I admire Jackie." Quickly Jack replied, "Here,
> take back your fucking watch."

The earlier version from Mexico also illustrates much of the
same gentle but sexually oriented anti-American feeling.

> An American is out on the range with a Mexican guide.
> He admires the Mexican's knife. The Mexican promptly
> gives it to him. Later, when the American is defecating,
> the Mexican says, "What beautiful white buttocks you
> have." The American promptly replies, "Here's your
> fucking knife."

A custom in one country must be translated and changed
when it goes to another where the custom does not persist.
This is the direction I feel this story took. A natural social situation in Mexico has to be translated into dream terms in order
to make any sense in our culture.

Each of these versions represents the effects of certain tropisms on what is basically the same story. In Mexico the story
is cast in two patterns, both of them extremely common. The
one, a confrontation of a Mexican and an American alone,

often leads to an implication of sodomy, as it does here. The other, having men of importance placed in awkward positions for purposes of burlesque or satire, also tends in the same direction, for the implications of sodomy or cuckoldry are equally humorous to the *machismo* (masculinity) oriented Mexican.

Similarly, the Hendrick text is characteristic of the anecdotes of famous personages popular from the Restoration until the present. (Libel laws have eliminated the printing of many legends that have attached themselves to living notables, though in as recent a writer as Alexander Wolcott the same process has been extremely active.)

The values of the audience affect the stories, too, as is obvious in stories concerning the relationship of the crafty Indian and the white man, with the white man outwitting the Indian.

Most important to our considerations, though, is the application of this widespread story ("The Dream Contest") to the conventions of the Negro narratives. In the Philadelphia text, our interest is shifted somewhat from the protocol arrangement to the ingenuity of the Negro millionaire in resolving the ruinous conflict to his benefit. The story in this form, as a contest between the Negro and the white man, is characteristic of Camingerly narratives and probably of most Negro groups in the United States.

This is a situation Richard M. Dorson found in regard to the changes in the Negro repertoire as it has moved from the South:

> Southern Negro lore had moved north, indeed, but only with migrants cradled and nurtured in the yeasty Southern traditions, or with the few still-living children of slaves. Northern-born Negroes, growing up among cities and factories, supercilious toward their Southern brothers, had severed and discarded their folk heritage, and new migrants grow farther from it as they take on Northern attitudes.[13]

13. Dorson, *Negro Folktales in Michigan,* p. 18.

It is quite true that the Negroes who have been born in Philadelphia or reared there know little of the tradition of animal stories that has flourished in the South. But judging by many of the stories presented here, they have retained many of the older stories from their Southern background. "The Coon in the Box" is one of the oldest and most ubiquitous stories collected among the Negroes of this country. The preacher tale is not only one of the oldest type of tale to be found among the American Negro but it is of broad international provenience.

But as Dorson points out, along with these older echoes a new voice is heard in Negro narratives.

> Unrecognized until very recently, a whole body of jests, some bitter, some mocking, some merely wry, have vented the hurt of colored Americans at their un-American treatment. These tales of protest frequently revolve about a generic character called "Colored Man," who is discomfited and humiliated by White Man, but whose very arrogance he can sometimes turn to account.[14]

The importance of this kind of story was examined briefly in Chapter 3. The germ of such stories certainly existed in the old cycle of Marster-John tales, which often had John, the slave, outwitting his master and either gaining his freedom or getting approval of his slothful work habits. The ones Dorson mentions are direct descendants of this sort of narrative, for the Negro in them turns the white man to account through verbal tricks. There are a number of this sort of story in this collection, notably the ones included under "Chinaman, Jew, Colored Man."

Now we come to the joke texts. I have used headnotes to introduce jokes to assist a comparative study, and I have included many of Gershon Legman's comments. Because certain books and journals are constantly referred to in the headnotes, I have used the following shorthand to refer to them:

14. Dorson, *American Folklore*, pp. 182–83.

Baugham	Ernest W. Baughman, A *Comparative Study of the Folktales of England and North America* (Unpublished thesis).
Botkin (*TAA*)	Ben A. Botkin (ed.), *Treasury of American Anecdotes.*
Brewer (*Brazos*)	J. Mason Brewer, *The Word on the Brazos.*
Dorson (*AF*)	Richard M. Dorson, *American Folklore.*
Dorson (*NFTM*)	Richard M. Dorson, *Negro Folktales in Michigan.*
Dorson (*NTPB*)	Richard M. Dorson, *Negro Tales from Pine Bluff, Arkansas, and Calvin, Michigan.*
Fauset	Arthur Huff Fauset, *Folklore from Nova Scotia.*
Hurston	Zora Neale Hurston, *Mules and Men.*
JAF	*Journal of American Folklore.*
Jones	Charles C. Jones, *Negro Myths from the Georgia Coast.*
MWF	*Midwest Folklore.*
Parsons (*Cape Verde*)	Elsie Clews Parsons, *Folklore from the Cape Verde Islands.*
Parsons (*FLSI*)	Elsie Clews Parsons, *Folk-Lore of the Sea Islands.*
PTFLS	*Publications of the Texas Folklore Society.*
Randolph (*Church House*)	Vance Randolph, *Who Blowed Up the Church House?*
Randolph (*Devil's*)	Vance Randolph, *The Devil's Pretty Daughter.*
Randolph (*Sticks*)	Vance Randolph, *Sticks in the Knapsack.*
Roberts	Leonard Roberts, *South from Hell-fer-Sartin'.*
SFQ	*Southern Folklore Quarterly.*
Southern Workman	*Southern Workman and Hampton School Record.*

| Tidwell | James N. Tidwell, *A Treasury of Ameri-can Folk Humor.* |
| WF | *Western Folklore.* |

Full reference notations for these works can be found in the bibliography.

Motif numbers refer to Stith Thompson, *Motif-Index of Folk-Literature;* tale type numbers to Aarne-Thompson, *The Types of the Folktale.*

These first two stories concerning the preacher emphasize his gluttony. Both seem to owe their existence more to the witty final lines than to the power of the narratives as a whole.

THE PREACHER AND THE PICKLES

Mrs. Jones, she was a widow. So the preacher, he'd come trying to get Mrs. Jones for a long time. So he come over one day. He said, "Mrs. Jones," he said, "I think I'll come over to your house for dinner if you would invite me. I'll come over there and we'll set down, and eat a little dinner, we'll sit down and talk. We'll talk 'bout the Bible." So she said, "O.K., well come on over on Sunday."

But she had a little boy, he had a bad habit. Of farting. You see, he drink a lot of milk, you know, and it would make him fart. His mother would try to stop him from drinking milk, you know, when she was going to have company, but he was sneaking and drinking anyhow. So this Sunday she was going to stop him, 'cause she knew he was going to sneak in and get it, 'cause she had a cow. If she didn't give it he'd go out to the cow and get it from the cow. So he drank this milk, so his mother said, "Well, I know what I'll do. I'll take a pickle and stuff it up his behind." So she told him to get dressed; he went and got washed. She called him in the room, she said, "Come here. Pull down your pants." So she took this pickle and stuck it up his behind. She said, "Now that'll keep you from farting." He said, "Yes ma'am."

Well, this here preacher liked pickles. So he ate all the food. So he started eating the pickles. So he said, "Unh,

I sure wish you had another one." So his mother said, "We haven't got another one in the house." Little boy hustling his mother. She said, "Stop, boy!" He went and got the pickle out of his asshole, washed it off, dipped it down in the pickle jar. Took it on the fork back there, he said, "Here's one more." Preacher he laid back in his chair and he said, "That was a whooper and a whopper." Little boy looked at him and said, "You a goddamn liar, it was my asshole stopper."

[Charley]

THE PREACHER IS CAUGHT

Now you know, captain's come home from a hard day's work, he peeked into his kitchen window and there was the preacher. There was the preacher taking one bite off of the chicken leg, throwing it away. Took a bite off a chicken wing, throwed it away. Took a bite off the breast and he throwed it away. The guy walked around the block and he came back again. He didn't see the preacher. Went in the front room, wasn't nobody in the parlor. Went down the cellar, nobody in the cellar. He went upstairs and opened the door, and there was deacon. But he wasn't at prayer meeting. But he was on his knees. He had whole mouth full of cotton. He said, "Hold it, deacon. Unnh unnh. You got to get up from there." He said, "I come by the first time, I didn't mind what I seen." He said, "Now look. I'ma put you straight. I don't mind you fucking up my eating, but goddamn, don't eat up my fucking."

[Kid]

THE PREACHER AND HIS SONG

Motif X 435 (The boy applies the sermon), X 410 (Jokes on parsons), related to J 1262.5.1 (Whoever gives alms in God's name will receive tenfold: preacher's wife gives sweetmeats away).

Little boy asked his father for fifty cents one day so he could take his girl to the movies. This boy's father was a preacher. Boy's father he had a little church. So he told his son, "O.K., son, here's fifty cents." He said, "Now you spend this fifty cents wisely. But I want you to come to church today before you go to the movies." "O.K., daddy, I'll be there."

So he was in church preaching. So the time for collection and he started hollering, "Oh, I want everybody to dig in their pockets deep, put some money in the church. Yes, sir." Everybody says, "Amen." Congregation hollered, "Amen." "'Cause if any one in my family was here and didn't put no money in the church, I'll skin 'em alive." But at the same time he was waving at his son not to put his money in the church.

His son being a young boy figured that his father meant to put the money in there, and when he get home he get fifty cents back. So when the basket got 'round to his son, he put his fifty cents in the basket.

So service was over, little boy went on him, said, "Dad, eruh, could I have my fifty cents back?" So he said, "What fifty cents?" He said, "Fifty cents I put in church. You was waving at me telling me to put my money in the church." Said, "Now I figured, when I get back home, eruh, you'd give my money back."

So his father said, "Look, boy. All you got to do is to have faith in the Lord. All you got to do is to have faith in the Lord, un hunh, and you get your money back." So he said, "You got to pray."

Well, the kid didn't know he'd messed, so he figured his father was right. Went up in the steeple. Start praying. Said, "Oh, Lord, please drop me my fifty cents. Lord, drop me my fifty cents." And every time he'd ask Him for fifty cents he'd hold his hand out. So just then a little bird flew over top him. He said, "Oh, Lord, would you drop me my fifty cents." So just then the bird shit in his hand. He said, "Lord, lookahere. I don't want this shit. All I want is my fifty cents."

[Charley]

The Preacher Is Lost

(Same punch line as the last but a different story.)

One day this preacher was taking a walk in the woods. Just walking, not concerned with where he was going or nothing. So he was walking and walking, started to turn to go back. When he went back, he couldn't find his way out. So he said, "Well, I'm not worried, God gonna show me my way out." So he kept on walking. Walked till night come. "I ain't worried, 'cause God's gonna show me my way out." So he walked all night. Bright and early next morning, he still walking. He walked up against this log, and he kneeled down. He hold his hands out, and he said, "God, please show me my way out." Just then a bird flew over and shit in his hand. He said, "God, don't hand me no shit, I'm really lost."

[Freddie]

The Preacher and the Farm Woman

Once again, the same idea is conveyed by the punch line. See Motifs Q 21.1 (Old Woman gave her only cow believing she would receive a hundred in return from God. A bishop hearing of her faith sends her 100 cows) and J 1262.5 (Parishioner hears preacher say that alms are returned "100 to 1"). This story is close to both.

This was another about a preacher. I don't know why they do this to preachers. There was this preacher going around and he was going to different people's houses saying, "Sister or brother, you contribute five or ten dollars to the church and the Lord's gonna see that you get it back and then some."

So he went to this woman. They lived in the country, you know. She had cows and things. You know, bulls and pigs all over her place. So this morning when the preacher come there, he said, "Sister say would you help the church get started by contributing five dollars?" So she said, "Well, I don't know." He said, "Well, Sister, if you do, you'll get your five back and about twenty-five more." So she said, "Well, O.K., reverend, I'll do that."

So, this was like maybe on a Friday, so Monday morning when she got up, sweeping her back porch up, old bull come up there and dumped his load on her steps. She swept it away and she didn't say anything. But that evening she set there, and she was waiting to get her five back and then this twenty-five.

So this went on every morning. She get up and sweep her porch, and she still never heard anything from this reverend. So next morning when she got up and she saw this pile down there, she looked up at the sky and she said, "Lord, I don't want no bullshit. I just want my five dollars back."

[Charley]

The Reverend and the Deacon's Contest

Stories on the sexual promiscuity of the clergy are legion. Boccaccio abounds with such stories, heightened in interest because of the supposed practice of priestly continence. Motifs J 1264 (Repartee concerning clerical incontinence), similar to J 1269.1 (The Parson's share and the Sexton's) in idea. *Legman* —The story, with the same details as here, appears in many French jest books of the 1920's.

The reverend and the deacon was sitting in church. The deacon said, "Reverend, I bet I have did it to more women in this congregation than you have." And the deacon said, "Shit, that what you think." He said, "Now I tell you what to do. When the church service starts, all that you did it to, say 'eeny meeny' and all that I did it to, I'm gonna say 'eeny meeny.'" "All right, that's a deal."

So the congregation started about eight o'clock, you know. They all started walking in. Reverend came in.

The first two sisters come in, the reverend said, "Eeny meeny." Second two sisters came in, deacon said, "Eeny meeny." So then long come 'round about ten o'clock, they still coming in, and the deacon's wife walked in. Reverend said, "Eeny meeny." The deacon said, "Hold it, reverend, I told all that you done did it to, you say 'eeny meeny.' But that's my wife." He said, "That's why I said 'eeny meeny.'" "And that's my mother in back of her, my four daughters, my granddaughter, my mother-in-law, my three aunts, and my great-great-grandmother." Reverend said, "Well, eeny, meeny, meeny, meeny, meeny, meeny, meeny, meeny." Other words, he done broke them all.

[Kid]

His Prayer Is Unheeded

One day a preacher was walking across a bridge. He was the kind of preacher that always cussed a lot. He was walking across the bridge and he heard the train coming. And when he turned, he slipped and hit the side of the bridge. Hanging on the bridge, he looked down to see the water below. So he started praying. He said, "God, don't let me fall in this water." Just then his left hand started to slip. He was hanging by his right hand, still praying. "God, don't let me fall in this water. I'll never say another cuss word." So his right hand slipped and he fell in the water. Water came up to his knees. He said, "Ain't this a damn shame, I done all this damn praying, and this water up to my motherfucking knees."

[Freddie]

Open Them Doors

Motif K 1961.1.2.1 (Parody sermon). Fauset, 93, has a similar brick-throwing incident in the middle of a sermon.

One time this preacher was preaching in the church on how the Holy Ghost came into church and enlightened the people. So he said,

> "Open them doors, and open them wide,
> Let the gospel come inside."

So they opened the door. So by-and-by he said it again:

> "Open them doors and open them wide,
> Let the gospel come inside."

So these two bums was coming past. So the preacher said,

> "Open them doors and open them wide,
> And let the gospel come inside."

The bums threw in there and hit him with a brick. He said,

> "Close them doors and close them quick.
> 'Cause some son of a bitch done hit me with a brick."

[Boots]

WHAT DID JOHN SAY?

This is Tale Type 1833 A, "The Boy Applies the Sermon," Motif X 435.1. For other American Negro texts of this popular story, see Dorson (*NTPB*), 255; Fauset, 94–95; *JAF* 47:314; Parsons (*FLSI*), 127–28; *SFQ*, 19:112. For a close variant where a sermon causes a thief to own thievery, see Dorson (*NFTM*), 170; Fauset, 98.

Once this preacher was preaching, and he drunk a lot. So he told this bootlegging son that he wanted him to go to his father and send him a pint of goathair. So the boy went over there to his father, John, and he told him, said, "Pop, reverend over there told me to tell you send him a pint of goathair." He said, "You tell that mother-fucker I ain't sending him shit till he pay me for that last pint."

So the boy went over and sat in back. The church had started. "Oh, damn. I got to wait till the sermon is over." It just so happened he was preaching about John. So he asked one time, "What did John say?" So the little boy was sitting there. Said, "I know daggone well the preacher didn't ask me what John say, and all these people in the congregation."

Preacher said, "What did John say? I ain't gonna ask you but one more time. I want to know." Little boy said, "Well, if he ask me again I'm gonna tell him."

He said, "What did John say?" Little boy said, "John say he ain't gonna send you a goddamn thing till you pay him for the last pint you got."

[Kid]

I'm Hauling Sand

This most nearly resembles the appearance of the ghost as it slowly drops down the chimney. As such, it can be considered with that story as a humorous outgrowth of Type 326 (or more precisely a humorous relative). Motifs J 1495 (Person runs from actual or supposed ghost); E 293 (Ghosts frighten people deliberately); H 1411 (Fear Test: staying in haunted house); E 281 (Ghosts haunt house). See Dorson (NTPB) for a similar story.

The reverend and the preacher they were in church, the congregation was talking 'bout ghosts, so they wanted to prove to them there wasn't no such thing as ghosts. So they picked the hauntedest house they could find, and they said they'd spend the night there.

So they was sitting down, reading, all of a sudden they heard someone say: "Coming up the back road, and I'm hauling sand."

Deacon looked out the window. He said, "You hear that, Rev?" Rev said, "It wasn't nothing." He turned the page in the Bible.

"Coming through the kitchen room, and I'm hauling sand."

Deacon said, "You hear that, Rev?" Rev said it wasn't nothing. He turned the page.

"I'm standing in the hallway, and I'm hauling sand."

Deacon said, "Did you hear that, Rev?" Rev said it wasn't nothing and he turned another page.

"I'm standing in the front, and I'm hauling sand."

Deacon said, "Rev, you see anything?" Rev looked around the room, he said, "I don't see nothing. Just somebody playing a trick on us."

"I'm standing in back of the reverend, and I'm hauling sand."

Deacon said, "Rev, I don't see nothing." Rev didn't say nothing.

"I'ma put my hand on the reverend's shoulder, and I'm hauling sand."

And the hand hit the reverend's shoulder, and he didn't see nothing. He got up, put his Bible down, put his hat and coat on, broke out the door. Deacon said, "Rev, where you going?" Said, "I'm going out the front door and I'm hauling ass."

[Kid]

BEAR MEETING AND PRAYER MEETING

This tale is common in the United States, both in song and story forms. As a minstrel type song it seems to have achieved some degree of popularity. The Frank C. Brown collection, Vol. III, 511–12, prints two variants; Dorson (*AF*), 196, alludes to a text; Parson (*FLSI*), 177, has one stanza from the South Carolina Sea Islands; White, *American Negro Folk Songs*, 210, prints it from Alabama; Ford, *Traditional Music of America*, 301–2 from the Ozarks; and it is mentioned both in Shearin and Combs, *A Syllabus of Kentucky Folk-Songs*, 31, and Davis, *Folk-Songs from Virginia*, 336. In tale form, we have texts from: Botkin (*TAA*), 120 (from *Wit and Humor of the American Pulpit* [Philadelphia, 1904], pp. 94–96); *PTFLS*,

10:36; *SFQ*, 18:129 (Ala.); Tidwell, 132 (from *SFQ*). Most of these are Negro texts. The verse-sermon in the story suggests its connection with the song. Jones, 66–68, prints a related exemplary story that may be the immediate ancestor of this.

Well, the deac and the rev was in the woods one day. The deacon and rev was breaking some wood together, taking it to the church to get the church warm before the service start. All of a sudden the rev heard a long noise. He whispered, "Hey, deacon." Deacon said, "What's the matter, brother?" He said, "Did you hear that?" "Hear what?" "That strange noise I just hear." "No, I didn't hear nothing." He said, "Sound like a bear." He said, "Look, reverend, we is members of the church. Leaders of the' flock. Prayer-giving men. Now if a bear come in this woods, the thing to do is to get down on your knees and pray that help be here and we be saved." He said, "Yeah, Rev, but suppose help don't get here on time?" "Don't worry 'bout it. The Lord watches over all his sheeps." "All right."

So they kept working. All of a sudden rev looks up and he seen this great big grizzly bear coming through the woods. Rev dropped the wood, dropped the ax, and he broke out. He ran about four or five of them old country miles. Them's long miles. And he sat down, just a-panting for breath [*pants*].

After a while he looked up, saw a cloud of dust coming down the road. And he looked real good, there goes old deacon. He said, "Hold it, deac." He said, "Wait a minute." Deac said, *panting*, "What's the matter, son? Don't hold me now. I'm in a hurry." He said, "What's your trouble? I thought you told me that if a bear come you would get down and pray?"

He said, "Well, son, it was like this; I got down and said the shortest, quickest, fastest prayer came to my mind." He said, "Just what did you pray, rev?" "It was like this. I said to the great man up above:

You delivered one man from the belly of the whale.
Delivered three from the fiery furnace.

That's what the good book say.
Then a body declare,
If you can't help me, Lord, please don't help that bear.

I kept on praying, brother, but there no help comes.
Next best thing to do was to get on 'way from there." He
said, "Yeah, but you didn't pray hard enough." He said,
"Brother, I come to one declusion. Praying's all right at
prayer meeting, but it ain't too good at bear meeting."

[Kid]

The Preacher and the Sinners

This is one of many stories here that could be classified under
K 1961.1.2.1 (Parody sermon). For another reporting of this
story, with the holdout a bootlegger, see *TFSB*, 24:110. *Legman*—This has various endings with far less antipreacher tone—
in particular where the preacher excoriates "he-ing and she-
ing," and all those sinners line up at the left; "he-ing and he-
ing," also "she-ing and she-ing," until finally only one little boy
is left, who quavers, "Reverend, how do you feel about me-
ing and me-ing?"

One day preacher was sitting up in church and he
looked down at the congregation. He said, "Brothers and
sisters, we are all gathered here in this church, we are
all gathered in this church today to pray. Be holy. Here
there still is among us some sinners, hypocrites. Today,
we gonna find the evil from the good. Pick out the good
from the bad. The one that's worthy of the flock, and
the ones that ain't. Now I say, all you faggots get up and
walk to the back of the room." All of the faggots got up
and they walked to the back of the room. "Now I say all
you bulldaggers, walk to the front of the room." All the
bulldaggers, they got up and they walked to the front of
the room. He said, "Now, I say, all you motherfuckers,
get over on the side of the hall." And all the motherfuckers
got over on the side of the hall. He said, "Now all you no-
good, you midnight ramblers, alcoholics, late players, out-

stayers, wife beaters, children deserters, get over on the other side of the room." So all them people got up and they walked to the other side of the room. He said, "Now all among you, these sinners is all around us. And there's not one man or woman or child in among us that is purified, and brother why are you sitting down on the front row?"

There was one little lonely brother sitting on the front row. He said, "Well, rev, you ain't called my name yet." He said, "Well, I said all the bulldaggers in the back." He said, "I ain't none of them." "I said all you motherfuckers on the side." "I ain't none of them." "I said all the midnight ramblers, the gamblers, the wife deserters and the wife. beaters get outside." He said, "I ain't none of them." "Then, brother, what is your sin?" He said, "I'm a cocksucker." "Come on up here with me, son."

[Kid]

THE PREACHER BENDS DOWN

This is once again K 1961.1.2.1 (Parody sermon). Dorson prints a text (NFTM), 170, and notes, "This suggests Type 1831 'The Parson and Sexton at Mass' where two connivers communicate by chanting." Legman—Charlie Chaplin based many of his early comedy routines on well-known jokes of this kind (for instance, the swallowed whistle of City Lights, which is an expurgated version of a sat-upon cane ferrule in a much older British joke). He clearly plays all sorts of cadenzas on the present story in his 1915 or 1916 comedy—which was very much resented—in which he is an ex- or escaped prisoner who has to pass himself off as the new minister. (In later theatrical pieces of this kind—for instance, Maugham's Rain—the minister has to be modified into an unspecified reformer with string necktie; also in burlesque stage anticlerical skits similar.) I have heard the present story given in the essentially more sacrilegious form of a burlesque quotation from Scriptures, in which the ex-prisoner who has become a minister in the West sees to his horror his former cellmate come into church just as

he had to begin the sermon. He swallows and begins: "Brethren and sistren, I take my text tonight from the sixteenth chapter of Habbakuk, where it says—uh, uh—'Thou who sees me,
and thinks that you knows me, ixnay-ackencray ["nix cracks,"
say nothing, in pig latin], and I will split with you later.' "

> This here preacher was in church doing his regular
> sermon. As you know, the regular ranting, up and down
> they go, kneeling down, standing up. Oh Lord this, and
> Oh Lord that. "My children, I want you to kneel down
> your head in prayer."
> As everyone kneeled down their head in prayer, this
> cat's wallet fell on the ground. Preacher reached down
> and picked it up and kept on preaching. "Well, Lord,
> Lord, if anyone saw me I'll split it with you later."

[Freddie]

GABRIEL BLOWS HIS HORN

This is Type 1785, Motif X 411 (Parson put to flight during his
sermon). This is a common story among American Negroes.
See Dorson *(NFTM)*, 169 (in notes lists two additional tales
very close to this); Brewer *(Brazos)*, 98–100; Fauset, 94; *JAF*
35:295; 41:552 (Phila.); Parsons *(FLSI)*, 58.

> This preacher had a church strictly for ladies. Every
> night about six o'clock the congregation of ladies would
> come in. The preacher he would preach and preach, get
> home about nine o'clock. It got so it kept up so long the
> men in the town was getting mad about this.
> So one day they went to church about six o'clock, the
> preacher was preaching. So the men in town they got
> together and they saw these two little boys. One of them
> had a bugle, and one was just running around playing. So
> he gave the boy that didn't have the bugle a match. He
> said, "Go play with these matches over there by the
> church." Boy said, "O.K." So he started playing with the
> match and set the church on fire. Church was just blaz-
> ing. They told the other boy to walk through the woods

and play the bugle. Church was just blazing. So the fire was coming up behind the preacher and he didn't see it. The ladies in the church started backing up heading for the door, just slowly back up. After awhile all the people were out, the preacher was standing on the platform.

> When Gabriel blows we all shall go.
> When Gabriel blows we all shall go.

The preacher looked around and saw the fire, headed for the door and a beam fell and blocked it. He turned to go for the window and his coat got caught on a nail. Just then the little boy started blowing the bugle. Toot, toot, toot, toot. Preacher simply replied, "Oh, Mr. Gabriel, don't play that shit yet."

[Freddie]

PREACHER WALKS THE WATER

This is included in K 1970 (Sham miracles) and is close to K 1961.1.3 (Sham parson; the sawed pulpit). Brewer *(Brazos)*, 46–47, prints a similar text.

This here reverend, he was preaching. "You know that Moses walked the water. So can I. What you think about that, deacon?" He hollered, "Yeah," 'cause they was in cahoots. But the deacon didn't like this preacher. He said, "Yeah, you can walk the water, brother." He said, "I tell you what I'ma do. Next Sunday, I'm gonna walk the water for you. I'm gonna smoke the water like Moses." Now everybody in church they wanted to see this. So he said, "Now look here, deac, early Sunday morning go out and put three boards out there. Tack 'em together, and I'll walk on the boards and it will look like I'm walking on the water." The deacon said, "O.K."

But instead of him putting three boards, he only put two boards. So the deacon came out there Sunday, the boards were nice and strong. He only tried out one, he figured the rest of them were the same way. So all the people coming 'round, he's already standing in the water. "Don't come no closer, 'less you all will knock the spirit off. I told you that Moses smoke the waters, didn't I?" Everybody looked and it looked like he standing on the water.

So he started walking out on his plank. He said, "Didn't Moses smoke the water?" The children hollered, "Yeah." He said, "I'm on the first one. Ain't that right, deac?" "That's right, preacher." He said, "I should be getting to the second one right now, shouldn't I?" "You're almost there." He said, "Well, pretty soon I'll be at the end of this journey." Deacon said, "Yes, you will." And by the time he said that, he had stepped off, he didn't step on the third board, but he fell down. He said, "Oh, Lord." Deacon looked at him and said, "What's the matter?" He said, "I wonder who moved that goddamned board?"

[Charley]

Who Believes?

This short anecdote is a vestige of Type 1826, Motif X 452 (Parson has no need to preach). For an Ozark text, see Randolph *(Sticks)*, 129–31.

You know Father Divine. Well, he was holding this big meeting up in Yankee Stadium, or Shibe Park or Carnegie Hall, and he had this big meeting. He was preaching and he said, "Who believes that I can walk the water?" Everyone shouted, "We do." "Who believes that I can walk the water?" "We do." So he just said, "Well, if you all believe it I don't have to do it."

[Anonymous informant]

Baptism and Belief

This could perhaps be included under Motif J 1260 (Repartee based on church or clergy). Dorson *(NFTM)* has a text of this on p. 173 from Michigan Negroes, and Brewer *(Brazos)*, 54–56, has one from Texas Negroes.

> You know Sunday service preachers have a baptizing. So the brother came down with his robe on, got down into the baptizing pit. Preacher put him down, grabbed him by the shoulder. He said, "Brother, I baptize you in the name, do you know?" He pushed him in the water and he held him down. Sister started talking to the preacher, he forgot he was holding the fellow. Pulled him up, he said, "Brother, I baptize you, do you know?" Pushed him down again. Guy was gasping for breath when he came up. Pulled him up. "Brother, do you know?" Pushed him down again. This time the guy could hardly get his breath, he was drinking water when he came up. Preacher said, "Brother, do you know?" Brother said, "I know goddamn well you trying to drown me."
>
> [Kid]

Cursing Cured

The next three stories are part of the large (but mainly unprinted) corpus of lore on how profanity can be eliminated from an offensive-tongued person's speech, and how it sometimes works. *Legman*—Mark Twain's story on himself about his wife trying to cure him of cursing by trying to outcurse him appears to be a modified version of some story related to this, now lost. His topper line is rather good, though; from memory: My dear, you have all the words right, but you just don't know the *tune.*" In another modified version the cursing is changed to dialect accent, which is to be cured by an elocution teacher; the humor here rises from the attempted cure backfiring and a week later the teacher assures the "improving" (that is, castratory) parents, "In a veek your liddle boy vil be spikking Henglish ez good like I'm spikking."

> There once was a little boy that was continuously always cussing. So his mother and father was puzzled by him always cussing seeing that they was people that never

used no foul language. So they asked the preacher to come over one night, give a suggestion how to stop the boy from cussing.

They had the preacher over for dinner. Preacher got there, everybody sat down at the table to eat. So the boy's mother went to say grace. Boy replied, "Damn, Ma, watcha doing?" So everybody started eating, so the boy wanted to season his food, so he called to the preacher, "Hey, bitch, pass the salt down here." Preacher didn't say nothing, just passed the salt.

So after they got finished eating, mother told the boy to go to bed. He put up a big squawk, but he went anyhow. The boy's mother asked the preacher what to do about the boy cussing. So the preacher told her late that night to take the boy out of his bed, don't awake him, and take him to the woods. Dig a hole and put the boy in it. In the morning when he wake up, he'll never cuss again.

So that night they took the boy out into the woods, dug a deep hole, and set the boy down in it. First thing, early the next morning, the boy woke up. See himself laying in the hole with blankets wrapped around him, and first thing he replied, "Damn, it's Judgment Day and I'm the first motherfucker to arise."

[Freddie]

THE CURSER OUTCURSED

Legman—There is a Negro protest story on this same situation, but I cannot retell it in rhyme, as I did not take it down many years ago when I heard it in Harlem. A Negro woman goes into a liquor store (thus dating it as mid-1930's?) and asks for some gin. The clerk hoity-toities her and says, "What kind of gin do you mean? We got Gilbey's gin at $2 a fifth; White Rose gin at $1 a quart; and plain ornery low-down nigger gin for 50¢." "Yes," she answers, "and there's three kinds of turd: there's mus-turd, horse-turd, and *you,* you plain ornery low-down piece of dogshit. Gimme the nigger gin for fifty cents." This didn't exactly rhyme but it went with a hell of a lilt to it.

There is also a "racially expurgated" white version of this—much less situational and more verbal, thus far weaker as humor—about the "three kinds of tea: f-a-r-t, with the delicate airy body; s-h-i-t with the heavy, heady odor; and c-u-n-t, the Tea of Teas, at (some-price-or-another) a pound."

The use of damn, etc., as intensives is the subject of an elegant passage by John Brophy, in Brophy and Partridge's *Songs and Slang of the British Soldier*, pp. 15–19, concerning the word "fucking"—which should actually be spelled "fucken," as it is the obsolete past particle (the modern "fucked-up") and not the present participle, as is usually thought; which also explains why the terminal "g" is invariably omitted: it does not belong there at all. The commonest expurgation 'of this is "bloody," as in "The Great Australian Adjective," of which my own interchangeable army version (with the last stanza omitted) is printed in Edgar Palmer's (i.e., Erich Posselt's) *G.I. Songs*, pp. 207–8, and reprinted—with a pretended Korean War provenance—in William Wallrich's *Air Force Airs* (New York, 1957), pp. 160–61.

This man used to walk in this grocery store every day. So one day he walked into the grocery store and said:

> "I want some motherfucking meat
> For my motherfucking cat.
> Not too motherfucking lean,
> Not too motherfucking fat.
> I want it packed very neat in a bag."

Pop was tired of having this happening every day. Every day when he wanted his meat for his cat. So the next day, Pop walking down this street and he seen this boy shooting crap. "Goddamn, I missed again." Pop looked down and looked at the boy. "That motherfucker got a seven again. Goddamn it, baby, Momma needs a new pair of shoes. Damn it, missed again. Motherfucking cocksucker." "Hey, son, you want a job?" "Goddamn right. How much money I'ma make, Pop?" "I'll give you twenty dollars a week." "Sure, what time you want me to come by? I'll be the fuck around three. Goddamn straight, I'll be there."

Next morning, early in the morning, little boy at the counter. So this stud walk in and said:

> "I want some motherfucking meat
> For my motherfucking cat.
> Not too motherfucking lean,
> Not too motherfucking fat.
> Pack it very neat in a bag.

Boy looked up at him, grabbed his bag, and here's what he said:

> "Here's the motherfucking meat
> For your motherfucking cat.
> Not too motherfucking lean,
> Not too motherfucking fat.
> Aim your feet at the motherfucking door
> And don't come back no motherfucking more."

[Petey]

THE JUDGE REPLIES

Legman—Much like the *cante fable* about the witness to a rape, reprimanded for using the word "fucking," who breaks into a rhyme about "His pants was down, his ass was bare/His you-know-what was you-know-where/His balls was dangling in mid-air/And if that wasn't fucking, then *I wasn't there.*"

This guy was standing on the corner, you know, he kept walking down the street. He said:

> "My name is Fucking Pete,
> I walk the fucking street.
> I fuck all the whores
> That think they're so fucking neat."

So the police walked up to him and said, "What you say?" Said:

"My name is Fucking Pete,
I walk the fucking street.
I fuck all the bitches
That think they're so fucking neat."

Cop said, "I'ma take you in. Disorderly conduct, 'citing a riot, disturbing the peace, resisting arrest." "I ain't did nothing." "You're going in anyway."

So next morning he got up. Judge said, "What's the charge?" "Disorderly conduct, 'sturbing the peace, 'citing a riot." "Um, what's your name?"

"My name is Fucking Pete,
I walk the fucking street.
I fuck all these bitches
Who think they're so fucking neat."

The judge said:

"Yeah, son. Well, I'm the fucking judge,
Who's give you some fucking time.
Here's fifteen years
To get that fucking off your mind."

[Kid]

ARGUMENT OF THE PARTS OF THE BODY

Legman—You have here a relic of an extremely ancient folk-tale—in fact a whole tale type. The family it belongs to is that of the argument in the *Arabian Nights* between the three sons, with the magic carpet, the all-seeing crystal ball, and the all-curing apple, who can't decide which of them is to get the princess cured by the combined powers of their three possessions. The specific argument between the parts of the body as to which is more important is very ancient indeed, and the rectum *always* wins, after the others pooh-pooh its claims (as I've heard this told in modern times myself!) when it says "Well, then, I'm gonna shut my mouth and not say another word." Whereupon all the other members of the body become deathly sick from constipation and agree the rectum is the most important. Your own story *begins* this tale, but does not give it, as your ending has clearly nothing to do with being "most important," and is a pure complaint. *That* form, or sub-form, is at least as old as the mid-seventeenth century, and I believe a rhymed form as a *dream* is given in one of the drolleries, with the testicles described as a hunter's dogs who stay by the side of the pond while he goes in swimming. There are also other forms of this complaint tale, where the complaining is done by fleas or other insects (symbolizing the child in the womb—who also sometimes does the complaining) who describe the penis as an intruder or one-eyed giant of the Polyphemus sort in the Homeric legend. I myself would not hesitate to classify the Polyphemus story as a symbolic form of this same vagina-as-cavern tale, all the more so since the P. story includes and ends with what is the *oldest recorded joke* in the world (where Ulysses tells the giant his name is "Nobody," so the giant later cannot explain who is hurting him), as pointed out by the Russian folklorist Afanasyev, in *Russian Secret Tales* in the 1860's. The element in your text, equating the rectum with an outhouse, also is found in a modern story about Henry Ford in heaven, who tells God that the creation of human beings was not well done because, in making Eve, "You put the exhaust too close to the intake."

> The parts of the body were all talking to themselves about which was the most important. Finally Peter rose up and spoke. He said, "I wear two stones tied around my neck. At night when I go to bed to take a little rest, I'm shoved in a dark hole, next door to a shithouse, and I stay till I puke. If I come out and stand up for my rights, I get shoved in again."
>
> [Kid]

HIMSELF DISCOVERED

This tale, along with a number that immediately follow, is reminiscent of Chaucer and Boccaccio in situation. As such it has much in common with many motifs: J 2136 (Numskull brings about own capture); J 582 (Foolishness of premature coming out of hiding); J 1805 (Other misunderstandings of words); X 111.7 (Misunderstood words lead to comic results). Baughman gives a motif (N 275.5.2—subdivision of Criminal confesses because he thinks himself accused) which nearest approximates the story. *JAF*, 32:372, has two stories in which a similar misunderstanding of words leads to the unmasking of hidden lover.

> Once there was a woman and man who were married, and the woman was a whore. Now the woman always cried broke when collectors came, so when the iceman came and asked for pay, she said, "Come into my bedroom," and she gave him a piece of cock. So then the husband came home and said why does she have to fuck the collectors instead of paying. So she said, "All right, I won't do it again."
>
> But as soon as her husband left, the colored insurance man came, so she told him, "I don't have any money but I can pay you with some cunt." So he accepted. Meanwhile the husband came home from work much earlier than usual and knocked on the door. The woman said, "Hide. That's my husband." So he hid in the closet.
>
> Her husband sat down and said, "You been messing around again, haven't you?" So he threw her down on the bed and started pulling the hairs on her cock. Meanwhile, remember the man is still in the closet. The husband gets down to two hairs, and they are hard to get out. So he starts cursing, "Come on out, you black bastards, damn it." The man in the closet starts shaking. The husband says again, "Come out of there, damn it, you black bastard." So the man comes running out of the closet with one shoe on and britches halfway up, running straight through the door.

> [Charley]

HIS EVENING KISS

This anecdote is one of the most amusing elements of Type 1361, which we know best through Chaucer's version, "The

Miller's Tale." For a full description of the tradition of the whole tale, see Bryan and Dempster, *Sources and Analogues of the Canterbury Tales,* pp. 106 ff. This one portion is Motif K 1225 (Lover given rump to kiss). See also J 1772.

Now look here. This fellow was going home, this guy was blind, you know. So every night when this guy would go past he would stop by and kiss this little old girl. So this night her old man was there. So he comes knocking on the window, he says, "Who's outside that window?" He said, "Look ahere." She said, "That's the blind man lives down the street. He always stop by here every night and he always kiss me." "Put your ass out the window, let that motherfucker kiss your ass. I've been trying to fuck him." So she puts her ass out the window, the old blind man hit her [*kissing sound*]. So he said, "Honey, what's the matter?" She said, "Honey, I'm sick." He said, "You sick?" She said, "Yes." "Let me kiss you 'gain." She puts her ass out the window, he smacks her one big long one [*long kissing sound*]. He said, "You ain't lying you sick, honey. You jaws are swollen like you have the mumps and your breath smells like shit."

[Kid]

Coming or Going

Remind me of the time I was sitting around this girl's house, friend of mine's wife, and I was going to give her a little bit, you know. Sitting up in her room. So all of a sudden I heard a door open. I said, "Who's that?" She said, "That's my husband." She said, "Kiss my titties, I'm coming." I said, "Shit, you kiss my ass, I'm going."

[Kid]

"Grandma, It's You!"

The substitution theme is legion in anecdotes of this sort. The Italian novelists of the late Renaissance made much of the theme. The substitution of older woman for younger is, however, fairly unusual. Thompson has a motif (K 1317.5—Woman substitutes for her daughter in the dark) but his reference to the Heptameron is misleading and belongs elsewhere, and Rotunda (from whom Thompson seems to have derived the motif) has a very different accent to his description. Certainly this story fits somewhere in the K 1317 area (Lover's place usurped by another) and should probably be around 1317.2.1 (Old woman as substitute for girl in man's bed) but should be constrasted with this latter because in the stories subsumed under it the woman is just a pawn of someone else, while here she is the schemer.

Now this is about a little old country boy. Yeah, this is about a little country boy. Little country boy lived waaay out in the woods. Man, he lived so far back in the woods he had to pack a lunch to go to the mailbox. Now anyway, he was going with this little old country girl. Now she told him, "Now listen here, you come 'round here 'bout nine o'clock, I'll cut the lights out, put the window up right after you whistle and you'll know that I'm all ready." He said, "All right." He said, "I be there." "All right."

So now her grandmother heard it. Grandmother, she was about sixty-eight, sixty-nine years old. She ain't had no joint since Grandpop died 'bout twenty-five years ago. Well, she thinking to herself, "I'ma get some of this young peter." So just about ten minutes of nine, she said, "Daughter, you run down to the store, get me some snuff." She said, "But Grandma, store's almost thirty-five miles from here. Can I use the buggy?" "No, the horse is sick, you walk." "Grandma, I won't be back till 'bout four o'clock in the morning." "You go 'head." "All right."

So the little daughter thought she'd cut through the woods and catch up with Johnny, but Johnny duck 'round the other way. Johnny came in, looked up at the window and whistled [*whistle*]. Grandma threw up the window, took off all her clothes, and throwed herself in bed. Johnny jumped up in the window, throwed off his clothes and jumped dead on that old-fashioned cock.

And Johnny started to work and whirling, after a while he said, "Damn." He come to life, looked down and saw [it] was Grandma. He said, "Grandma, it's you!" She said "Yes, son. It's me." He said, "Grandma, it stinks." She said, "Well, son, I'ma tell you, it's like this: it was just so goddamn good. I'm too old to come, so I just went on ahead and shit."

[Kid]

THE NIGHTLY RITUAL

This is basically the same story as above with a slightly different scene, technique, and punch line.

This old guy, you know, he was sitting home, you know. He was coming home every night, certain time, all he did, he had a routine, he'd did it so long. His mother— mother-in-law, rather—father-in-law lived with him. And his wife. And every night he'd go to bed, his wife'd go to bed, rather, and his mother-in-law and father-in-law, they'd go to bed, they lived under them. And you know, when he come home from work, 'bout two, three o'clock, he'd just get in bed, lay there for an hour or two. Then he'd get up and go on and work out. And his wife be hollering, "Oh, honey, you know I love you. You sweet thing, you. Ooh, you do it so good."

So his mother-in-law was lying there one night, said, "I'ma get me some of that young peter. First chance I get." So Thursday night come up, was a cabaret, so her husband had left for work early so she couldn't ask him. So mother-in-law said, "You go on, I'll watch the kids." So the father-in-law said, "Well, I'll take her to the cabaret, you know, so somebody be with her." She said, "Yeah, that be fine." She said, "Now I'll sneak upstairs while they're gone. I'll jump in bed."

She snuck upstairs, got undressed, got in bed, same side his wife lay on, you know. He came home from work that night, jumped in bed, you know. Routine. He didn't pay her no mind. He just crawled on over, got in bed. Laid there 'bout half an hour, got a little sleep. Rolled over, and you know, started to work it out. He sweating and pushing, sweating and pushing. She wasn't saying nothing. He was wondering why his wife, you know usually she tells him how much she loves him and everything, tonight she quiet. It was windy that night, you know, getting ready to rain. The wind blowing real hard, summer night. And the front door was open. Ma, she wanted to say something so bad, she could scream. So all of a sudden the wind blew the door slammed. She thought it was her husband. So she jumped up, she said, "You dirty motherfucker, you. Why you riding son-of-a-bitch. My own son-in-law, laying up on top of me like this here. Laying up here just a doing it to me. And knowing good and well that you're married to my daughter. Now look here, boy, you hit this thing one or two more time and get on down from here."

[Kid]

THE HAIRY SCOREBOARD

This is, as the informant points out, one of the standard traveling salesman stories which, with the milkman jokes, gives greatest evidence of being the modern successor to the novelle.

This fellow was one of these traveling salesmen. That's what all these jokes are about. Traveling salesman riding along in the woods one night, that's when one of these storms come up. So he said, "I guess I'll stop in this little old shack here and see who's home." So he knocks on the door. Pop comes, says "Yeah." He says, "Pardon me, dad, my car broke down. I'd like to know could I spend the night here tonight?"

"Sure. Look here now, you got a choice. You could sleep out the barn with my pet bear or you could sleep upstairs [with] me and my daughter." "I'd ruther sleep with you and your daughter." "All right. Dinner's at six and we going to bed at nine." "All right."

So he ate dinner, you know, talked to the daughter, got tight. Nine o'clock he went to bed. Ten-thirty she rolled over and said, "How 'bout us getting a little piece?" He said, "I don't know. Suppose your father wake up?" "Don't worry about him. Pull a hair out of his ass, see is he woke." He reached over and pulled one—boinggg! "He's 'sleep." So they started working. Hour later she said, "Better stop, see is Dad woke." He pulled 'nother hair. Boinggg! So they worked 'nother fifteen, twenty minutes, she said, "Stop. See is Daddy woke." He pulled 'nother hair. Boing!

So they fucked for four or five hours and every ten minutes they stopped, pulled a hair out of Dad's ass. At last, woke up. He reached over, said, "Wait a minute. Lemme tell y'all something. You paid your rent, you paid your board and mo'. Paid for your dinner, gave me twenty dollars extra. Now I don't mind you fucking my daughter, but be damned if I don't mind you 'bout using my ass for a scoreboard."

[Kid]

Washday in the Woods

The man who has had to do without seems to interest the Camingerly group, as is illustrated by the next two stories.

Now you 'magine yourself in the woods. This old lady out there washing clothes, and a fellow walking through the woods about two blocks away. There's a clear field now, and he can see everything. Now this old lady was washing wool, and she was bending over just rubbing in the bowl. Rubbing her old clothes in the bowl, down South, you know. This old guy come walking past. He just come out of jail doing seven and a half. He ain't had no kind of cock for I don't know when. Got blisters on his dick from jerking off so much. He looks through the woods and he spots the old lady rubbing down, he says, "Ummh, hmmh, the keast of the beast." Breaks down and charge through the woods where Ma is stroke down in the tub. He hit her. He hit her—zhagoop! She hollered,

"*Ummmmh, hmmmmh,* Lord have mercy. Ummh. Son, I don't know your name. I can't see your face. Now get it, child, for you'll find me *every* Monday morning at the same old place."

[Kid]

George Is Upstairs

This story is very current in joke-telling sessions, Negro and otherwise. Since collecting this version, I have heard it a number of times, generally with the same details.

Now this here fellow, you know, he was in the navy. He was in the navy, you know. Stone sailor. He been out on the sea for 'bout a year. He ain't had nothing like a woman. So he came in 'bout four o'clock in the morning, got his pass, ran into city, come to this house he heard about. Knocked on the door, the guy said, "Yeah?" Said, "Look here, how's the chance of a man getting something did for me?" Said, "But, Dad, it's four o'clock in the morning and all the girls done split, man. But we got George upstairs." "I don't play that motherfucking shit." The guy leaves.

Next night he had KP so he had to stay a little late. Comes in late again. Knocked on the door. "Yeah?" "Look here," he said, "I just got in town, man, I got to have something done to me now. How's the chance in a fellow getting fixed up?" He said, "You keep coming late. The girls are gone, but we got George upstairs." "I don't play that motherfucking shit." Said, "You come 'round here tomorrow right, and I'll have you five girls, you can take your pick." "All right."

So next day they got to joking 'round, joking 'round, joking 'round 'bout two o'clock in the morning. He comes out of there ass shoving out like fire. Come by, said, "Look here, man, I hope you saved me a girl." "The girls, they waited till ten-thirty, they went out and made some money. But we still got George upstairs." "Man, I don't play that shit." He said, "Wait a minute, I got to get some-

thing. How much is George?" "Three hundred dollars."
"Three hundred dollars? How is it three hundred dollars?" He said, "Well, see, lemme 'splain it to you. Now
there's a hundred for George. There's a hundred for me.
And a hundred for Al." "Wait a minute. Why Al got to get
a hundred?" "Well, see, Al gitta help me hold George,
'cause George don't play that shit neither."

[Kid]

THE WATCH

Here is another tale about a signifying monkey whose guile is
defeated by a show of strength. One of the important coun-
terparts to the Marster-John stories, and often told in conjunction with them, is the "kind Marster" type in which the faith-
ful servant is rewarded for his service and encounters the
wide world for the first time. A story I heard often but never
recorded concerned just such a situation, but the servant
worked out a way of telegraphing his master for more money
until this practice was brought to a halt through a humorous
cryptic telegram.

One day Sam's boss, Mr. Charlie, walked up him and
said to old Sam, "Sam, you have been slaving for me ever
seen you came out of your mammy's cock. And since tomorrow is a special holiday and all the niggers will be
in town, because that is just about the only time that
you people can come to town, unless us white folks is
with y'all. I am going to let you wear my gold chain and
twenty-dollar gold piece to town and let those poor niggers gaze at my Sam." So Sam scratched his head, and
sweating all the same time, said thank you Mr. Charlie,
boss man, and went on down to his shack.

When Sam got home and told his wife what his boss
had give him to go to town with, she said that Sam was
the richest nigger in these parts of the South. So Sam
put on his suit that his brother had sent him from up
North; Sam had to hide the suit, because his boss wouldn't
let him wear it, because he would have taken it from him.

When Sam hit the edge of town, the poor niggers, as his boss put it, started looking and running up to Sam and ask, who did he kill, did he shoot his boss, or who did he rob, and one said that Sam had better high-tail it to the hills before they find out and get a posse started looking for him. Sam said, "Hold on a minute, you poor niggers. I didn't rob or kill anyone. My boss Mr. Charlie let me wear his gold chain and twenty-dollar gold piece to come to town and be a rich nigger, and show you poor niggers up." They all started to scratch their heads, and talking to one another, saying that they wish they had a boss as good as Mr. Charlie was to Sam.

Then Old Sam spotted something come his way with something on a chain, and started to run when the crowd called him back and told him that it was a monkey on a chain, and that box that the music came out of was an organ, and the man was an organ grinder. And the man tell hot numbers if you put something in the monkey's cup. They told Sam to go and see for himself, so he did. Sam went up to the monkey and said, "Good morning, Mr. Monkey," so the monkey looked at Sam and said to him that he was the prettest nigger that he had seen all day, so Old Sam told the monkey how long he had been working for his boss man, and that his boss loved him and let him wear his chain and twenty-dollar gold piece to town for the holiday. So the monkey looked Sam over and then asked Sam where did he get the suit, so Sam told him that his brother had sent it to him from up North. So Old Sam reached in his pocket and pulled out a dime and said, "Mr. Monkey, I want you to tell me a hot number."

Mr. Monkey looked at Sam and said, "Hey, nigger, I'll tell you what I will do, I will give you two hot numbers and show you a trick too." So Old Sam said, "O.K., Mr. Monkey," so the monkey told him to let him hold the watch, so he took the watch off the chain and let the monkey hold it. The monkey put the watch in his mouth, and swallowed it, which Sam did not know, so Sam waited for a half an hour, and said, "Mr. Monkey, when are you

going to tell me the numbers and show me the trick?"
The monkey said, "Hold on, nigger, it takes time to do
wonders like this, and more time for a nigger, and this is
special for you." Sam waited, and he asked again. The
monkey told Sam, "Nigger, you have to watch stuff like
that, coming up to me and asking me for a hot number
with a dime, don't you know that me and my boss are city
slickers, and you a black nigger coming up to me, why the
very idea. The reason I took you for the okey-dok is because you was the sharpest nigger in town and after you
told me that story I lead you in this hole," and he also told
Old Sam, "Nigger, that is the SHIT you have to WATCH."
So Old Sam looked at him and didn't say a word, but
reached in his pocket and put out his switchblade, and
grab the monkey by the neck, and put down his side of
the story. He told the monkey that he was old, was true,
but he wasn't going to fall for that shit, "So that is the
WATCH he had to SHIT."

[from Javester's Manuscript]

A Party

The following is basically the same story as the one explored
in its relation to its Uncle Remus antecedent in Chapter 3.
Here the ending is quite different, but the tone remains the
same.

One day while Bro Lion and Bro Monkey was walking
along in the jungle, they spied a poster tacked on a tree,
with a few of the home animals standing around in a
bunch saying that they were going, going. "Where?"
Bro Lion say to Bro Monkey. Bro Monkey shoke his
head and said that he didn't know what was going on. So
they walked up to the tree, and everyone of the animals
that were standing there move aside for Bro Lion and Bro
Monkey because Bro Lion was the king of the jungle, and
Bro Monkey was his side kick, and every little thing that
Bro Monkey would do the lion would take up for him,
he was a nasty little son-of-a-bitch, he would fuck his

mother, if she was living, thought Bro Lizard. The poster read, "To all the Brothers and the Sisters of this jungle, you are invited to attend a party given by Mr. and Mrs. Stip Tiger and Etc. on the twelfth day of the month."So the lion and the monkey said that they would go and turn it out, so the monkey agreed like he always did.

Came the night of the party, every brother and every sister in the jungles were there, Bro Deer with his wife, Bro Lizard and his wife, Bro Cheetah and his wife, etc. They had a band, and the place was decorated, they had all kinds of goodies, a bib cake, punch, whiskey, wine, woman, and song. Bro Monkey looked at Bro Lion and said that he was going to tear his little ass tonight, with all those whores there and the other brothers' wives, behind, all those drinks, and music, so the lion told him to go ahead and have a good time. Bro Monkey started off by trying to pull Mrs. Baboon, she was the prettiest bitch at the party, he started dancing with her, on a slow record, and was trying to do the barrow house with her, in other words the mooch. He had to give that up because he was too short to grind with her. When he did let her go when the music stopped, his little prick had gotten hard, he didn't give damn, he was so bold that he took it out and said stop the music, and cried out to all the bitches in the house, and said look what you can get for nothing, all the respectakle women in the house scream, while all the whores in the house hollowed "Daddy" and ran over to him and made Bro Monkey cream, then at that moment Bro Tiger came running through the crowd and grab the monkey by the collar and was going to throw him out, when Bro Lion said, no you are not, with his head all bad, and tight, and told Bro Tiger to put his buddy down and said the monkey was his cut, and no mother should put his hands on him, and to let the party carry on.

So the party started again, until Mrs. Tiger had heard a noise from behind the couch that said, "Come on, bitch, and eat my dick." She jumped up and got her husband, when they looked the couch, there was Bro Monkey lay-

ing there with two whores, one was sucking his little dick
and the other was kissing him. Mr. Tiger said to leave
him be, because he was scared of Bro Lion. The next
little thing that they caught him doing was pissing in the
punch bowl, so all they could do was to remove the
punch, and Bro Tiger was taking the wine away, because
all the whiskey had ran out, as you know. Bro Lion shouted
for Bro Monkey to get the wine, Bro staggered over to
Mrs. Tiger and took the wine, then the guest had
started to leave, when Bro Lion and Bro Monkey went
over to the door and told everyone that he had caught
trying to leave to set their ass down in a corner, or fuck,
dance and be merry, because this was now his party, and
Bro Monkey agreed.

Bro Lion had gotten so drunk that he said that he
wanted to fuck, he didn't want a whore because that wasn't
good enough for him. So he looked at Mrs. Tiger, she
was still young and good-looking so he grabbed her and
threw her down on the foot of the couch and spread her
legs and fell in, then someone told Bro Tiger that they
would all get them and gang them, so that they would
stop all that horseshit, and even throw them out. Bro Lion
said no, because he would come back with his family,
herd, gang, and not only fuck his wife but everyone's
wife, so they let him be. Then Bro Lion rolled off and fell
asleep from the wine. Bro Monkey walked up to Mr.
Tiger and asked him what kind of party it was, because
the cake wasn't decorated. Mr. Tiger said that it was a
birthday party. Bro Monkey said that he worked in a
bakery before and said that he could decorate a cake, so
he went over to the table and pulled up a chair a climb
on the table and started to shit on the cake. So all the
brothers and sisters said that they were fed up with that
shit that Bro Lion and Bro Monkey was putting down, so
they grab monkey and told him that he was going to eat
that shit. The monkey told them that he wasn't and to go
fuck themselves and then said that Bro Lion would get
them and kick all their asses when he got sober. By that
time Bro Lion had a woke up from all the noise that they

were making, and he had to close one eye to see what everyone was doing. He heard them say to Mr. Tiger to make Bro Monkey eat that shit, so the monkey put up a fight and broke away from them and ran over to Bro Lion and told him that they were trying to make him eat some shit that he had dropped on Mr. Tiger's birthday cake, and Bro Lion looked at him from one eye and told Bro Monkey that he was too drunk to help him. Bro Monkey told him again that they were trying to make him eat some shit, Bro Lion looked at him again through one eye and told Bro Monkey that he heard what the man said, "You are going to eat that SHIT."

[from Javester's Manuscript]

A Sleeve Job

This is perhaps the most widely known story of the "Lady and the Tiger" type, often collected in less suggestive form as "The Purple Passion." It is in classic shaggy-dog form with the familiar letdown ending. Brunvand ("A Classification for Shaggy Dog Stories," *JAF* 76 [1963], p. 67) lists it as D 510.1 (misprinted 501.1), and lists only the twelve texts in the Indiana University Archives as his sources. *Legman*—This story is apparently first printed, as having been an *original* recitation by Henry Monnier, the French Mark Twain, under the title "*La Diligence de Lyon*" ("The Lyons Stagecoach") in a letter giving several such jokes and recitations, signed "Marquis de C." in Jules Gay's bibliographical magazine *Le Fantaisiste* (San Remo, 1873), Vol. I, pp. 176–185. As there given, the text is very long and precise as to its sexual details, but with a clear humorous intention throughout, and ends (p. 181) with the woman on her deathbed while the "sucker," who has been searching for her, and the chimera of the "*Diligence de Lyon*," actually gets in with her so that she should show him how it is done with dying breath. "*Mais, une crise se declare, elle retombe. . . . et expire, emportant son secret dans la tombe!!!!*"

One day a nigger was standing on the corner, and up walked a white woman and said to him, did he want a sleeve job. The nigger rub his head and repeated, a sleeve job, and asked her what was a sleeve job. She said to him, "Don't ask questions, just say yes or no." The nigger rubbed his head again and said, "Yes mam," because she look so good to him and furthermore, because she was white, and he didn't know what a sleeve job was and mainly because he wanted to find out what it was, and he thought it was something good. So she gave him an address, and told him to be there at seven o'clock sharp, and don't be late, and don't bring any company with him, because if he did he wouldn't get the sleeve job. So he told the white woman, yes mam, and said that he wouldn't be late. He went on down the street and met a buddy of his named Jack, he asked Jack what was a sleeve job. Jack told him that he didn' know what it was, or is.

He still had some time to kill before he had to be there to get his sleeve job, so he went in the bar, had a few drinks, and still he was wondering what a sleeve job could possibly be, so he asked the bartender what it was. He said that he had never heard of it, so he left there and strolled on down the street and met old dirty Slim. He called old dirty Slim and asked him. Old dirty Slim was what you would call a bushwacker, a nose diver, a canyon yodler, well, in other words a cocksucker, or just say that he ate pussy. He was also a puck lover, and a whore mongler. In other words he was just plain dirty Slim to everyone. So he asked old dirty Slim, and even Slim couldn't tell him.

So he fucked around till it got close to seven. So he had money enough to hop a cab, so he got the cab and rode to the corner from where she had given the address, so he got out of the cab and walked to the woman's house, being very careful that no one would catch him going in. He went to the front door and rang the bell. He heard a buzzer ring, he did have sense enough to know that it meant to turn the knob and enter, he went in looking all around with his hat in his hands twisting and ruffing his hat up.

He heard a voice coming from the next room, saying to

him to come in, where she was. When he went in to the
other room, he saw a beautiful white woman laying on
the couch, with white pinkish tits, with red nipples, and
a firm white body, and one leg thrown up on the top of
the couch, this spreading her legs, showing her pussy,
with reddish-brown hairs running from the crack of her
ass to her nable, and around her thighs, this made him
start to sweat and also made his heart beat, and to think,
and to know that he was going to endure her, to seduce
her, and to be love by her, not just to be love by her, but
just because she was a white woman, and he had never
experienced this sort of a thing with a white woman, and
mainly a sleeve job.

She told him to come over to her and [not to] be scared
because she lived there by herself and she had no husband and they were alone. He went to her and all he
could do was to stare at her taking pictures of her to remember her, and to remember the violent moments
that he would spend with. She said to him, did he still
want the sleeve job. He answered her, and said yes mam,
so she told him to go upstairs to the bathroom and take a
shower, because he had to be very clean for a sleeve, and
she told him that she always like the man to be clean
when she was giving out a job.

So the nigger went upstairs and was taking the shower
when he heard her call to him to hurry up because she
on edge and waiting for him. He said yes mam, and came
running out of the bathroom, and down the stairs steps,
and he was breaking a record until he hit that second step
from the bottom and fell down and broke his neck, and he
never did find out what a "Sleeve Job" was.

DO YOU KNOW WHAT A SLEEVE JOB IS?

[from Javester's Manuscript]

GOOD MANNERS

This is one of many stories (the next story is also a variant)
of daughters reporting on sexual performance. The point of

these stories often turns on the naiveté of the girls and result-
ant comic sexual misunderstandings.

One time there was this woman, she had three daughters. Her daughters got big, about eighteen, mother sent
them out to sell some pussy. So they all went out together. All got tricks so they came home. They all went
in different rooms. So they stayed in there 'bout fifteen
minutes. The mother tiptoed upstairs, listened at each
door. So one girl, her room she heard squeaking of the
bed. So she tipped to the next room. She heard loud
screaming. All right, she went to the next room. She ain't
hear a motherfucking thing there. She was kind of
curious. So she tipped back downstairs.

When they all got finished they come back downstairs.
So she asked the first daughter, she said, "Why was the
bed squeaking so much?" She said, "Mama, he was doing it to me so good that I had to move a lot." So she accepted that.

Then she went to the next girl. She said, "What was all
the screaming about?" Said, "Mama, that man was fucking so good."

So she went to the next girl. She said, "What was happening in your room? I didn't hear nothing." She said,
"Well, Mama, you always beat me about talking when I
have a mouthful."

[Kid]

GOOD MORNING, THIS MORNING

For a similar code story, see "The Reverend and the Deacon's
Contest." This is one of many stories (others follow immediately) overtly placing a Negro in contest with others (usually
two others). *Legman*—This "code" story is also told of a woman
whose twin daughters get married simultaneously and who report to her in the morning how their respective husbands performed. The whorehouse version is evidently a more rational
situation, and probably the original—the marriage form being
then intended as more polite. (See remarks on last story.)

This woman had a whorehouse, you know. She had four girls that lived there. But the police was getting on them so bad that it was hot. Every time the police would come in they would trick with one of them, soon as they gave the girls money they would lock her up. The woman told them, she said, "Now girls, tonight is Friday night and everybody will be getting paid. Big business. Now y'all ain't gonna see no money. When they first come there they gonna give me the money. Then you just count how many tricks you have. In the morning when you come down, every time you say 'morning' that means how many tricks you have." They said all right.

So one of the girls said, "I'm sick, I can't work tonight." "All right. I tell you what. Mary, Susie, y'all work." Three girls, one was a Puerto Rican girl, other was an Irish girl, other was a colored girl there.

So they went on that night and business was pretty fair. Next morning come downstairs. Puerto Rican girl come down, she said, "Nice morning, this morning." So she gave her enough for two tricks. This Irish girl come down, she said, "Good morning, this morning, how are you this morning?" Gave her money for three tricks. 'Bout two hours passed, then the colored girl come down. So everybody looked at her. They said, "How you doing?" She said, "Good morning, this morning. If every morning was like this morning, have a good morning every morning, wouldn't we?"

[Kid]

THE DEVIL LETS THEM DREAM

A number of jokes refer to the exoteric view of the Negro (his traits as seen by outside groups). In the most common of these jokes, also collected by the Negro, he attempts to buy something from the devil and to defer payment. See Dorson (*NFTM*), p. 77. This comment on his supposed laziness is the only reference to this attribute I have found, and I was surprised to find the story in this group, as its tone is frankly anti-

Negro. *Legman*—Your feeling about this story is clearly correct: it is an anti-Negro story—in fact, anti-Jewish at the same time—and it is surprising that it was collected from a Negro informant. (Of course, dreaming one's way to riches is a fair enough dream.) Negro stories and Jewish stories both show—in their authentic forms—the most extreme difference from the usual dialect stories told about these two peoples, which are almost always crude attacks, though the persons re-telling them imagine them to be humorous. The present "laziness" story is also told about the Marseillais, in the form of a prize for laziness, which the winner refuses to accept with his hand, saying, "Mind shoving it in my pocket, boss?" See a similar story, obviously a "whopper" and not Negro in origin, in Botkin *(TAA)*, p. 92. A closer analogue of your story—and one which perhaps explains what is really involved in this laziness—is about two hoboes who find a packet of heroin tossed out of a train window during a raid. They each take a sniff and begin explaining to each other what they are dreaming. One dreams he has a million dollars, mountain of gold, etc. The other says, "Say, bo, if you got a million bucks, willya give me half?" "Ah gwan," says the other, "dream up yer own fuckin' mountain of gold!" This comes very close to the punch line of your text.

> One time there was a Jew, an Irishman, and a colored man. So this man was going to give away a million dollars. So he wanted to see who was the smartest of all. Who-ever was the smartest he was going to give him the million dollars. So he asked this Irishman, "What would you do if you went to sleep and dreamt that you had a million dol-lars and woke up and found that you had a million dol-lars?" The Irishman being a wise man he jumped up and said, "I guess I'd invest it. Get me a business of some sort, try to get me another million." So he said, "All right."
>
> So he went to the Jew. So he asked the Jewish fellow, he said, "Uh, supposing you went to sleep, woke up, dreamt about a million dollars, woke up and found you had a million dollars? What would you do?" So the Jew

jumps up all excited. He said, "I'd buy me a couple of meat markets, kosher markets, and so forth, try to get *me* another million."

So he came to this colored guy, he said, "Uh, if you went to bed and dreamt about a million dollars, woke up and had a million dollars, what would you do?" So the colored guy jumped up and said, "Shit, I'd go back to sleep and try to dream me up another million."

[Kid]

THE DEVIL'S CHOICES

The next two stories are really one, and come from the same informant who saw them as one with two different endings. They are both a variation on "Chinaman, Jew, Negro" without any trickery involved. The situation of the second version is related to the widely told jest of the person (often a cowboy) finding a hat in the mud, only to find a rider and his horse under it.

This guy went to hell and the devil gave him his choice. He had these three rooms. He said, "Whatever room you go in, you'll have to stay for all eternity." So they went up to the first door, and he heard "Prrrrpp, prrrrpp, brack." Said, "Shit, I don't know what they're doing in there. I don't want to go in there." Second room, he heard a bed squeaking, moaning, and groaning. He said, "Shit, I know they fucking in there. I don't want to be fucking rest of my life." So this third room he didn't hear nothing, just "Ssshooo, splash, ssshooo, splash" [*whispered*]. Said, "Shit, I wonder what's happening in there?" So he said, "Well, I'll go in the last one."

So the devil took him up on a stepladder, opened this trap door, and kicked him in real fast. Here go another guy, standing up to his neck in shit, hollering, "Please don't wave, please don't wave."

[Freddie]

The devil gave this guy three rooms to go into to stay for all eternity, but he gave him his choice. Well, the guy, listening at the doors, first door he heard this "Brrrrpp, brack." Second door he heard a bed squeaking, moaning, and groaning. He said, "Shit, they probably fucking in there. I better let that slide. I don't want to do that for all eternity." So he goes to the third room and he hears "Ssshooo, splash, ssshooo, splash." So he said, "O.K., I'll take this one." So he goes in the last one and the Devil takes him up on the trap door and pushes him in, falls down in all this shit, starts swimming to stay on top. He sees this other person standing in the shit up to his neck, laughing his ass off. Cat said, "You up to shit in your neck and you're laughing. What's wrong with you?" He said, "You'd be laughing too if Joe was down on the bottom holding you up."

[Freddie]

THE OLD WISE KING

A further variation on the devil's choices, here cast in a slightly different setting.

This here's about this old wise king, man. King Richard and all that shit. He told these guys, he said, "Lookahere." He caught these guys stealing, these three men. He said, "Goddamn it, next time I catch y'all son of bitches stealing, I'ma kill all you." So these motherfuckers say, "We ain't gonna steal no more. We ain't gonna steal no more." So they said, "Shit. That son of a bitch." So they went up the palace. They fucked the queen, man, they fucked the queen's maids, the chambermaids. They fucked every woman they could see. They all but fucked the king, but he got away a little bit.

Anyway, the king caught 'em. He said, "Goddamn it, I'ma kill y'all." He said, "But being as y'all don't do it so bad, I'ma . . . what I do to y'all, I'ma let y'all die 'cording to the way you want to die." So they said, "O.K."

"Man, I want to die," he said, "I want to *eat* myself to death." The king's all right, so the king said, "Put this motherfucker in a room there by hisself with nine guards and give him all the food he wants. Let him eat hisself to death." Asked this other guy, "What you wanta do?" Other guy said, "Well," said, "I want to cut paper dolls till I die." He figuring maybe he'll live a little longer than the rest of them. King have pity on them. Some shit he was talking about. He said, "All right. Put him in there with all the paper he can, and nine more guards to watch him to make sure he can't escape."

Got down to the last guy, he said, "All right, you, how do you want to die?" He said, "Well, king, old boy," said, "I want to fuck myself to death." King said, "All right," he said, "Put him in another room with a hundred women, and nine guards so this motherfucker won't escape." So they stayed in there.

So three months, king comes back to this motherfucker, to this place. So he said, "All right. Open this first door. What this guy doing?" Said, "This guy's eaten hisself to death." Said, "All right. Nine guards can come out and go on back to your old duties." Said, "All right." So open the next door and this guy was in there, he had paper dolls all over the motherfucking wall, dead. Eyes looked like paper. So goddamn it, he opened the door, he said, "What the fuck! Here's these women laying all in the corner fucked to death." The hundred women he put in there all fucked to death, guards standing over there, their ass all red, this motherfucker over there beating the meat. "Now ain't that some shit. Ain't that the most."

[Kid]

We Go by What You See

One day a man and a woman were fighting in the street. There was an old lady out there, she seen the man and the woman fighting. This woman, she was cutting her husband all up. So the old woman that seed the fight, she told the lady that lived next door that didn't see the fight, she said, "This woman was out there, cutting her husband like nobody's business." So the old lady said, "Yeah?" So the cops come and got the woman and the man. So they took 'em to court.

So the old lady that didn't see the fight, she come to court. She was sitting down, so the Judge say, "Anybody in the courtroom see what happened?" So the old lady that didn't see what happened, she said, "Yeah." "Will you please take this witness stand?" She got up on the witness stand. Judge say, "What happened at the fight?" No, the judge say, "Did you see the fight?" Lady said, "No, I didn't see it but I heard about it." So the judge said, "Well, we don't go by what you hear, we go by what you see, up here. Will you please get down off the witness stand?"

The old lady she went to get down off the witness stand, she had a shawl on. So the old lady, she farted. So the judge said, "Who done that?" The old lady said, "I did." "Give her ninety days in jail." She said, "For what, judge?" " 'Cause you farted." Old lady said, "Did you see it?" Judge said, "No." "Did you hear it?" Judge said, "Yeah." "Well, judge, you said you can't go by what you hear, you got to go by what you see."

[Kid]

He Gets the Tank Filled

Legman points out that this theme was used by the Marx Brothers in one of their early movies ("Out West"?) where one of the challengers says, "You see that fly out there?" making the other give up because of the great eyesight of the first man. I have heard this same story told in joke form many times.

This fellow, you know, came down South. And you know it was in this town, you know, it was prejudiced. He rolled in, had one of these big, long Cadillacs, one of these

$400 suits thrown on, diamond rings. A colored fellow.
When he ran on up, white fellow sitting down chewing
tobacco. "Fill the tank, will you, chief?" "You talking to
me, boy?" "Yeah, I'm talking to you." "You know where
you at, son?" "Yeah, I know where I'm at." He said, "Well,
down here, you say 'mister' and you say it snappy, you
hear." "Now I don't say 'mister' to nobody." He said, "You
see that bush out there 'bout two hundred yards? Fly on
top of it." He said, "I see it." So the old white fellow
reached up and pulled the trigger, blew the fly clear off
the bush. Didn't even touch the bush. He said, "That's
what happens when you don't say 'mister,' boy."

He said, "Well, you trying to show off? You got a saucer
on you?" "Yeah, I got a saucer." "Throw it in the air." This
old fellow throwed the saucer in the air, other fellow
reach in the car, got an apple, throwed it in the air, took
a straight razor, whipped it out, 'fore the apple hit the
ground, peeled, cut the core out, sliced it up so thin that
it land in the saucer, hit the ground, it was apple sauce.
White fellow jumped up and said, "What you want,
sonny?" "Just regular."

[Kid]

Too Much Grief

This is another ghost story common among American Negroes.
For other texts, see Dorson (*NTPB*), 81; *JAF*, 40:270; *SFQ*,
18:130; Tidwell, 132 (from *SFQ*). It is one of a large group of
stories about those who dress up a ghost in order to scare someone. The most common of these stories among American
Negroes is the one in which Marster scares John for praying
for death insistently. See Jones, 66–68, for an early reporting
of this type of story.

This lady and this man, their son just when he got to be
twenty-one years old, he was in a gang fight and he got
killed. So every night they prayed. "If I could only see
Junior one more time. Please, Lord, let me see him one
more time." They prayed loud. Two, three hours.

So the fellow that lived on the third floor, he couldn't ever sleep. "Now if I hear them praying tonight," he told his old lady, "I'ma put on a sheet. I'ma walk down there and stop all this. If they think they see their son, maybe they'll stop all this noise." She said, "That's a good idea."

So that night 'bout eight o'clock they started praying. "Just let me see Junior one more time. Please let me see Junior." So about twelve o'clock he decided to put his sheet on. He walked down and knocked on the door. Tap, tap. She said, "Paw, did you hear that?" Dad said, "I didn't hear nothing. Keep on praying." Tap, tap. She said, "Paw, Junior's knocking." Said, "Ain't nobody come back from the dead, woman. That ain't Junior." So she said, "See who's at the door." So he said, "Maw. It's meeee." "That's Junior, Paw." "Don't you open that door, woman. Don't open that door."

There he was, guy tied up, you know, with sheet over his head. Looked just like a ghost. Hallway was dark. She said, "Junior, you come back." He said, "Yes, Maw." She said, "Don't he look good, Paw?" He looked at him, he said, "Yes, you look good, son." He said, "You look good, son, now go on back." She said, "Go shake your father's hand, son." He said, "You look good, son, now go on back." Pop kept on backing up. Junior kept a-coming towards him. He said, "You look good, boy, now go on back." He kept a-walking. Pop kept backing up. He said, "You look good, son, now go on back, will you?" So he walked over and touched Pop on the shoulder. He said, "Dad." Pop said, "That's why your motherfucking ass is dead now. You're so goddamned hard-headed."

[Kid]

THE DRUNK DOES PUSHUPS

Jokes about drunks are legion. Thompson leaves a whole section for stories about drunks, though he does not include many references within the section (X 800). I include here three representative stories, plus a close relative, the "junkie" or "head" joke, concerned with addicts. Both kinds are variations on the numskull or noodle pattern.

> This here sailor, he got drunk. So he was going to the bar, there was 'nother sailor already in there. So the guy said, "Eruh, you can't get nothing to drink, 'cause you're drunk." He said, "No, I'm not drunk. I know what I'm doing. I can do some pushups, far as that's concerned." So the guy said, "O.K., lemme see you do twenty-five pushups." So here comes this other drunk sailor. "Give me a drink." "You can't have nothing to drink in here, you're too drunk." He said, "You think I'm drunk. Look at that guy. He don't even know his girl left him."
>
> [Charley]

The Drunk Goes Around to the Side Door

> Well you know how sailors is. Sailors, they get drunk all the time. Well, this here sailor, he went in the bar, er uh, guy said, "What would you like?" So he stayed in there and he got drunk. Tried to go to another bar. Guy put him out. So he went 'round the side door. Guy kicked him in the mouth and threw him out on his ass. Still wasn't satisfied. He go around the back and come in. Guy beat him up, threw him out again. Get up off the ground, brush his clothes off. Brush his hat off. Walk right back 'round the front and come back in. So the guy said, "Didn't I . . ." He said, "Hold it. Goddamn it, you don't own every bar in town, now." (He thought he was going in different bars.)
>
> [Charley]

Going Fishing

Though this story is put in the form of a drunk joke, it really is one of the "madmen" cycle, a series of some antiquity, as Tom O Bedlam in *King Lear* testifies.

You know, these here fellows were out there walking
New York. The fellow was up on a building, everybody was
looking up in the air. "I say, what's going on up there?"
So the guy, you know, cop walked up to these three fellows on a ledge, you know. He said, "What y'all doing?"
"All going crazy." They was high. Look here, boy, they
was high. He said, "Officer, them two fellows, they is
crazy." He said, "Now that guy sitting there throwing that
wheel out like he's fishing, and that boy's sitting there with
the net." He said, "They stone mad." He said, "Now officer,
that one sitting on the roof, he think he's fishing. Now
look at him. He's throwing the wheel out, he's winding
it back. And the fellow with him, he's crazy, too. He got
the net down there like he's catching a fish." So the officer said, "Well, you go out there and stop 'em." So the
fellow said, "All right." " 'Cause you look like you're the
only one sober." So the guy reached out and got two sticks
and made like he was rowing and said, "I'm coming,
captain."

[Kid]

The Junkie Referee

Most junkie jokes, as with this one, make reference to the ad-
dict's inability to interpret actions realistically. (See "The
Drunk Does Pushups" above.)

Junkie's walking down the street. A car came up and
hit a trailer-truck. Guy flew through the window, head
was cut in half, his leg was broke, jaw was busted. Land in
front of the junkie. Junkie looked down on him and said,
"Safe."

[Kid]

A Remedy for Snakebite

Country origin is the basis for numskull decisions or observations in the next few stories. J 1919.5 (Genitals cut off through
ignorance).

You know, this old cat was down on the farm. He went over to this guy, he said he seen this woman in this window, she putting a broomstick in herself. So he said, "Instead of doing that, you cut a hole in the floor and I'll get under there, and then me and you can do it together." She said, "All right." So he was doing that for a long time. One day this other cat he come, he say he want some. So he say to this guy, "I'll give you some tips on how to get some, see. Now, son, you go under there, you stick your thing up in there, woman come and lay on you, and you get what you want." All right, he did it. Did like that so Mom come in there, seen her throwing the lid on the floor. So she had a shotgun. She come from out in the yard 'cause she thought she heard something out there. She said, "Get up from that floor. Didn't I tell you about getting down there. Snakes could be down there." Girl is down there, scratching her face and everything, as if she was scared or something had bit her. So when she got up, Mom said, "Oh, my God, the snake done bit my daughter and is spitting his poison at me." She shot his head right off his shoulders.

[Kid]

SOME JAWS

J 1772.9 (One object thought to be another: excrement).

This guy was riding along with the train. He was riding and riding. He was looking for a bathroom. Couldn't find a bathroom. This guy thought, "Stick your ass out the window." Stuck his ass out the window, took a shit and two farmers are standing along the side of a road, hit one farmer in the face. Squash! He said, "Damn, those city slickers sure do chew some nasty smelling tobacco." The other one replied, "But did you see the jaws on that motherfucker?"

[Petey]

HE'S A POET

One day this country boy was in school, you know. Asked this boy something like this. He was standing up against the thing, he said:

> "Right between them big beautiful clouds
> With the pass, you know, the pass allows."

He looked at him. He says:

> "Right between them two big trees
> There is beauty, please."

So he looked at him, he said, "Here?" "Yeah."

So the guy went home to his girlfriend. Said:

> "Right between your big, beautiful eyes
> Is where your beauty lies.
> Right between them two big thighs
> Make my passion rise."

[Victor]

I WON'T DO IT!

The immigrant numskull is an important figure in American folklore, but not among this group, perhaps because of a difficulty with dialects.

Now, this guy was walking down the street, and he said, "I won't do it. I just won't do it." Cop said, "What's the matter, fellow?" "I just won't do it. I'm not going to do it. I just refuse to do it." Cop said, "You all right?" Said, "Yeah, I'm all right. I just won't do it." "Boy, I'ma take you in." He said, "Well, take me in." Took him down.

Next morning they got up in front of the judge. Judge said, "What's your problem?" Said, "I just ain't gonna do it, that's all. Just won't do it." Judge said, "You know you're in the courtroom now. Give you some time. Explain your problem to me." "I won't do it. Lock me up. Give me twenty years. I won't do it." He said, "What's the matter?" He said, "What's the matter?" He said, "Well, look—a-tirty-five-a years I come-a to dis country. I'se a good man, I get me a good job, and I make-a me a good business. I do everything a-right. But I won't do it." The judge said, "You won't do what?" He said, "I give-a my love to my wife, my heart to my children, I give my freedom to my country, and they got a nerve to put up a sign, 'Give your nuts to the squirrels.' I just won't do it."

[Kid]

DOWN UNDER THE TREE

You know this little girl, she lived in the country. She wasn't no little girl. 'Bout seventeen years old. Now her father and her uncle had a farm, but her uncle died and left three fourths of the farm to her that when she was beturned seventeen she could do anything she wanted with it. Well, she was seventeen now. Now the farmer next door, he had a nice little young boy. He was nineteen. Very nice little boy. Little girl was stone in love with him, but he never said nothing to her. His father wanted the land of this little girl, but her father wouldn't sell it to him.

So the little boy was down by the lake one day. She called and she said, "Tommy." He said, "Yeah. What you want? Why you always bother me?" She said, "I just want you to talk tc me." "I don't want to talk to you." She said, "Well, look. Will you come over and kiss me, please?" "No, I ain't gonna kiss you." "I'll give you $100." "All right, I'll kiss you and that's all." She said, "All right." He kissed her. She gave him $100 and he went on home.

Father said, "Where you been, son?" "I been down there playing. Little girl from across the road, she came over bothering me. Give me $100 just to kiss her." "All right."

Next day he goes down. She come, says, "Tommy."

"What you want now?" "Feel my titties, play with my stomach." "For what?" "I'll give you $500." "That's all I'ma do then." "All right." She paid him, he went on home. "What you do today, sonny?" "I was down there playing, little girl asked me to feel her titties, play with her stomach. She gave me $500. And I did it, so she gave me $500. But that's all I did." Father said, "Umm, you going down there tomorrow?" "Yes sir." "All right."

So his father jumped up that morning, eased down to the woods, jumped up in a tree 'bout where they play at. So the little girl come down there playing. Tommy come down. She said, "Tommy, come over here." Took off her panties. "Do it to me?" "No." She said, "I'll give you $1,000." "All right. That's all I'ma do. Just gonna put it in." "All right." He put it in, got ready to get up. She said, "Tommy, don't get up now. Just move a little bit." "No, I ain't gonna move a little bit." Father up in the tree, he's looking down listening to all the conversation. She said, "You know that land your father's been wanting?" "Yeah, what about it?" She said, "If you move one more time I give it to you. You know that house your father's been wanting that's on my land?" "Yeah." "You move two more times and I add that in. You know that orange grove over there your father's been wanting?" "Yeah." "You move three more time and I throw that in." She said, "I got two million dollars. Now if you work real easy and take your time for 'bout an hour and a half, give that to you, too." Father said, "Go on, son, shake ass, son, shake ass."

[Kid]

A PARABLE

You know these two bulls were standing upon the field, you know, way up on the hill. Down in the valley was a whole lot of cows. Now the young bull looked at the old bull—you know, this old bull he had been in the bull-fighting ring in his day and he was a very old bull—so the young bull he was spry, jumping around and healthy. All full of pep. He said, "Look here, old bull, let's run down in the valley and fuck a few of those cows." Old bull looked at him and said, "Son, if you take your time, we *walk* down, we might fuck 'em all."

[Kid]

THE OLD DOG AND THE YOUNG DOG

Another in parable form. *Legman*—This story was told in the U. S. Army, almost as an item of indoctrination, during World War II, especially by the soldiers in Italy, and as then told represented their repugnance against the wholesale prostitution of the defeated Italians, as frighteningly recorded in Curzio Malaparte's *The Skin*.

You know this young dog was standing there talking to the old dog. He said, "Young dog, you ain't been out in the world yet, is you?" Dog said, "No sir." He said, "I'ma show you what life there is out here." He said, "All right." "Everything I do, you just come along behind me and do the same thing." "Yes sir."

So the dogs they walked out and walked down the street and old dog got to a pole, smelt the pole, cocked the leg and he peed on it. So young dog cocked *his* leg and peed. So they walked along and old dog came to a car. He walked around the car, he looked at it, smelt the car, cocked his leg up and he peed on that. So the young dog, he walked up, smelt the car, cocked his leg and *he* peed on it. The old dog he walked down to the garbage can, looked over the side, got himself a bone and ate it. The young dog, he walked over to the garbage can, looked over the side, got himself a bone. So they walked on for maybe ten or fifteen minutes, they saw a she-dog. Old dog smelt her, kissed her, walked around, jumped up on her, knocked himself off a piece out. So the young dog he walked up to her, kissed her and he smelt her, jumped up on her, knocked *him*self a piece out.

So they went on down, you know, to the yard. Old dog

said, "Well, son, how you like the world?" He said, "It's complicated." "What you mean?" He said, "Well, now, eruh, we went down, walked, came to a pole, smelt the pole, then we peed on it. Came to a car, we looked it over, smelt the car and peed on that. Then we walked down, seen girl, kissed her and even smelled her. Then we did it to her. That was all right. Even when we went to the garbage can, got something to eat. I guess it was all right. But what's the basis of being out in the world? I don't see no future in it." He said, "Well, son, take the advice of an old dog. Anything in this world that you can't smell, eat, kiss, or fuck, piss on it."

[Kid]

MR. BUZZARD AND MR. RABBIT

This story has been popular at joke sessions for a number of years, though I have never seen it in print. It is a humorous complaint against the upward mobile. I think the names are prefaced by "Brother" because I had just asked the informant if he knew any of the Brother Rabbit stories. *Legman*—I have collected it with the rabbit having *two* friends: Mr. Buzzard, and also the turtle, who later becomes Mr. Tur-*toole*. Your text has also—except in the final line—lost the rhyming done on the names, in which the butler tells the returned rabbit, "Mr. Buz-*zard* is out in the yard" and "Mr. Tur-*toole* is in the swimming pool."

I have also collected toppers like this used in stories, mocking pretentiousness. One in particular is of a woman in a beer joint who wants to make an impression on a handsome man she sees at the bar and who tells the waiter, in a flutey voice, to bring her "an egg-whip cream, soft as a maiden's kiss, and ask that gem-man in the corner," and so forth; to which the man she is trying to impress counters by ordering, "Waiter, gimme a tall beer, strong as a donkey's piss, with the foam farted off, and ask that damn whoor in the corner what's her charge."

Brother Rabbit was out on the job one day, you know, and he was spreading fertilizer 'round his garden. So Brother Buzzard came by and he said, "Hey, Brother Rabbit." "Yeah, Brother Buzzard." "Whatcha doing?" "Spreading fertilizer." "Fertilizer, what's that?" "Nothing but horse, cow manure." "What it do?" "Makes the soil better. Makes the soil, grass, and crops grow." He said, "Look, I got a little small garden in the back of my house." He said, "How 'bout bringing me some of that over, Saturday night?" "I'll bring you a wagon load." "How much you charge me?" "I'll just charge you half price." Said, "All right."

So Brother Buzzard he went on home. Brother Rabbit got on up Saturday morning, load the wagon up, took it over to Brother Buzzard's house. Brother Buzzard, he'd got into a whole lot of money. He'd bought a big mansion. You know, he had a chauffeur, butler, and they was having a cocktail party that night. All these here rich animals from the forest were there, you know. So here comes the rabbit with his dungarees, full of shit, you know, hat broke down, rings the bell. Butler come to the door. Said, "I come to see Brother Buzzard." Said, [*haughtily*], "I'm sorry, sir, but there is no Brother Buzzard here. Mr. Buzz*ard* is the resident." He said, "Wait a minute, now. This is Brother Buzzard's house." "No, sir. Buzz*ard* is the resident." He said, "Look now. Brother Buzzard tole me to bring him round a load of fertilizer. He told me to bring it today, right here. Now I know he lives here, 'cause I been here thousand times." Said, "I'm sorry sir, Mr. Buzz*ard* live here."

By that time, all the confusion, all them rich animals come to the door. They looking. So the rabbit's getting mad. He said, "Tell Brother Buzzard I want to see him. I ain't gonna tell you no more." "Yes, sir, Mr. Buzz*ard* live here." He said, "Well you go tell Mr. Buzz*ard* that Mr. Rab*bit* is here with the shit."

[Petey and Freddie—A Collaboration]

TARZAN'S HOLLER

This modern etiological story is one of the many grotesques
that have been floating around adolescent circles. The recent
forms have conformed more closely to the sick joke pattern.

You know practically everybody goes to the movies
once or twice a night. Now I know everybody and them
been to see "Tarzan." Well you see, I'ma give you the dead-
line on Tarzan. See, everybody wondering where he get
that big holler, you know that "Aaaaaaowaaah." Well, you
see, I'ma tell you the true story 'bout that. Now see, when
Tarzan was young, that's when he first found Jane. And
him and Jane 'cided they was going to get married, 'cause
they's in jungle by 'selves, and she went for him and he
went for her. But see, in these days, he didn't wear no
bathing suit like they got in the movies, see. He didn't
wear a nair of clothes.

So one day they was walking, and Jane 'cided she'd go
one way and he'd go 'nother, you know, hunting food and
stuff. So meantime the hunters had been by that way and
they had digged a big round hole. Deep. Catch this big
ape. Well, they didn't catch the ape but they caught a gorilla. And, you know, how the wind blowing in the middle
of the night, leaves had covered the hole back up. So Jane
fell down in the hole. And when she fell down she started
screaming when she saw this big gorilla. "Tarzan, Tarzan."
Tarzan ran and he ran. He ran up on this here big high
mountain. He looked down. He said, "Jane." He said,
"Are you all right?" She said, "Yes, but there's an ape down
here." Ape woke up and looked at her, said, "Ummh,
hmmh." So he decided he was going to go on, knock, see
what Tarzan'd been getting. So Tarzan said, "Well, you
hold on, Jane. Me reach up and grab vine. Me swing down
through hole, you grab vine, we swing out together." Jane
said, "All right."

So Tarzan jumped up off the cliff, took one of these here
beautiful swan dives, about three or four hundred yards,
and got hold of this here, when he went down he grabbed

this vine. He was coming down beautifully. He swung down through the hole, and Jane reached for the vine and missed and grabbed his dick. Just when all that weight hit down on Tarzan's dick that's when he hollered "Aaaaaaowaaah!" Deep down in the jungle you hear the scream of the constipated ape [*grunting, defecating noises*].

[Kid]

SHE CALLS HIS NAME

This is the first kind of joke a child learns and remembers, only with adolescent content. The unfortunate-name story leading to amusing action, as here, or to embarrassing situation (Have you seen my Hynee?) was legion among my friends during grammar school. See Wolfenstein, *Children's Humor*, 64–65, for a discussion of the psychology of this joke.

You hear about Johnny Fuck-a-little-faster? Once there was this boy named Johnny Fuck-a-little-faster. So his mother went out to the store. He had a box of cakes in the wagon. Little girl said, "Johnny. Can I have a ride in your wagon?" He said, "Yeah, you can have a ride in my wagon and a cookie too if you go home with me." She said, "For real?" He said, "Yeah." So he gave her some cookies and pulled her all around, that kind of thing. She got out. When he got her out, he opened the door and let her in the house. He said, "You want some more cookies?" He said, "I'll give you some more cookies if you'll pull down your panties." She said, "O.K. So she pulled off her pants, he gave her some more cookies and she ate them. She said, "Could I have some more cookies?" He said, "I'll give you some more cookies if you'll open your legs." "O.K." She opened her legs. So he got on there and he started, he started. Mother came in and said, "Fuck-faster!" That's what she was calling him. So he started fucking faster. So she said, "Fuck-faster!" So he started fucking faster. She said, "Fuck-faster, boy." He said, "I'm fucking as fast as I can, Ma."

[Charley]

A Ride in His Wagon

Another one almost the same. This little boy, he was riding around in his car. Said, "Johnny, can I have a ride in your wagon?" He said, "No." He rode around the block again, came back, she said, "Johnny, can I have a ride in your wagon?" He said, "No!" So he rode around the block and come back again. She said, "Johnny, please can I have a ride in your wagon?" So he said, "If I give you a ride in my wagon, will you give me some ?" She said, "Unh hunh." So he said, "O tay." So she rode around and she came back and they both rode to the alley. So he said, "I'll give you a penny too." So he gave her a penny and a cookie. She said, "O.K." She pulled her little panties down and he said, "Oh, no. I don't want no—you ain't got no hair." She said, "What the hell do you want for two cents and a cookie?"

[Charley]

The Iceman Cometh

The iceman is to the working man what Jody is to the soldier and convict. Consequently, he appears in many similar stories.

This little boy was tongue-tied. So he asked his ma, he said, "Mama, how tum my talk 'ike 'is here?" So she said, "Oh, boy, I don't know." Said, "I don't know why you talk like that." So he asked his father. He said, "Daddy, how tum I tal' 'ike 'is here?" Father said, "Boy, it's a mystery to me. I wonder myself." So the iceman came, and he said, "Mi'man, how tum I tal' 'ike 'is here?" Iceman said, "Get away f'om here, boy, I don't know how tum 'ou 'alk 'ike 'at."

[Charley]

BOASTS, BRAGS, EXAGGERATIONS

The next few pages of boasts and exaggerations fit into Motif section X 1600. The boast is the greatest connecting link with the proverb and other shorter verbal forms. It is impossible to draw the line where a boast is a tale and where it is a proverb, so I have included them all in this chapter. The first is obviously a story. After that they descend from conversational gambits to one-liners. These latter are commonly used in contest situations similar to the dozens, but where the idea is to deprecate oneself humorously rather than to boast.

Legman—Most of the same stories were told as recently as the 1940's in the nineteenth-century framework of "heights"; that is to say, as replies to the formula question, "What is the height of speed?" and so forth. A German collector of similar heights is cited in *The Limerick* (Paris, 1953), p. 427, note 917, dated 1892; and both polite and erotic collections of them were published in French in the nineteenth century.

I'll tell you about the coldest day. It was in '58, look ahere, it was colder than nine icebergs. I was standing on this corner, and I only had this short jacket on, and it was cold and the wind was blowing about 215 miles an hour. And the snow was falling, sleet was dropping, the rain was drizzling. Now you know it was cold. I was standing up on Broad and Market. I was going to New York that weekend of all weekends. The buses kept zooming by and zooming by, zoom. I never seen the Greyhound bus. So all of a sudden this big gray bus stopped. "Say, chief, you waiting for a bus?" I said, "Yeah." He said, "Well, this is the Greyhound bus stop." I said, "Well, there ain't no Greyhound bus here." He said, "Well, this is a Greyhound bus, get on." I said, "No, it ain't." He said, "Yes, it is." I said, "It's not." He said, "Why you say that?" I said, "Well, the Greyhound is got a dog on the side of the bus." It was cold. After a while the window flew up and a dog put his head out, said, "Shit, cold as it is out there, I better come in here."

[Kid]

I used to be bad. I can remember a time I took a short stick and beat a cat down so low that he had to reach up to tie his shoes. That's no lie. I put my nose to a guy's face that weigh 240 pounds on a Wednesday and told him he better not move till Thursday morning. But I don't know what he said. I hung up.

[Kid]

I was fighting a guy in the ring and I swung at him with a straight right and missed. And the wind was so strong that the breeze gave his manager pneumonia and he died.

[Kid]

I've seen it so hot that a man was driving his horse and carriage by a field, and it was so hot the corn was popping, and the horses dropped dead thinking it was snowing. (X 1633.1)

I've seen it so hot that when hens layed, they came out hard-boiled. (X 1633)

I've seen it so cold that a nigger talked and it took him two weeks to thaw out the words. (X 1623.2.1)

I've seen it so dark that I was in my room and I heard a knock on the door. You know who it was? A raindrop asking me for a match so he could see how to hit the ground.

I've seen a man so fast that he was getting some water at the well and the bottom fell out the bucket and he went in the house and got another bucket and caught the water before it hit the ground. (X 1740 and X 939.1—*Lie: person of remarkable speed*)

When I was young, I could run a rabbit down in a fast-footed race.

I'm so broke, I couldn't buy a crippled crab a crutch if I had a forest of small trees.

I'm so broke I couldn't buy a dick a derby, and that's a small fit.

I'm so broke I couldn't buy a mosquito a wrestling jacket, and that's a small fit.

My soles are so thin that if I stepped on a dime I could tell whether it's heads or tails.

I'm so hungry my backbone is almost shaking hands with my stomach.

I'm so hungry I could see a bow-legged biscuit walk a crooked mile. (*Cf. the nursery rhyme beginning, "There was a crooked man . . ."*)

I'm so broke, if they were selling Philadelphia for a penny, I'd have to run, afraid they would sell it to the wrong person.

THE BIG WATERMELON

Some of the best boasts have become associated with the Texas jokes. One of that type, this might fit either Motif X 1411.1 (*Lie: the great melon*) or X 1420 (*Lies about vegetables*).

Fellow from Texas, he was telling how big Texas was. "In Texas, we got miles and miles and miles. Nothing but miles and miles and miles. Well, partner, I tell you, in Texas, when you get up in the morning, comb your hair, stick your comb down on the ground and you strike oil. Yes, suh."

So this Southern fellow said, "Well, has you all been up in New York?" "New York?" "Partner, New York is just the northeast side of Texas. That's all it is now." He said, "Gee whiz, wow, that's a big watermelon over there. Must be about fifteen feet in diameter. Must weigh a good bit. Ooh, it's a big watermelon." So the Southern fellow said, "You all talking about that cucumber laying there?"

[Kid]

BRAND-NAME STORIES

These final two pieces are not stories so much as routines; they give a story line, but the object is to use as many brand names as possible. The first plays on names of alcoholic beverages, the second on cigarettes.

This here little boy was coming out of the store one night. This cop picked him up. The cop told him, "Say, little boy, what's your name?" "Calvin." "What's your father's name?" "J. W." He said, "What's his last name?" "Dant." "What's your mother's name?" "Schenley Vacco." He said, "Where do you live at?" He said, "Well, I live all the way up in Valley Forge." He said, "Where about in Valley Forge?" "Around Four Roses." "Who's in that place with you?" "Must I tell?" He said, "Yeah! I asked you, didn't I?" "Tokay."

Cavalier took a ride across the desert on a Camel, just 'cause he was in love with somebody called Fatima. Philip was blasting off to Morris. Now Raleigh decided since he had made a Lucky Strike he was going down to Chesterfield's. He had a whole pocketful of Old Gold. And so, last but not least, he decided to go on a Holiday.

[Kid]

Unusual Terms and Expressions

Included in this section are words and expressions that may be unfamiliar to the readers and a few terms that were current in Camingerly of singular interest. I have made some effort to support my definitions from other sources, most notably the *Dictionary of American Slang* by Harold Wentworth and Stuart Berg Flexner. Peter Tamony and G. Legman have been especially helpful in the compiling of this glossary. As in the past, I shall refer to Legman's contributions by prefacing them with his name and a dash.

BALL—Widely used in the sense of a dance, but used here in reference to an orgy. See Wentworth and Flexner, p. 16. *Legman*—It does not refer to dancing but to sexual intercourse, especially in a secret, orgiastic way, as in the similar song widely known in Scotland, "The Ball of Kirriemuir." These erotic "balls" are remnants of Witches' Sabbat—sex cults in the late middle ages—and were a paramount element in the witch persecutions in Scotland, and later in America. The word is plainly glossed only once, but very significantly, in Pepys's *Diary*, in the late seventeenth century, where he is invited to an orgiastic party held by a group who called themselves The Ballers, apparently the group for whom Rochester's obscene play *Sodom* was written for naked presentation. . . . The first use of the word *in print* . . . is in Grose's *Classical Dictionary of the Vulgar Tongue* where he describes the same sort of dances and orgies under the term "Buff-Ball(ers)," the word "buff" meaning one's naked skin. The survival of this word, entirely underground and (except for Grose) absolutely without the advantages of print, for three hundred years now is almost unparalleled in philological history.

BITCH—Any woman. As used here, usually without usual pejorative connotations. Wentworth and Flexner, p. 39.

BLANSHED—Knocked, ruined.

BOOLHIPPER—Slick black leather coat, usually found, as here, with a belt in the back. Pronounced somewhere between boolhipper and boodlehipper or boodlipper.

BOOTY—As used here, an extension of "body," specifically the body of a woman. Oliver, p. 189, prints a blues verse in which the word is used in this way. On the other hand, "boot" has had a history of sexual connotation and may have affected the formation of this word. The term "Buckinger's Boot" meant the cunt in eighteenth-century England, see Grose, *Classical Dictionary. Legman*—The reference to Grose here is interesting but does not cover the term itself, since that was a real boot (of a man without legs), where this is clearly as you say, an extension of "body." Actually it is merely a variant pronunciation of it.

BULLDAGGER—A lesbian. Variant pronunciation, bulldiker. *Legman*—The actual origin of bulldagger is simply a long series of mispronunciations and corruptions of the word hermaphrodite, extraordinary as that may seem at first sight. The series is even more extraordinary in that *all* the corruptions of the original word still co-exist simultaneously, namely: *harumphodite, morphodite, dike, dyker;* and *bull-dyker* or *bull-dagger* with the addition of the male *bull* element. Such very male-imitating lesbians are also called *diesel-dykes.*

BUSTED MY NUTS—Had an orgasm.

CAMEL-HAIR BENNY—In eighteenth-century British slang, "Joseph" meant coat. Cf. *Genesis:* coat of many colors and Joseph's cloak left in the grasp of Potiphar's wife. Benjamin was, of course, Joseph's younger brother. In the early nineteenth-century British slang, *Benjamin* or *Benny* came to mean a smaller or close-fitting coat.

CASHMERE—Any sweater.

CHICKENSHIT—A corruption of "chicken feed"—that is, insubstantial, small, insignificant—but in this case referring to a person rather than to the usual material things. The addition of shit as a suffix is wholly in line with other such additions to animal names, *bullshit, apeshit, horseshit,* etc. Cf. Wentworth and Flexner, p. 99.

COCK—Most commonly the female genitalia.

COOLING—Doing a cool thing, in other words, performing in complete control of oneself in the midst of a potentially explosive situation. Used much in jazz talk. Obvious derivation: cool as opposite of getting heated up, as in "cool as a cucumber," which is found as early as 1732 (Oxford, 109). Wentworth and Flexner, p. 121.

COONCAN—A corruption of the Mexican *Con Quien*, a card game in the rummy family.

COTTON—The hair on a woman's pudendum.

CUE—Used here to mean tip in the sense of money given for services.

CRABS—Crab lice.

CRAZY—Good, or highest good in jazz talk. See Wentworth and Flexner, p. 129.

CRAZY RIM—Very good looking hat. May simply be descriptive of its good looks, with the addition of designation of the object by one of its parts for the whole (*rim* for *hat*).

CRUT—Variant of *crud;* originally, dried semen which sticks to clothes, body, etc., after emission, but more generally referring to anything base. Cf. Wentworth and Flexner, pp. 132, 133.

CUTTING MAN—Best friend. "Cut" has always been associated with contest of some sort. Cutting cards is a common way of sudden-death gambling. Competition between jazz bands has been referred to as cutting. This expression may refer to the one you choose to do the cutting for you, thus someone you trust, thus a friend. Wentworth and Flexner, p. 136.

DICK—The penis. Perhaps a variant of "prick." Cf. Wentworth and Flexner, p. 146.

DOWN—To place someone at a verbal disadvantage. Used both as a verb and adjective. You can down someone, or you can put someone down. Word may have sexual derivation, in that putting someone underneath you during the sexual act indicates that he is playing the female role, that he is by inference a homosexual. This parallels the use of the word "mount" which means to best someone physically or verbally, but which derives from the expression of animals having intercourse, the male mounting the female.

DOZENS—Short for "playing the dozens" (see Chapter 2). Synonyms are "sounding" and "woofing," these being the more common way of referring to the game today. Dozens is not even understood by some Negroes now. There has been some speculation as to the origin and history of the game under the name playing the dozens. John Dollard in "The Dozens: The Dialect of Insult," feels that the name may have come from one of the rhymes that went from one to twelve describing the obscenities "mother" engaged in. C. S. Johnson (*Growing Up*, pp. 184–85) suggests that the name owes its origins to the unluckiness of throwing a twelve in craps. Newman Ivey White, *American Negro Folk Songs*, p. 364, seems to agree implicitly with this, as he gives a dozens reference (I don't play the dozen/And don't you ease me in.") among songs about gambling. Paul Oliver in *Blues*, p. 128, says of its history, " 'Putting in the Dozens' developed as a folk game in the late nineteenth century, . . ." but he gives no documentation for this.

William Griffin has suggested, in a personal communication, that the name may come from "dozen," v., to stun, stupefy, daze, which can be used both transitively and intransitively (OED). If this were true, its etymology would concur with many other Negro words which come ultimately from English parlance of the eighteenth century. This would attach an English name to a phenomenon possibly brought from Africa. Newbell Niles Puckett, *Folk Beliefs*, p. 23, quoting Kingsley, says, "The dominant affection in the home is the intense devotion of the African for his mother, more fights being occasioned among boys by hearing something said in disparagement of their mothers than by all other causes put together." This would place the game, or something like it, quite far back historically.

The first mention I have found of the game with this name is from the popular magazine *Current Opinion* (September, 1919) in an article on Gilda Gray, a white blues singer. The chorus of a song is printed called "The Dirty Dozens." This song is different from the one sung by "Speckled Red" (Rufus Perryman) as quoted in Oliver, *Blues*, p. 128. The white reference above could be considered an even earlier one.

The songs concerning the dozens creates a problem quite separate from that considered here. Briefly, the record referred to above seems to have achieved sufficient popularity that a number of others were subsequently issued. Paul Oliver has kindly sent me a list of the following: "The Dirty Dozens," Lonnie Johnson, OK 8775; "Double Dozens," Sweet Peas Spivey, Decca 7204; "Twelve," Kokomo Arnold, Decca 7083; "Dirty Dozen," Leroy Carr, Vocalion 1454; "The Dozing Blues," George Noble, Melotone 70605; "Dirty Mother for You," Shuffling Sam, Vocalion 03329; "Mother Fuyer," Dirty Red, Aladdin 194. All of these have some relationship to the earlier record.

Mack McCormick, in the notes to his record *Unexpurgated Songs of Men*, Arhoolie ????, gives the most compelling source, a formulaic song routine about the subject which began "I fucked your mother one, . . ." going up to twelve.

FAG—Male homosexual. Wentworth and Flexner, p. 176, point out that speculation has been that fag meaning homosexual came from fag meaning cigarette in that cigarettes were considered effeminate by pipe and cigar smokers pre-World War I. But fag has meant boy servant or schoolboy in England since before 1830 and the term probably derives ultimately from there. (Fag is for faggots or the sticks of wood the boys had to gather.)

Fix—In proper position, in pool slang.

Freak—A male homosexual. Cf. Wentworth and Flexner, p. 199.

Fuck—See *Jive*.

Gat—A firearm, probably a corruption of Gatling Gun. Cf. Wentworth and Flexner, p. 209.

Georgia Skin—A card game in the rummy family.

Gig—Job, situation. May have sexual origin, as gig or gigi means vagina or rectum. A gig may have originally meant a sex date and expanded in meaning to a date of any kind, but usually a playing date for musicians. If sexual originally, much like many other jazz terms, see *Jazz*, *Jive*. Wentworth and Flexner, p. 214.

Goathair—Bootleg liquor.

Grinding—Sexual intercourse. Descriptive of movement during act. Wentworth and Flexner, p. 230. The movement used metaphorically in terms of striptease dance. This latter use is more common.

Herbs—Marijuana. Probably descriptive of common properties of feel, smell, and texture.

Hoorah—Probably a corruption of "I roar" or "I rule."

Hung to—Very attached to, addicted.

Hustling—Making nervous signs at. Very different from common slang sense of the term.

Jazz—See *Jive*.

Jibs—Teeth.

Jive—A whole lot of talk. Originally and still used in the sense of "fuck" and "jazz," i.e., the sexual act. All three have achieved similar changes, jazz being synonymous with jive in the realm of talk, fuck referring more to actions. Synonyms: "shuck" and "shive."

Joint—Male sex organs.

Lobstertoes—Some sort of venereal disease, perhaps simply a bad case of crabs.

MAIN WHO' (pronounced like "hoe")—Best girlfriend.

ME AND YOU—Short for "There's just me and you and we're going to fight."

MOUNT—See *Down*.

PASSION—When used in sense of "passion rising," a euphemism for the penis becoming erect.

PIECE—Short for piece of ass, or sexual intercourse, or referring directly to the woman involved. Cf. Wentworth and Flexner, p. 388.

PIMP—Originally a procurer, but because of the style of this profession, now used among this group to refer to any "smart" person.

PUNK—Young male companion of homosexual. Wentworth and Flexner, 411 (punk 4). More specialized than usual meaning of young, fresh person.

RAGS—Clothes. Used in this sense since 1855. Wentworth and Flexner, p. 416.

RAISE—Stop, or "hold it." Shortening of the order to raise your hands when pointing a gun at someone, with a more general application.

RAP—Conviction of a crime. Wentworth and Flexner, p. 419, print a possible derivation, the rap referring to the tap on the shoulder in a police line-up indicating the implication of the culprit.

RAUNCHY—Bad, especially overly loose, careless, or inept. Cf. Wentworth and Flexner, p. 420.

REAL DOWN—Very good. Real is a synonym of very; down a synonym of cool, but only in this one expression. The usual meaning of down is quite different (see *Down*).

ROCKETS—Bullets. Descriptive of shape and speed.

ROLL—A double-breasted suit.

SASHAY—Move (usually fast). May come from the dance step, which itself comes from the idea of courting. See Wentworth and Flexner, p. 443.

SATCH—As yet undetermined type of jacket, perhaps designated by its use by Negro pitcher Satchel Paige or trumpeter Louis "Satchmo" Armstrong.

SHIVE—jive. See *Jive*.

SHUCK—Fuck (mostly sound-alike), usually only in terms of talk and action rather than the sex act. Expression is usually "shuck" and "shive." See *Jive*.

SIGNIFY—To imply, goad, beg, boast by indirect verbal or gestural means. A language of implication. This use is quite broadened from that expressed by Wentworth and Flexner, p. 477, "to pretend to have knowledge; to pretend to be hip, especially when such pretentions cause one to trifle with an important matter."

SISSY—Young homosexual, or effeminate. Derives from "sister." Wentworth and Flexner, p. 478.

SLICK—One who is very adept. In this area can refer to any kind of endeavor. Cf. Wentworth and Flexner, p. 486–87.

SOUND—Play the dozens. Word descriptive of activity. Wentworth and Flexner, p. 504, give a somewhat broader interpretation of the word.

STAKE—A sum which is gambled. See Wentworth and Flexner, p. 515.

STINGY BRIM—Small-brimmed hat, often of the porkpie variety. Name is a euphonistic description of object.

STOMPED—Corruption of "stamp," grind under one's feet. Perhaps just a common Negro pronunciation. See Wentworth and Flexner, p. 522.

STONE—An adjective or adverb indicating a greater degree of whatever the noun or verb which it modifies originally meant. A stone sailor is a sailor who has all sailors' characteristics. May have come from such expressions as "stone cold," and "stone dead," which took actual attributes from stones as elements of description. "Stone blind" is an early extension that shows such a development of the word as used here.

STUD—Any male, especially one in the know. Obvious sexual origin. Cf. Wentworth and Flexner, p. 526.

SWITH—Smell. (variant of "sniff"?)

TIGHT—Good friends.

TRICK—Legman: The act of intercourse, usually in the whorehouse phrase "to turn a trick."

VINE—A suit of clothing. Name perhaps descriptive of the hang of the clothes. Cf. Wentworth and Flexner, p. 565.

WHORE—See *Main who'*.

Bibliography

Aarne, Antti, and Stith, Thompson. *The Types of the Folktale*. Suomalainen Tiedeakatemia, 1928. Revised and enlarged edition, 1961.

Abrahams, Roger D. *Negro Folklore from South Philadelphia*. Dissertation, Department of English, University of Pennsylvania, 1962.

———. *Positively Black*. Prentice-Hall, 1969.

Adams, E. C. L. *Nigger to Nigger*. Charles Scribners, 1928.

Addy, Sidney Oldall. *Household Tales with Other Traditional Remains*. David Nutt, 1895.

Baughman, Ernest W., *A Comparative Study of the Folktales of England and North America*. Unpublished thesis.

Beck, Horace (ed.). *Folklore in Action*. American Folklore Society, 1962.

Becker, Howard C. (ed.) *The Other Side*. Free Press, 1964.

Beckwith, Martha Warren (coll., Roberts, Helen H.). *Jamaica Folk-Lore*. 1928.

Billingsley, Andrew. *Black Families in White America*. Prentice-Hall, 1968.

Botkin, B. A. (ed.). *Folksay*. University of Oklahoma Press, 1930.

———. *A Treasury of American Anecdotes*. Random House, 1959.

267

————. *A Treasury of American Folklore*. Crown, 1944.

————. *A Treasury of Southern Folklore*. Crown, 1949.

————. *A Treasury of New England Folklore*. Crown, 1947.

Brand, Oscar. *Bawdy Songs and Backroom Ballads*. Dorchester Press, 1960.

Brewer, J. Mason. *Dog Ghosts*. University of Texas Press, 1958.

————. *The Word on the Brazos*. University of Texas Press, 1952.

Brophy, John and Eric Patridge. *Songs and Slang of the British Soldier*. Eric Patridge, 1930.

Burke, Kenneth. *A Rhetoric of Motives*. Prentice-Hall, 1953.

Burt, Olive W. *American Murder Ballads*. Oxford University Press, 1958.

Cazden, Norman (ed.). *A Book of Nonsense Songs*. Crown, 1961.

California Folklore Quarterly. 1942–46.

Chase, Richard. *American Folk Tales and Songs*. Signet Editions, 1956.

Davis, A., and John Dollard. *Children of Bondage*. Harper, 1960.

Dollard, John. "The Dozens: The Dialect of Insult," *American Imago I* (1939), 3–24.

Dorson, Richard M. *American Folklore*. University of Chicago Press, 1959.

————. *Negro Folktales in Michigan*. Harvard University Press, 1956.

————. *Negro Tales from Pine Bluff, Arkansas, and Calvin, Michigan*. Indiana University Press, 1958.

Elliott, Robert C. *The Power of Satire*. Princeton University Press, 1960.

Fauset, Arthur Huff. *Folklore from Nova Scotia*. American Folklore Society, 1931.

Finger, Charles J. *Frontier Ballads*. Doubleday, Page, 1927.

Ford, Ira W. *Traditional Music of America*. E. P. Dutton, 1940.

Frazier, E. Franklin. *The Negro Family in the United States*. University of Chicago Press, 1939.

Friedman, Albert. *The Viking Book of Ballads.* Viking Press, 1956.

Funk and Wagnalls Standard Dictionary of Folklore, Mythology and Legend (eds., Maria Leach and Jerome Fried), 2 Vols. Funk and Wagnalls, 1949, 1950.

Fuson, Harvey H. *Ballads of the Kentucky Highlands.* Mitre Press, 1931.

Gardner, Emelyn Elizabeth. *Folklore from the Schoharie Hills, New York.* University of Michigan Press, 1937.

Gordon, Robert W. *Folk Songs of America.* National Service Bureau, 1938.

Grose, ?????. *Classical Dictionary of the English Tongue.* London, 1788.

Grotjahn, Martin. *Beyond Laughter.* Blakiston, 1957.

Harris, Joel Chandler. *Nights with Uncle Remus.* Century, 1883.

———. *Uncle Remus and His Friends.* Houghton, Mifflin, 1892.

Henry, Mellinger E. *Folksongs from the Southern Highlands.* J. J. Augustin, 1938.

———. *Songs Sung in the Southern Appalachians.* Mitre Press, 1933.

Herskovits, Melville J. *The Myth of the Negro Past.* Beacon Press, 1958 (paperback reprint).

Herskovits, Melville J. and Frances. *Dahomean Narrative.* Northwestern University Press, 1958.

Hinsie, Leland E., and Roberts, Jean Campbell. *Psychoanalytic Dictionary.* Oxford University Press, 1958.

Hoosier Folklore. 1942–50.

Hughes, Langston, and Arna Bontemps. *The Book of Negro Folklore.* Dodd, Mead, 1958.

Huizinga, Johann. *Homo Ludens, A Study of the Play Element in Culture.* Beacon Press, 1950, 1955 (paperback reprint).

Hurston, Zora Neale. *Mules and Men.* Lippincott, 1935.

Johnson, Charles S. *Growing Up in the Black Belt.* American Council on Education, 1941.

————. *Shadow of the Plantation.* University of Chicago Press, 1934.

Johnson, Guy B. *Folk Culture of Saint Helena Island, South Carolina.* University of North Carolina Press, 1930.

Jones, Charles C. *Negro Myths from the Georgia Coast.* State Co., 1888.

Journal of American Folklore. 1888–.

Keil, Charles. *Urban Blues.* University of Chicago Press, 1966.

Kennedy, R. Emmet. *Black Cameos.* A. C. Boni, 1924.

————. *Mellows.* A. C. Boni, 1925.

Leach, MacEdward. *The Ballad Book.* Harper, 1955.

Logue, Christopher (ed.). *Count Vicarion's Book of Bawdy Ballads.* (Paris), 1956.

Lomax, Alan. *Folk Songs of North America.* Doubleday, 1960.

————. *The Rainbow Sign.* Duell, Sloan and Pearce, 1959.

Lomax, John and Alan. *American Ballads and Folk Songs.* Macmillan, 1934.

————. *Best Loved American Folk Songs.* Macmillan, 1947.

————. *Negro Folk Songs as Sung by Leadbelly.* Macmillan, 1936.

————. *Our Singing Country.* Macmillan, 1949.

Lord, Albert. *The Singer of Tales.* Harvard University Press, 1960.

New York Folklore Quarterly. Ithaca, 1945–.

Odum, Howard W. *Rainbow Round My Shoulder.* Bobbs-Merrill, 1928.

————. *Wings on My Feet.* Bobbs-Merrill, 1929.

Odum, Howard W., and Guy B. Johnson. *The Negro and His Songs.* University of North Carolina Press, 1925.

Oliver, Paul. *Blues Fell This Morning.* Cassell, 1960.

Palmer, Edgar. *G. I. Songs.* Sheridan House, 1944.

Parrish, Lydia. *Slave Songs of the Georgia Sea Islands.* Heritage House, 1942.

Parsons, Elsie Clews. *Folk-Lore of the Sea Islands, South Carolina.* American Folklore Society, 1923.

———. *Folklore from the Cape Verde Islands,* 2 Vols. American Folklore Society, 1923.

Propp, Vladimir. *Morphology of the Folktale.* University of Texas Press, 1968.

Publications of the Texas Folklore Society. 1916–.

Puckett, Newbell N. *Folk Beliefs of the Southern Negro.* University of North Carolina Press, 1926.

Radin, Paul. *The Trickster.* Philosophical Library, 1956.

Randolph, Vance. *The Devil's Pretty Daughter.* Columbia University Press, 1955.

———. *Sticks in the Knapsack.* Columbia University Press, 1958.

———. *Who Blowed Up the Church House?* Columbia University Press, 1952.

Roberts, Leonard. *South from Hell-fer-Sartin'.* University of Kentucky Press, 1955.

Rohrer, John H., and Munro Edmondson, (eds.). *The Eighth Generation.* Harper, 1960.

Sandburg, Carl. *The American Songbag.* Harcourt, Brace, 1927.

Saxon, Lyle, Edward Dreyer, and Robert Tallant. *Gumbo Ya-Ya.* Houghton, Mifflin, 1945.

Scarborough, Dorothy. *On the Trail of Negro Folk Songs.* Harvard University Press, 1925.

Sebeok, Thomas (ed.). *Style in Language.* The M.I.T. Press, 1960.

Shearin, Habert G., and Josiah Combs. *A Syllabus of Kentucky Folk-Songs.* Transylvania Printing Co., 1911.

Simpson, G. E., and Y. M. Yinger. *Racial and Cultural Minorities.* Harper, 1953.

Southern Workman and Hampton School Record, Vols. 20–23. Hampton, Virginia, 1904.

Southern Folklore Quarterly.

Spaeth, Sigmund. *Weep Some More, My Lady.* Doubleday, Page, 1927.

Stout, Earl J. *Folklore from Iowa.* American Folklore Society, 1936.

Sypher, Wylie (ed.). *Comedy.* Doubleday, 1956.

Tennessee Folklore Society Bulletin. Maryville, 1936–.

Thompson, Harold W. *Body, Boots and Britches.* Lippincott, 1940.

Thompson, Stith. *The Folktale.* Dryden Press, 1951.

———. *Motif-Index of Folk-Literature,* 6 Vols. Indiana University Press, 1955–58.

Thorp, N. Howard (Jack). *Songs of the Cowboys.* Houghton, Mifflin, 1921.

Tidwell, James N. *A Treasury of American Folk Humor.* Crown, 1956.

Von Sydow, C. W. *Selected Papers on Folklore.* Rosenkilde and Bagger, 1948.

Wallrich, William. *Air Force Airs.* Duell, Sloan and Pearce, 1957.

Wentworth, Harold, and Stuart Berg Flexner. *Dictionary of American Slang.* Thomas Y. Crowell, 1960.

Western Folklore. 1946.

Wheeler, Mary. *Steamboatin' Days.* Louisiana State University Press, 1944.

White, Newman I. *American Negro Folk Songs.* Harvard University Press, 1928.

White, Newman Ivey (ed.). *The Frank C. Brown Collection of North Carolina Folklore,* 5 Vols. Duke University Press, 1952 and after.

Whitney, Annie Weston, and Caroline Canfield Bullock. *Folklore from Maryland.* Memoirs of the American Folklore Society XVIII, 1925.

Wittke, Carl. *Tambo and Bones.* Duke University Press, 1930.

Wolfenstein, Martha. *Children's Humor.* Free Press, 1954.

Tale Types and Motifs

Tale type numbers are from Antti Aarne and Stith Thompson, *The Types of the Folktale* (Helsinki, 1961).

Motif numbers are from Stith Thompson, *Motif-Index of Folk-Literature* (Copenhagen and Bloomington, Indiana, 1955–1958), 6 volumes.

273

MOTIFS REFERRED TO OR INCLUDED IN TEXT

K1970	*Sham miracles*
K2131.2	*Envious jackal makes lion suspicious of his friend the bull*
N275.5.2	*Criminal confesses because he thinks himself accused*
N688	*What is in the dish: "Poor Crab"*
Q21.1	*Old woman gives her only cow believing she will receive a hundred in return from God*
X111.7	*Misunderstood words lead to comic results*
X410	*Jokes on parsons*
X435	*The boy applies the sermon*
X435.1	*"What says David?" Boy: "Pay your old debts"*
X452	*The parson has no need to preach*
X800	*Humor based on drunkenness*
X939.1*	*Lie: person of remarkable speed*
X1411.1	*Lie: the great melon*
X1420	*Lies about vegetables*
X1623.2.1	*Lie: frozen words thaw out in the spring*
X1633	*Lie: effect of heat on animals*
X1633.1	*Lie: weather so hot that corn pops in fields, animals freeze to death thinking it has snowed*
X1740	*Absurd disregard of natural laws*

Index

276

The Trouble with Uncle

For Alan, the coolest skipper under the sun!

William Heinemann Ltd
Michelin House
81 Fulham Road
London SW3 6RB

LONDON   MELBOURNE   AUCKLAND

First published 1992
Copyright © Babette Cole 1992

ISBN 0 434 96128 0

Printed and bound in Italy by L.E.G.O. S.p.A., Vicenza

The Trouble with Uncle

Babette Cole

Heinemann

The trouble
with Uncle is…

He doesn't just play around with boats.

Uncle found his own club.

One of the members sold him a *real* treasure map...

"Come on. Now we can get rich quick!"
said Uncle.

Uncle tried to work out the way to the island,
but he couldn't do the sums.

"Load of rubbish!" he said.
So we set sail anyway.

We were lost at sea for ages.

Eventually…
"Land ahoy!" shouted Uncle.

But when we dropped anchor,
the land started to move!

"Take that hook out of my nose at once!" said the whale, "and then I'll take you to your beastly island."

We set off at top speed.

"Good riddance!" said the whale.

"This must be it," said Uncle.

It was the
right island,
of course.

But someone had built a hotel on top of the treasure.

The hotel was full of film stars.

Then some real
pirates came
alongside.

They kidnapped Lovelace L'amour, the famous film star and took all her jewels.

Rescuing Lovelace was easy for Uncle.

The pirates left all her jewels behind.

She gave Uncle
a reward.

But back at sea it fell
overboard.

Luckily a mermaid
caught it.

She taught Uncle sea sums.
Uncle fell in love!

They were married
by the parrot!

NAVIGATION
YACHTMASTER
TREASURE ISLAND
SEAMANSHIP

Sailing home was no
trouble at all.

But now I've got trouble with Aunty!